ABOUT THIS PUBLICATION

FOR SERVICE ASSISTANCE

Customer Service
1.704.898.0770

North Carolina General Statues is published by The Muliti-Media Group of Greater Charlotte in Charlotte, North Carolina. Copyright 2015 by the Multi-Media Group of Greater Charlotte. This book or parts thereof may not be reproduced in any form, stored in a retrieval system, or transmitted in any form by any means—electronic, mechanical, photocopy, recording or otherwise—without prior written permission of the publisher, except as provided by United States of America copyright law.

The records required by U.S. Code 2257(a) through (c) and the pertinent regulations 28 C.F.R. Cli. 1, Part 75 with respect to this publication and all materials associated with such records are maintained by The Multi-Media Group of Greater Charlotte, Publisher and available for review by Attorney General.

www.visionbooks.org

Copyright © 2015 by MMGGC
All rights reserved!

TID: 5107866
ISBN (10) digit: 1503244156
ISBN (13) digit: 978-1503244153

123-4-56789-01239-Paperback
123-4-56789-01239-Hardback

First Edition

090520140547

Printed in the United States of America

2015 EDITION

North Carolina Criminal Law And Procedure-Pamphlet # 81

Printed In conjunction with the Administration of the Courts

North Carolina Criminal Law and Procedure
Pamphlet Reference Guide

Chapters	Pamphlet
Chapter 1 Civil Procedure	1
Chapter 1 Civil Procedure (Continue)	2
Chapter 1A Rules of Civil Procedure	2
Chapter 1B Contribution.	2
Chapter 1C Enforcement of Judgments.	2
Chapter 1D Punitive Damages.	2
Chapter 1E Eastern Band of Cherokee Indians.	2
Chapter 1F North Carolina Uniform Interstate Depositions and Discovery Act.	2
Chapter 2 - Clerk of Superior Court [Repealed and Transferred.]	3
Chapter 3 - Commissioners of Affidavits and Deeds [Repealed.]	3
Chapter 4 - Common Law	3
Chapter 5 - Contempt [Repealed.]	3
Chapter 5A - Contempt	3
Chapter 6 - Liability for Court Costs	3
Chapter 7 - Courts [Repealed and Transferred.]	3
Chapter 7A – Judicial Department	3
Chapter 7A – Continuation (Judicial Department)	4
Chapter 7A – Continuation (Judicial Department)	5
Chapter 7B - Juvenile Code	5
Chapter 8 - Evidence	6
Chapter 8A - Interpreters for Deaf Persons [Recodified.]	6
Chapter 8B - Interpreters for Deaf Persons	6
Chapter 8C - Evidence Code	6
Chapter 9 - Jurors	6
Chapter 10 - Notaries [Repealed.]	6
Chapter 10A - Notaries [Recodified.]	6
Chapter 10B - Notaries	6
Chapter 11 - Oaths	6
Chapter 12 - Statutory Construction	6
Chapter 13 - Citizenship Restored	6
Chapter 14 - Criminal Law	7
Chapter 14 –Criminal Law (Continuation)	8
Chapter 15 - Criminal Procedure	9
Chapter 15A - Criminal Procedure Act (Continuation)	10
Chapter 15A - Criminal Procedure Act (Continuation)	11
Chapter 15B - Victims Compensation	11
Chapter 15C - Address Confidentiality Program	11
Chapter 16 - Gaming Contracts and Futures	11
Chapter 17 - Habeas Corpus	11

Chapter 17A - Law-Enforcement Officers [Recodified.]	11
Chapter 17B - North Carolina Criminal Justice Education and Training System [Recodified.] Chapter 17C - North Carolina Criminal Justice Education and Training Standards Commission	11 11
Chapter 17D - North Carolina Justice Academy	11
Chapter 17E - North Carolina Sheriffs' Education and Training Standards Commission	11
Chapter 18 - Regulation of Intoxicating Liquors [Repealed.]	12
Chapter 18A - Regulation of Intoxicating Liquors [Repealed.]	12
Chapter 18B - Regulation of Alcoholic Beverages	12
Chapter 18C - North Carolina State Lottery	12
Chapter 19 - Offenses against Public Morals	12
Chapter 19A - Protection of Animals	12
Chapter 20 - Motor Vehicles	13
Chapter 20 - Motor Vehicles (Continuation)	14
Chapter 20 - Motor Vehicles (Continuation)	15
Chapter 20 - Motor Vehicles (Continuation)	16
Chapter 21 - Bills of Lading	17
Chapter 22 - Contracts Requiring Writing	17
Chapter 22A - Signatures	17
Chapter 22B - Contracts Against Public Policy	17
Chapter 22C - Payments to Subcontractors	17
Chapter 23 - Debtor and Creditor	17
Chapter 24 – Interest	17
Chapter 25 – Uniform Commercial Code	18
Chapter 25 – Uniform Commercial Code (Continuation)	19
Chapter 25A – Retail Installment Sales Act	20
Chapter 25B - Credit	20
Chapter 25C - Sales of Artwork	20
Chapter 26 - Suretyship	20
Chapter 27 - Warehouse Receipts [Repealed.]	20
Chapter 28 - Administration [Repealed.]	20
Chapter 28A - Administration of Decedents' Estates	20
Chapter 28B - Estates of Absentees in Military Service	20
Chapter 28C - Estates of Missing Persons	20
Chapter 29 - Intestate Succession	21
Chapter 30 - Surviving Spouses	21
Chapter 31 - Wills	21
Chapter 31A - Acts Barring Property Rights	21
Chapter 31B - Renunciation of Property and Renunciation of Fiduciary Powers Act	21
Chapter 31C - Uniform Disposition of Community Property Rights at Death Act	21
Chapter 32 - Fiduciaries	21
Chapter 32A - Powers of Attorney	21
Chapter 33 - Guardian and Ward [Repealed and Recodified.]	21

Chapter 33A - North Carolina Uniform Transfers to Minors Act	21
Chapter 33B - North Carolina Uniform Custodial Trust Act	21
Chapter 34 - Veterans' Guardianship Act	22
Chapter 35 - Sterilization Procedures	22
Chapter 35A - Incompetency and Guardianship	22
Chapter 36 - Trusts and Trustees [Repealed.]	22
Chapter 36A - Trusts and Trustees	22
Chapter 36B - Uniform Management of Institutional Funds Act [Repealed.]	22
Chapter 36C - North Carolina Uniform Trust Code	22
Chapter 36D - North Carolina Community Third Party Trusts, Pooled Trusts	23
Chapter 36E - Uniform Prudent Management of Institutional Funds Act	23
Chapter 37 - Allocation of Principal and Income [Repealed.]	23
Chapter 37A - Uniform Principal and Income Act	23
Chapter 38 - Boundaries	23
Chapter 38A - Landowner Liability	23
Chapter 39 - Conveyances	23
Chapter 39A - Transfer Fee Covenants Prohibited	23
Chapter 40 - Eminent Domain [Repealed.]	23
Chapter 40A - Eminent Domain	23
Chapter 41 - Estates	23
Chapter 41A - State Fair Housing Act	23
Chapter 42 - Landlord and Tenant	23
Chapter 42A - Vacation Rental Act	23
Chapter 43 - Land Registration	23
Chapter 44 - Liens	24
Chapter 44A - Statutory Liens and Charges	24
Chapter 45 - Mortgages and Deeds of Trust	24
Chapter 45A - Good Funds Settlement Act	24
Chapter 46 - Partition	24
Chapter 47 - Probate and Registration	25
Chapter 47A - Unit Ownership	25
Chapter 47B - Real Property Marketable Title Act	25
Chapter 47C - North Carolina Condominium Act	25
Chapter 47D - Notice of Settlement Act [Expired.]	25
Chapter 47E - Residential Property Disclosure Act	25
Chapter 47F - North Carolina Planned Community Act	25
Chapter 47G - Option to Purchase Contracts	25
Chapter 47H - Contracts for Deed	25
Chapter 48 - Adoptions	26
Chapter 48A - Minors	26
Chapter 49 - Bastardy	26
Chapter 49A - Rights of Children	26
Chapter 50 - Divorce and Alimony	26
Chapter 50A - Uniform Child-Custody Jurisdiction and	

Enforcement Act	26
Chapter 50B - Domestic Violence	26
Chapter 50C - Civil No-Contact Orders	26
Chapter 51 - Marriage	26
Chapter 52 - Powers and Liabilities of Married Persons	27
Chapter 52A - Uniform Reciprocal Enforcement of Support Act [Repealed.]	27
Chapter 52B - Uniform Premarital Agreement Act	27
Chapter 52C - Uniform Interstate Family Support Act	27
Chapter 53 - Banks	27
Chapter 53A - Business Development Corporations and North Carolina Capital Resource Corporations	28
Chapter 53B - Financial Privacy Act	28
Chapter 54 - Cooperative Organizations	28
Chapter 54A - Capital Stock Savings and Loan Associations [Repealed.]	28
Chapter 54B - Savings and Loan Associations	29
Chapter 54C - Savings Banks	29
Chapter 55 - North Carolina Business Corporation Act	30
Chapter 55A - North Carolina Nonprofit Corporation Act	31
Chapter 55B - Professional Corporation Act	31
Chapter 55C - Foreign Trade Zones	31
Chapter 55D - Filings, Names, and Registered Agents for Corporations, Nonprofit Corporations, and Partnerships	31
Chapter 56 - Electric, Telegraph and Power Companies [Repealed.]	31
Chapter 57 - Hospital, Medical and Dental Service Corporations [Recodified.]	31
Chapter 57A - Health Maintenance Organization Act [Recodified.]	31
Chapter 57B - Health Maintenance Organization Act [Recodified.]	31
Chapter 57C - North Carolina Limited Liability Company Act.	31
Chapter 58 - Insurance.	32
Chapter 58 - Insurance (Continuation)	33
Chapter 58 - Insurance (Continuation)	34
Chapter 58 - Insurance (Continuation)	35
Chapter 58 - Insurance (Continuation)	36
Chapter 58 - Insurance (Continuation)	37
Chapter 58 - Insurance (Continuation)	38
Chapter 58A - North Carolina Health Insurance Trust Commission [Recodified.]	38
Chapter 59 - Partnership.	39
Chapter 59B - Uniform Unincorporated Nonprofit Association Act.	39
Chapter 60 - Railroads and Other Carriers [Repealed and Transferred.]	39
Chapter 61 - Religious Societies	39
Chapter 62 - Public Utilities	39

Chapter 62 - Public Utilities (Continuation)	40
Chapter 62A - Public Safety Telephone Service And Wireless Telephone Service	40
Chapter 63 - Aeronautics	40
Chapter 63A - North Carolina Global TransPark Authority	40
Chapter 64 - Aliens	40
Chapter 65 – Cemeteries	40
Chapter 66 - Commerce and Business	41
Chapter 67 - Dogs	41
Chapter 68 - Fences and Stock Law	41
Chapter 69 - Fire Protection	41
Chapter 70 - Indian Antiquities, Archaeological Resources and Unmarked Human Skeletal Remains Protection	42
Chapter 71 - Indians [Repealed.]	42
Chapter 71A - Indians	42
Chapter 72 - Inns, Hotels and Restaurants	42
Chapter 73 - Mills	42
Chapter 74 - Mines and Quarries	42
Chapter 74A - Company Police [Repealed.]	42
Chapter 74B - Private Protective Services Act [Repealed.]	42
Chapter 74C - Private Protective Services	42
Chapter 74D - Alarm Systems	42
Chapter 74E - Company Police Act	42
Chapter 74F - Locksmith Licensing Act	42
Chapter 74G - Campus Police Act	42
Chapter 75 - Monopolies, Trusts and Consumer Protection	42
Chapter 75A - Boating and Water Safety	43
Chapter 75B - Discrimination in Business	43
Chapter 75C - Motion Picture Fair Competition Act	43
Chapter 75D - Racketeer Influenced and Corrupt Organizations	43
Chapter 75E - Unlawful Activities in Connection With Certain Corporate Transactions	43
Chapter 76 - Navigation	43
Chapter 76A - Navigation and Pilotage Commissions	43
Chapter 77 - Rivers, Creeks, and Coastal Waters	43
Chapter 78 - Securities Law [Repealed.]	43
Chapter 78A - North Carolina Securities Act	43
Chapter 78B - Tender Offer Disclosure Act [Repealed.]	43
Chapter 78C - Investment Advisers	43
Chapter 78D - Commodities Act	43
Chapter 79 - Strays [Repealed.]	43
Chapter 80 - Trademarks, Brands, etc.	44
Chapter 81 - Weights and Measures [Recodified.]	44
Chapter 81A - Weights and Measures Act of 1975.	44
Chapter 82 - Wrecks [Repealed.]	44
Chapter 83 - Architects [Recodified.]	44

Chapter 83A - Architects	44
Chapter 84 - Attorneys-at-Law	44
Chapter 84A - Foreign Legal Consultants	44
Chapter 85 - Auctions and Auctioneers [Repealed.]	44
Chapter 85A - Bail Bondsmen and Runners [Recodified.]	44
Chapter 85B - Auctions and Auctioneers	44
Chapter 85C - Bail Bondsmen and Runners [Recodified.]	44
Chapter 86 - Barbers [Recodified.]	44
Chapter 86A - Barbers	44
Chapter 87 - Contractors	44
Chapter 88 - Cosmetic Art [Repealed.]	44
Chapter 88A - Electrolysis Practice Act	44
Chapter 88B - Cosmetic Art	45
Chapter 89 - Engineering and Land Surveying [Recodified.]	45
Chapter 89A - Landscape Architects	45
Chapter 89B - Foresters	45
Chapter 89C - Engineering and Land Surveying	45
Chapter 89D - Landscape Contractors	45
Chapter 89E - Geologists Licensing Act	45
Chapter 89F - North Carolina Soil Scientist Licensing Act	45
Chapter 89G - Irrigation Contractors	45
Chapter 90 - Medicine and Allied Occupations	45
Chapter 90 - Medicine and Allied Occupations (Continuation)	46
Chapter 90 - Medicine and Allied Occupations (Continuation)	47
Chapter 90 - Medicine and Allied Occupations (Continuation)	48
Chapter 90A - Sanitarians and Water and Wastewater Treatment Facility Operators	48
Chapter 90B - Social Worker Certification and Licensure Act	48
Chapter 90C - North Carolina Recreational Therapy Licensure Act	48
Chapter 90D - Interpreters and Transliterators	48
Chapter 91 - Pawnbrokers [Repealed.]	48
Chapter 91A - Pawnbrokers Modernization Act of 1989	48
Chapter 92 - Photographers [Deleted.]	48
Chapter 93 - Certified Public Accountants	48
Chapter 93A - Real Estate License Law	49
Chapter 93B - Occupational Licensing Boards	49
Chapter 93C - Watchmakers [Repealed.]	49
Chapter 93D - North Carolina State Hearing Aid Dealers and Fitters Board.	49
Chapter 93E - North Carolina Appraisers Act	49
Chapter 94 - Apprenticeship	49
Chapter 95 - Department of Labor and Labor Regulations	49
Chapter 95 - Department of Labor and Labor Regulations (Continuation)	50
Chapter 96 - Employment Security	50
Chapter 97 - Workers' Compensation Act	50
Chapter 97 - Workers' Compensation Act (Continuation)	51

Chapter 98 - Burnt and Lost Records	51
Chapter 99 - Libel and Slander	51
Chapter 99A - Civil Remedies for Criminal Actions	51
Chapter 99B - Products Liability	51
Chapter 99C - Actions Relating to Winter Sports Safety and Accidents	51
Chapter 99D - Civil Rights	51
Chapter 99E - Special Liability Provisions	51
Chapter 100 - Monuments, Memorials and Parks	51
Chapter 101 - Names of Persons	51
Chapter 102 - Official Survey Base	51
Chapter 103 - Sundays, Holidays and Special Days	51
Chapter 104 - United States Lands	51
Chapter 104A - Degrees of Kinship	51
Chapter 104B - Hurricanes or Other Acts of Nature	51
Chapter 104C - Atomic Energy, Radioactivity and Ionizing Radiation [Repealed and Recodified.]	51
Chapter 104D - Southern States Energy Compact	51
Chapter 104E - North Carolina Radiation Protection Act	51
Chapter 104F - Southeast Interstate Low-Level Radioactive Waste Management Compact [Repealed]	51
Chapter 104G - North Carolina Low-Level Radioactive Waste Management Authority Act of 1987 [Repealed]	51
Chapter 105 - Taxation	51
Chapter 105 - Taxation (Continuation)	52
Chapter 105 - Taxation (Continuation)	53
Chapter 105 - Taxation (Continuation)	54
Chapter 105A - Setoff Debt Collection Act	55
Chapter 105B - Defaulted Student Loan Recovery Act	55
Chapter 106 - Agriculture	55
Chapter 106 - Agriculture (Continue)	56
Chapter 106 - Agriculture (Continue)	57
Chapter 107 - Agricultural Development Districts [Repealed.]	57
Chapter 108 - Social Services [Repealed and Recodified.]	57
Chapter 108A - Social Services	57
Chapter 108B - Community Action Programs	58
Chapter 108C Medicaid and Health Choice Provider Requirements.	58
Chapter 108D Medicaid Managed Care for Behavioral Health Services.	58
Chapter 109 - Bonds [Recodified.]	58
Chapter 110 - Child Welfare	58
Chapter 111 - Aid to the Blind	58
Chapter 112 - Confederate Homes and Pensions [Repealed.]	58
Chapter 113 - Conservation and Development	58
Chapter 113 - Conservation and Development (Continuation)	59

Chapter 113A - Pollution Control and Environment	59
Chapter 113A - Pollution Control and Environment (Continuation)	60
Chapter 113B - North Carolina Energy Policy Act of 1975	60
Chapter 114 - Department of Justice	60
Chapter 115 - Elementary and Secondary Education [Repealed.]	60
Chapter 115A - Community Colleges, Technical Institutes, and Industrial Education Centers [Repealed.]	60
Chapter 115B - Tuition and Fee Waivers	60
Chapter 115C - Elementary and Secondary Education	60
Chapter 115C - Elementary and Secondary Education (Continuation)	61
Chapter 115C - Elementary and Secondary Education (Continuation)	62
Chapter 115C - Elementary and Secondary Education (Continuation)	63
Chapter 115D - Community Colleges	63
Chapter 115E - Private Educational Facilities Finance Act [Recodified]	63
Chapter 116 - Higher Education	63
Chapter 116 - Higher Education (Continuation)	63
Chapter 116A - Escheats and Abandoned Property [Repealed.]	64
Chapter 116B - Escheats and Abandoned Property	64
Chapter 116C - Continuum of Education Programs	64
Chapter 116D - Higher Education Bonds	64
Chapter 116E - Education Longitudinal Data System	64
Chapter 117 - Electrification	64
Chapter 118 - Firemen's and Rescue Squad Workers' Relief and Pension Funds [Recodified.]	64
Chapter 118A - Firemen's Death Benefit Act [Repealed.]	64
Chapter 118B - Members of a Rescue Squad Death Benefit Act [Repealed.]	64
Chapter 119 - Gasoline and Oil Inspection and Regulation	64
Chapter 120 - General Assembly	65
Chapter 120 - General Assembly (Continuation)	66
Chapter 120 - General Assembly (Continuation)	67
Chapter 120C - Lobbying	67
Chapter 121 - Archives and History	67
Chapter 122 - Hospitals for the Mentally Disordered [Repealed.]	67
Chapter 122A - North Carolina Housing Finance Agency	67
Chapter 122B - North Carolina Agricultural Facilities Finance Act [Repealed.]	67
Chapter 122C - Mental Health, Developmental Disabilities, and Substance Abuse Act of 1985	67
Chapter 122C - Mental Health, Developmental Disabilities, and Substance Abuse Act of 1985 (Continuation)	68

Chapter 122D - North Carolina Agricultural Finance Act	68
Chapter 122E - North Carolina Housing Trust and Oil Overcharge Act	68
Chapter 123 - Impeachment	69
Chapter 123A - Industrial Development [Repealed.]	69
Chapter 124 - Internal Improvements	69
Chapter 125 - Libraries	69
Chapter 126 - State Personnel System	69
Chapter 127 - Militia [Repealed.]	69
Chapter 127A - Militia	69
Chapter 127B - Military Affairs	69
Chapter 127C - Advisory Commission on Military Affairs	69
Chapter 128 - Offices and Public Officers	69
Chapter 128 - Offices and Public Officers (Continuation)	70
Chapter 129 - Public Buildings and Grounds	70
Chapter 130 - Public Health [Repealed.]	70
Chapter 130A - Public Health	70
Chapter 130A - Public Health (Continuation)	71
Chapter 130A - Public Health (Continuation)	72
Chapter 130B - Hazardous Waste Management Commission [Repealed.]	72
Chapter 131 - Public Hospitals [Repealed.]	72
Chapter 131A - Health Care Facilities Finance Act	72
Chapter 131B - Licensing of Ambulatory Surgical Facilities [Repealed.]	72
Chapter 131C - Charitable Solicitation Licensure Act [Repealed.]	72
Chapter 131D - Inspection and Licensing of Facilities	72
Chapter 131E - Health Care Facilities and Services	72
Chapter 131E - Health Care Facilities and Services (Continuation)	73
Chapter 131F - Solicitation of Contributions	73
Chapter 132 - Public Records	73
Chapter 133 - Public Works	74
Chapter 134 - Youth Development [Recodified.]	74
Chapter 134A - Youth Services [Repealed.]	74
Chapter 135 - Retirement System for Teachers and State Employees; Social Security; Health Insurance Program for Children	74
Chapter 135 - Retirement System for Teachers and State Employees; Social Security; Health Insurance Program for Children	75
Chapter 136 - Transportation	75
Chapter 136 - Transportation (Continuation)	76
Chapter 137 - Rural Rehabilitation [Repealed.]	76
Chapter 138 - Salaries, Fees and Allowances	76
Chapter 138A - State Government Ethics Act	76

Chapter	Page
Chapter 139 - Soil and Water Conservation Districts	76
Chapter 140 - State Art Museum; Symphony and Art Societies	76
Chapter 140A - State Awards System	76
Chapter 141 - State Boundaries	76
Chapter 142 - State Debt	76
Chapter 143 - State Departments, Institutions, and Commissions	77
Chapter 143 - State Departments, Institutions, and Commissions (Continuation)	78
Chapter 143 - State Departments, Institutions, and Commissions (Continuation)	79
Chapter 143 - State Departments, Institutions, and Commissions (Continuation)	80
Chapter 143A - State Government Reorganization	80
Chapter 143B - Executive Organization Act of 1973	80
Chapter 143B - Executive Organization Act of 1973 (Continuation)	81
Chapter 143B - Executive Organization Act of 1973 (Continuation)	82
Chapter 143C - State Budget Act	83
Chapter 143D - The State Governmental Accountability and Internal Control Act	83
Chapter 144 - State Flag, Official Governmental Flags, Motto, and Colors	83
Chapter 145 - State Symbols and Other Official Adoptions.	83
Chapter 146 - State Lands	83
Chapter 147 - State Officers	83
Chapter 148 - State Prison System	84
Chapter 149 - State Song and Toast	84
Chapter 150 - Uniform Revocation of Licenses [Repealed.]	84
Chapter 150A - Administrative Procedure Act [Recodified.]	84
Chapter 150B - Administrative Procedure Act	84
Chapter 151 - Constables [Repealed.]	84
Chapter 152 - Coroners	84
Chapter 152A - County Medical Examiner [Repealed.]	84
Chapter 153 - Counties and County Commissioners [Repealed.]	84
Chapter 153A - Counties	84
Chapter 153A – Counties (Continue)	85
Chapter 153B - Mountain Resources Planning Act	85
Chapter 153C - Uwharrie Regional Resources Act	85
Chapter 154 - County Surveyor [Repealed.]	85
Chapter 155 - County Treasurer [Repealed.]	85
Chapter 156 Drainage	85

Chapter 156 – Drainage (Continuation)	86
Chapter 157 - Housing Authorities and Projects	86
Chapter 157A - Historic Properties Commissions [Transferred.]	86
Chapter 158 - Local Development	86
Chapter 159 - Local Government Finance	86
Chapter 159 - Local Government Finance (Continuation)	87
Chapter 159A - Pollution Abatement and Industrial Facilities Financing Act [Unconstitutional.]	87
Chapter 159B - Joint Municipal Electric Power and Energy Act	87
Chapter 159C - Industrial and Pollution Control Facilities Financing Act	87
Chapter 159D - The North Carolina Capital Facilities Financing Act	87
Chapter 159E - Registered Public Obligations Act	87
Chapter 159F - North Carolina Energy Development Authority [Repealed.]	87
Chapter 159G - Water Infrastructure	87
Chapter 159H - [Reserved.]	87
Chapter 159I - Solid Waste Management Loan Program and Local Government Special Obligation Bonds	87
Chapter 160 - Municipal Corporations [Repealed And Transferred.]	87
Chapter 160A - Cities and Towns	88
Chapter 160A - Cities and Towns (Continuation)	89
Chapter 160B - Consolidated City-County Act	89
Chapter 160C - Baseball Park Districts [Repealed.]	90
Chapter 161 - Register of Deeds	90
Chapter 162 - Sheriff	90
Chapter 162A - Water and Sewer Systems	90
Chapter 162B Continuity of Local Government in Emergency.	90
Chapter 163 Elections and Election Laws.	90
Chapter 163 Elections and Election Laws. (Continuation)	91
Chapter 164 Concerning the General Statutes of North Carolina.	92
Chapter 165 Veterans.	92
Chapter 166 Civil Preparedness Agencies [Repealed.]	92
Chapter 166A North Carolina Emergency Management Act.	92
Chapter 167 State Civil Air Patrol [Repealed.]	92
Chapter 168 Persons with Disabilities.	92
Chapter 168A Persons With Disabilities Protection Act.	92

§ 143B-109. Historic Murfreesboro Commission - reports.

The Historic Murfreesboro Commission shall submit an annual report of its activities, holdings, and finances, including an audit of its accounts by a certified public accountant, to the Secretary of Cultural Resources. In the event such annual report is not received by the Secretary, or if such report does not indicate the need for the continuation of the Commission, the Secretary of Cultural Resources is authorized to recommend to the next General Assembly the abolition of the Commission. (1973, c. 476, s. 107.)

§ 143B-110. Historic Murfreesboro Commission - members; selection; quorum; compensation.

The Historic Murfreesboro Commission shall consist of 30 members appointed by the Governor plus, ex officio, the mayor of the Town of Murfreesboro, the Chairman of the Board of Commissioners of the County of Hertford, the President of Chowan College, and the Secretary of Cultural Resources or designee. The initial appointed members of the Commission shall be the members of the present Historic Murfreesboro Commission who shall serve for a period equal to the remainder of their current terms on the Historic Murfreesboro Commission. At the end of the respective terms of office of the initial members of the Commission, the appointments of their successors, with the exception of ex officio members, shall be for terms of five years and until their successors are appointed and qualify. Any appointment to fill a vacancy on the Commission created by the resignation, dismissal, death or disability of a member shall be for the balance of the unexpired term. The Commission shall elect its own officers. Members of the Commission shall serve without pay and without expense allowance from State funds. The Commission shall determine its requirements for a quorum. (1973, c. 476, s. 108.)

Part 23. John Motley Morehead Memorial Commission.

§ 143B-111. John Motley Morehead Memorial Commission - creation, powers and duties.

There is hereby recreated the John Motley Morehead Memorial Commission. The John Motley Morehead Memorial Commission shall have the following powers:

(1) To acquire title to or interests in property, both real and personal, and to solicit, collect, and expend funds for the acquisition, restoration, maintenance, and operation of a memorial to John Motley Morehead in the City of Greensboro; and to carry on other activities, including research and publications, reasonably related to this purpose;

(2) To convey, lease, mortgage, and otherwise dispose of real and personal property and interests therein, as well as to accept deeds, bills of sale, and other instruments conveying and investing title in it; and

(3) To offer such memorial to the State of North Carolina, which memorial, if accepted by the Department of Cultural Resources and Council of State, may be administered as a State historic site subject to existing covenants and agreements. (1973, c. 476, s. 110.)

§ 143B-112. John Motley Morehead Memorial Commission - status.

The John Motley Morehead Memorial Commission is hereby declared not to be a State agency within the meaning of the Executive Organization Act of 1973 and shall be exempt from all provisions of the Executive Organization Act of 1973 except G.S. 143B-111 through G.S. 143B-115. (1973, c. 476, s. 111.)

§ 143B-113. John Motley Morehead Memorial Commission - authorization for counties to assist.

The special approval of the General Assembly is hereby given to all appropriations of surplus or non-ad-valorem tax funds that should be made and paid over to said Commission by all counties and municipalities and the same are declared to be for a public purpose and the special approval of the General Assembly is given for such appropriations. Upon the request of the Commission hereby created, the governing body of Guilford County or of the City of Greensboro may, in its discretion, make appropriations from non-ad-valorem tax revenues to the Commission. (1973, c. 476, s. 112.)

§ 143B-114. John Motley Morehead Memorial Commission - reports.

The John Motley Morehead Commission shall submit to the Secretary of Cultural Resources an annual report of its activities, holdings, and finances, including an audit of its accounts by a certified public accountant. In the event such annual report is not received by the Secretary, or if the report indicates that there is no further need for the Commission, the Secretary of Cultural Resources is authorized to recommend to the next General Assembly the abolition of the Commission. (1973, c. 476, s. 113.)

§ 143B-115. John Motley Morehead Memorial Commission - members; selection; quorum; compensation.

The John Motley Morehead Memorial Commission shall consist of 19 members as follows: nine members appointed by the Governor; three members appointed by the Board of Commissioners of Guilford County; three members appointed by the City Council of Greensboro; and four ex officio members, as follows: the Secretary of Environment and Natural Resources or designee, the Superintendent of Public Instruction or designee, the State Treasurer or designee and the Secretary of Cultural Resources or designee. The initial members of the Commission shall be the members of the present John Motley Morehead Memorial Commission who shall serve for a period equal to the remainder of their current terms on the John Motley Morehead Memorial Commission. At the end of the respective terms of office of the initial members, the appointments of their successors, with the exception of the ex officio members, shall be for terms of six years and until their successors are appointed and qualify. Any appointment to fill a vacancy on the Commission created by the resignation, dismissal, death, or disability of a member shall be for the balance of the unexpired term. The Commission shall elect its own officers. Members of the Commission shall serve without pay and without expense allowance from State funds. The Commission shall determine its requirements for a quorum. (1973, c. 476, s. 114; 1977, c. 711, s. 4; 1989, c. 727, s. 218(124); 1997-443, s. 11A.119(a).)

§§ 143B-116 through 143B-120. Reserved for future codification purposes.

Part 24. Grassroots Arts Program.

§ 143B-121. Program established.

The Department of Cultural Resources shall establish a program to be known as the Grassroots Arts Program, by which funds shall be distributed among the counties of this State for the purpose of assisting the counties in the development of community arts programs. The Grassroots Arts Program shall be established within the "Community Art Development Section" (North Carolina Arts Council) of the Division of the Arts. (1977, c. 1008, s. 1.)

§ 143B-122. Distribution of funds.

Of the funds available under the Grassroots Arts Program, twenty percent (20%) of the total shall be distributed among the counties equally, and the remaining eighty percent (80%) shall be distributed among the counties on a per capita basis. (1977, c. 1008, s. 2; 2007-323, s. 21.1(a).)

§ 143B-123. Rules and procedures; standards for qualification for funds.

The Department of Cultural Resources shall be authorized to adopt rules and procedures necessary to implement this program and shall adopt standards which must be met by organizations within the counties in order to qualify for funds under the Grassroots Arts Program. The standards adopted shall include, but not be limited to the following:

(1) The organization must show that it exists primarily to aid the arts and that it aids the arts in all its forms including the performing, visual and literary.

(2) The organization must show that its programs are open to the entire community.

(3) The organization must show that it is a nonprofit, tax-exempt corporation, governed by a citizen board which is not self-perpetuating, and that it has been in existence and active for at least one full year.

(4) The organization must show that it can match funds available under the Grassroots Arts Program with public or private funds from within the county in which it is located at a ratio of one-to-one. (1977, c. 1008, s. 3.)

§ 143B-124. Designation of organization as official distributing agent; duties.

Guided by the standards set out in G.S. 143B-123, the board of county commissioners of each county shall designate to the Department of Cultural Resources an organization to serve as its distributing agent for Grassroots Arts Program funds. Upon the approval of the Department of Cultural Resources, the designated organization shall become the official distributing agent for that county and shall remain so until such time as it no longer meets the necessary standards. To receive its per capita funds, the official distributing agent must annually submit to the Department of Cultural Resources for its approval a plan for the expenditure of the funds allotted to that county and must account for the funds after they have been expended. Funds may be used for programming, administrative and operating expenses, and should assist in the total development of the arts within that county. (1977, c. 1008, s. 4.)

§ 143B-125. Disposition of funds for counties without organizations meeting Department standards.

Funds for counties without organizations which meet the necessary standards set by the Department of Cultural Resources shall be retained by the department and used for arts programming within these counties. Where feasible, the department shall maintain the same per capita rate for the distribution of funds to these counties and shall require the same matching ratio. (1977, c. 1008, s. 5; 1993, c. 321, s. 33.)

Part 25. Historical Military Reenactment Groups.

§ 143B-126. Voluntary registration; designation of names; registration symbol.

The Department of Cultural Resources shall establish a program for the voluntary registration of historical military reenactment groups. The Department shall require, as part of the registration procedure, the filing of a copy of the various bylaws governing the groups. The Department shall designate the names to be used by the groups to ensure a lack of duplication or confusion between the groups and shall, in the case of duplicate name requests, decide the use of a particular name based on the longest period of existence as shown by the dates of the bylaws or other evidence of creation. The Department shall create a seal or other logo which shall indicate registration with the Department and shall be authorized for use only by groups properly registered pursuant to this part. (1981, c. 523, s. 1.)

§ 143B-127. Contracts with registered groups.

The Department of Cultural Resources, Office of Archives and History shall sign contracts for the performance of military historical dramas on State-owned property only with historical military reenactment groups properly registered pursuant to this Part. (1981, c. 523, s. 2; 2002-159, s. 35(j).)

Part 26. Advisory Committee on Abandoned Cemeteries.

§ 143B-128: Repealed by Session Laws 2011-266, s. 1.1, effective July 1, 2011.

Part 27. Roanoke Voyages and Elizabeth II Commission.

§§ 143B-129 through 143B-131: Repealed by Session Laws 1993 (Reg. Sess., 1994), c. 769, s. 12.5(c).

Part 27A. Roanoke Island Commission.

§ 143B-131.1. Commission established.

There is established the Roanoke Island Commission. The Commission shall be an independent, self-supporting commission, but shall be located within the Department of Cultural Resources for historic resource management, organizational, and budgetary purposes. (1993 (Reg. Sess., 1994), c. 769, s. 12.5(a); 1995, c. 507, s. 12.6(a); 2011-145, s. 21.2(g).)

§ 143B-131.2. Roanoke Island Commission - Purpose, powers, and duties.

(a)   The Commission is created to combine various existing entities in the spirit of cooperation for a cohesive body to protect, preserve, develop, and interpret the historical and cultural assets of Roanoke Island. The Commission is further created to operate and administer the Elizabeth II State Historic Site and Visitor Center, the Elizabeth II, Ice Plant Island, and all other properties under the administration of the Department of Cultural Resources located on Roanoke Island having historical significance to the State of North Carolina, Dare County, or the Town of Manteo, except as otherwise determined by the Commission.

(b) The Commission shall have the following powers and duties:

(1) To advise the Secretary of Transportation and adopt rules on matters pertaining to, affecting, and encouraging restoration, preservation, and enhancement of the appearance, maintenance, and aesthetic quality of U.S. Highway 64/264 and the U.S. 64/264 Bypass travel corridor on Roanoke Island and the grounds on Roanoke Island Festival Park. However, the local government that has jurisdiction over the affected portion of the travel corridor shall process the applications for and issue the certificates of appropriateness and shall be responsible for the enforcement of those certificates and any rules adopted pursuant to this subdivision that apply to the portion of the travel corridor within the jurisdiction of the local government. No reimbursement shall be made by the Commission to the local government for the processing of applications or issuance of certificates of appropriateness, or the enforcement of those certificates or the rules.

(2) To operate the Elizabeth II State Historic Site and Visitor Center and the Elizabeth II as permanent memorials commemorating the Roanoke Voyages, 1584-1587.

(3) To supervise the development of Ice Plant Island and to manage future facilities.

(4) To advise the Secretary of the Department of Cultural Resources on matters pertinent to historical and cultural events on Roanoke Island.

(5) With the assistance of the Department of Cultural Resources, to identify, preserve, and protect properties located on Roanoke Island having historical significance to the State of North Carolina, Dare County, or the Town of Manteo consistent with applicable State laws and rules.

(6) To establish and collect a charge for admission to any property or event operated by the Commission.

(7) To solicit and accept gifts, grants, and donations.

(8) To cooperate with the Secretary and Department of Cultural Resources, the Secretary and Department of Transportation, the Secretary and Department of Environment and Natural Resources, and other governmental agencies, officials, and entities, and provide them with assistance and advice.

(9) To adopt and enforce such bylaws, rules, and guidelines that the Commission deems to be reasonably necessary in order to carry out its powers and duties. Chapter 150B of the General Statutes does not apply to the adoption of rules by the Commission.

(10) To accept monies, gifts, donations, grants, or devises, which funds will be used by the Commission for purposes of carrying out its duties and purposes herein set forth. The Commission may establish a reserve fund to be maintained and used for contingencies and emergencies. The Friends of Elizabeth II, Inc., shall use the balance of any unencumbered funds that were transferred to it pursuant to this subdivision only for expenses of the Commission or the properties operated by the Commission that are identified as operating or for maintenance costs by the Commission and that are requested by the Commission.

(11) By cooperative arrangement with other agencies, groups, individuals, and other entities, to coordinate and schedule historical and cultural events on Roanoke Island.

(12) Make recommendations to the Secretary of Cultural Resources concerning personnel and budgetary matters.

(13) To acquire real and personal property by purchase, gift, devise, and exchange.

(14) To administer the Historic Roanoke Island Fund as provided in G.S. 143B-131.8A.

(15) To procure supplies, services, and property as appropriate and to enter into contracts, leases, or other legal agreements to carry out the purposes of this Part and duties of the Commission. The provisions of G.S. 143-129 and Article 3 of Chapter 143 of the General Statutes do not apply to purchases by the Roanoke Island Commission of equipment, supplies, and services. However, the Commission shall: (i) submit all proposed contracts for supplies, materials, printing, equipment, and contractual services that exceed one million dollars ($1,000,000) authorized by this subdivision to the Attorney General or

the Attorney General's designee for review as provided in G.S. 114-8.3; and (ii) include in all proposed contracts to be awarded by the Commission under this subdivision a standard clause which provides that the State Auditor and internal auditors of the Commission may audit the records of the contractor during and after the term of the contract to verify accounts and data affecting fees and performance. The Commission shall not award a cost plus percentage of cost agreement or contract for any purpose. (1993 (Reg. Sess., 1994), c. 769, s. 12.5(a); 1995, c. 507, s. 12.6(b); 1997-443, ss. 11A.119(a), 30.1; 1998-212, ss. 21.1(a), 21.1(b); 2006-259, s. 25; 2010-194, s. 26; 2011-145, s. 21.2(d), (e), (h); 2011-284, s. 98; 2011-326, s. 15(aa).)

§ 143B-131.3. Assignment of property; offices.

Upon request of the Commission, the head of any State agency may assign property, equipment, and personnel of such agency to the Commission to assist the Commission in carrying out its duties under this Part. Assignments under this section shall be without reimbursement by the Commission to the agency from which the assignment was made. (1993 (Reg. Sess., 1994), c. 769, s. 12.5(a).)

§ 143B-131.4. Commission reports.

Before July 1, 1995, the Commission shall submit to the General Assembly a comprehensive report incorporating specific recommendations of the Commission for development and promotion of the Elizabeth II State Historic Site and Visitor Center. After the initial report, the Commission shall submit a quarterly report to the Chairs of the House Appropriations Subcommittee on General Government and the Chairs of the Senate Appropriations Committee on General Government and Information Technology and to the Fiscal Research Division of the General Assembly. The report shall include:

(1) A summary of actions taken by the Commission consistent with the powers and duties of the Commission set forth in G.S. 143B-131.2.

(2) Recommendations for legislation and administrative action to promote and develop the Elizabeth II State Historic Site and Visitor Center.

(3) An accounting of funds received and expended. (1993 (Reg. Sess., 1994), c. 769, s. 12.5(a); 2012-142, s. 18.1.)

§ 143B-131.5. Roanoke Island Commission - Additional powers and duties; transfer of assets and liabilities.

(a) The Commission shall also have the powers and duties established by Chapter 1194, Session Laws of 1981, as amended.

(b) Effective October 1, 1994, all lawful standards, rules, regulations, guidelines, contracts, agreements, permits, bylaws, and certificates of appropriateness of or issued by the Roanoke Voyages Corridor Commission or the Roanoke Voyages and Elizabeth II Commission shall remain in effect until modified, amended, revoked, repealed, or changed (as appropriate) by the Roanoke Island Commission in accordance with law.

(c) All the assets and liabilities of the Roanoke Voyages and Elizabeth II Commission are vested in the Roanoke Island Commission. (1993 (Reg. Sess., 1994), c. 769, s. 12.5(a).)

§ 143B-131.6. Roanoke Island Commission - Members; terms; vacancies; expenses; officers.

(a) The Commission shall consist of 24 voting members appointed as follows:

(1) Six members appointed by the Governor;

(2) Six members appointed by the General Assembly upon the recommendation of the President Pro Tempore of the Senate, at least two of whom reside in Dare County;

(3) Six members appointed by the General Assembly upon the recommendation of the Speaker of the House of Representatives, at least two of whom reside in Dare County; and

(4) The following persons, or their designees, ex officio:

a. The Governor;

b. The Attorney General;

c. The Secretary of the Department of Cultural Resources;

d. The Secretary of the Department of Transportation;

e. The Chair of the Dare County Board of Commissioners; and

f. The Mayor of Manteo.

(b) Members shall serve for two-year terms, with no prohibition against being reappointed, except initial appointments shall be for terms as follows:

(1) The Governor shall initially appoint three members for a term of two years and three members for a term of three years.

(2) The General Assembly upon the recommendation of the President Pro Tempore of the Senate shall initially appoint three members for a term of two years and three members for a term of three years.

(3) The General Assembly upon the recommendation of the Speaker of the House of Representatives shall initially appoint three members for a term of two years and three members for a term of three years.

Initial terms shall commence on October 1, 1994.

(c) The Governor shall appoint a chair biennially from among the membership of the Commission. The initial term of the chair shall commence on October 1, 1994. The Commission shall elect from its membership a vice-chair, a secretary, and treasurer to serve two-year terms. The Commission in its discretion may appoint a historian to serve at its pleasure. Initial terms shall commence on October 1, 1994.

(d) A vacancy in the Commission resulting from the resignation of a member or otherwise, shall be filled in the same manner in which the original appointment was made, and the term shall be for the balance of the unexpired term. Vacancies in appointments made by the General Assembly shall be filled in accordance with G.S. 120-122.

(e) The Commission members shall receive no salary as a result of serving on the Commission but shall receive per diem, subsistence, and travel expenses in accordance with the provisions of G.S. 138-5 and G.S. 138-6, as applicable. When approved by the Commission, members may be reimbursed for subsistence and travel expenses in excess of the statutory amount.

(f)   Members may be removed in accordance with G.S. 143B-13 as if that section applied to this Part.

(g)   The chair shall convene the Commission. Meetings shall be held as often as necessary, but not less than two times a year.

(h)   A majority of the members of the Commission shall constitute a quorum for the transaction of business. The affirmative vote of a majority of the members present at meetings of the Commission shall be necessary for action to be taken by the Commission.

(i)   The Commission shall make its recommendations by March 15 of each year that terms expire for appointments for terms commencing July 1 of that year; provided the initial appointments for terms commencing October 1, 1994, shall be made upon recommendation of the Roanoke Island Historical Association. (1993 (Reg. Sess., 1994), c. 769, s. 12.5(a); 2000-181, s. 2.4.)

§ 143B-131.7. Roanoke Island Commission - Counsel.

The Attorney General shall assign legal counsel to the Commission. (1993 (Reg. Sess., 1994), c. 769, s. 12.5(a).)

§ 143B-131.8: Repealed by Session Laws 2011-145, s. 21.2(c), effective July 1, 2012.

§ 143B-131.8A. Historic Roanoke Island Fund.

(a)   The Historic Roanoke Island Fund is established as a nonreverting enterprise fund and shall be administered by the Roanoke Island Commission. All operating revenues generated by the Roanoke Island Commission, including revenues collected from any property operated by the Roanoke Island Commission, together with all gifts, grants, donations, or other financial assets of whatever kind received or held by the Roanoke Island Commission shall be credited to the Historic Roanoke Island Fund and shall be used only (i) for the expenses of operating and maintaining the Roanoke Island Commission and the properties managed by the Roanoke Island Commission, (ii) to carry out any of the other duties and purposes set out by this Part, or (iii) for capital expenditures for the properties operated by the Commission.

(b)   The Department of Cultural Resources shall pay to the Commission on a monthly basis a pro rata share of the utilities, maintenance, and operating expenses of the Outer Banks History Center, which is located in the facility owned by the Commission. The funds received pursuant to this subsection shall be credited to the Historic Roanoke Island Fund.

(c)   The Department of Cultural Resources shall credit to the Historic Roanoke Island Fund all rental proceeds received by the Department from the rental properties located near the Outer Banks Island Farm. (2011-145, s. 21.2(j).)

§ 143B-131.9. Roanoke Island Commission staff.

The Commission shall appoint and fix the salary of an Executive Director to serve at its pleasure and may hire other employees. Employees of the Commission who were transferred from the Department of Cultural Resources as of July 1, 1995, and who were subject to the North Carolina Human Resources Act, Chapter 126 of the General Statutes, at the time of the transfer shall continue to be subject to that act. Employees of the Commission who were transferred but were not subject to the North Carolina Human Resources Act at the time of transfer are not subject to the North Carolina Human Resources Act. Employees of the Commission who were not transferred are not subject to the North Carolina Human Resources Act unless the Commission designates the employee's position as subject to the North Carolina Human Resources Act when the employee is hired. Once designated, a position remains subject to the North Carolina Human Resources Act unless exempted in accordance with that act. (1995, c. 507, s. 12.6(c); 2013-382, s. 9.1(c).)

§ 143B-131.10. Exceptions.

Notwithstanding G.S. 143C-1-1, the following provisions do not apply to this Part: G.S. 143C-6-4, 143C-6-5, and 143C-6-9. (1995, c. 507, s. 12.6(c); 2006-203, s. 102.)

Part 28. Andrew Jackson Historic Memorial Committee.

§ 143B-132: Repealed by Session Laws 2011-266, s. 1.3, effective July 1, 2011.

Part 29. Veterans' Memorial Commission.

§ 143B-133. Commission established.

(a) There is created within the Department of Cultural Resources the Veterans' Memorial Commission.

(b) The Veterans' Memorial Commission shall consist of 15 members, none of whom shall be members of the North Carolina General Assembly. The appointments shall be made as follows:

(1) Five persons shall be appointed by the General Assembly upon the recommendation of the Speaker of the House of Representatives in accordance with G.S. 120-121.

(2) Five persons shall be appointed by the General Assembly upon the recommendation of the President Pro Tempore of the Senate in accordance with G.S. 120-121.

(3) Five persons shall be appointed by the Governor.

Vacancies in appointments made by the General Assembly shall be filled in accordance with G.S. 120-122. Other vacancies in appointive terms shall be filled by appointment by the Governor.

(c) The members of the Commission shall serve for the life of the Commission.

(d) The members of the Commission shall receive necessary travel and subsistence expenses in accordance with the provisions of G.S. 138-5.

(e) The majority of the Commission shall constitute a quorum for the transaction of business.

(f) The members of the Commission shall select a chairman and vice-chairman.

(g) The Commission shall meet at least once during each calendar quarter upon the call of the chairman. The initial meeting shall be called by the Secretary of Cultural Resources to be held no later than August 31, 1987.

(h) The Department of Cultural Resources shall provide administrative and support staff to the Commission to assist it in performing its duties.

(i) The Commission shall terminate and this Part expire upon dedication of the monument. (1987, c. 779, s. 1; 1995, c. 490, s. 62.)

§ 143B-133.1. Powers of Commission.

(a) The Commission shall cause to be erected on the Capitol Grounds a monument to the veterans of World War I, World War II, and the Korean War.

(b) The Commission may, in its discretion, hire any person or persons to design, construct, and erect the monument, and shall choose its location on the Capitol Grounds, in accordance with the review procedures of the North Carolina Historical Commission as set forth in Chapter 100 of the General Statutes, and without regard to Article 8 of Chapter 143 of the General Statutes, G.S. 143B-373, or G.S. 147-12(12).

(c) Further, when a designer is selected and awarded a contract by the Commission to construct and erect the memorial, the Commission shall so advise, in writing, the Office of State Budget and Management of the total amount of the contract, a schedule of payments to be executed, if required, including any particular conditions upon which final acceptance of the Memorial and payment to the designer shall be made. Upon receipt of this document, the Office of State Budget and Management shall cause disbursements to be made from the Reserve established by Section 3 of Chapter 971, Session Laws of 1983, in accordance with the Commission's contractual obligations. (1987, c. 779, s. 1; 2000-140, s. 93.1(a); 2001-424, s. 12.2(b).)

§ 143B-134. Reserved for future codification purposes.

Part 30. African-American Heritage Commission.

§ 143B-135. Commission established.

(a) Creation and Duties. - There is created the African-American Heritage Commission in the Department of Cultural Resources to advise and assist the Secretary of Cultural Resources in the preservation, interpretation, and promotion of African-American history, arts, and culture. The Commission shall have the following powers and duties:

(1) To advise the Secretary of Cultural Resources on methods and means of preserving African-American history, arts, and culture.

(2) To promote public awareness of historic buildings, sites, structures, artwork, and culture associated with North Carolina's African-American heritage through special programs, exhibits, and publications.

(3) To support African-American heritage education in elementary and secondary schools in coordination with North Carolina Public Schools.

(4) To build a statewide network of individuals and groups interested in the preservation of African-American history, arts, and culture.

(5) To develop a program to catalog, preserve, assess, and interpret all aspects of African-American history, arts, and culture.

(6) To advise the Secretary of Cultural Resources upon any matter the Secretary may refer to it.

(b) Composition and Terms. - The Commission shall consist of 10 members who shall serve staggered terms. The initial board shall be selected on or before October 1, 2008, as follows:

(1) Four appointed by the Governor, two of whom shall serve terms of three years, one of whom shall serve a term of two years, and one of whom shall serve a term of one year. At least one appointee shall be a member of the North Carolina Historical Commission.

(2) Three appointed by the General Assembly upon the recommendation of the President Pro Tempore of the Senate, one of whom shall serve a term of three years, one of whom shall serve a term of two years, and one of whom shall serve a term of one year.

(3) Three appointed by the General Assembly upon the recommendation of the Speaker of the House of Representatives, one of whom shall serve a term of three years, one of whom shall serve a term of two years, and one of whom shall serve a term of one year.

Upon the expiration of the terms of the initial Commission members, each member shall be appointed for a three-year term and shall serve until a successor is appointed.

(c)   Vacancies. - A vacancy shall be filled in the same manner as the original appointment, except that all unexpired terms appointed by the General Assembly shall be filled in accordance with G.S. 120-122. Appointees to fill vacancies shall serve the remainder of the unexpired term and until their successors have been duly appointed and qualified.

(d)   Removal. - The Commission may remove any of its members for neglect of duty, incompetence, or unprofessional conduct. A member subject to disciplinary proceedings shall be disqualified from participating in the official business of the Commission until the charges have been resolved.

(e)   Officers. - The chair shall be designated by the Governor from among the members of the Commission to serve as chair at the pleasure of the Governor. The Commission shall elect annually from its membership a vice-chair and other officers deemed necessary by the Commission to carry out the purposes of this Article.

(f)   Meetings; Quorum. - The Commission shall meet at least semiannually to conduct business. The Board shall establish the procedures for calling, holding, and conducting regular and special meetings. A majority of Commission members shall constitute a quorum.

(g)   Compensation. - The Commission members shall receive no salary as a result of serving on the Commission but shall receive per diem, subsistence, and travel expenses in accordance with the provisions of G.S. 120-3.1, 138-5, and 138-6, as applicable. (2008-107, s. 19A.2.)

Article 3.

Department of Health and Human Services.

Part 1. General Provisions.

§ 143B-136: Repealed by Session Laws 1997-443, s. 11A.2.

§ 143B-136.1. Department of Health and Human Services - creation.

There is created a department to be known as the "Department of Health and Human Services," with the organization, duties, functions, and powers defined in this Article and other applicable provisions of law. (1997-443, s. 11A.3.)

§ 143B-137: Repealed by Session Laws 1997-443, s. 11A.2.

§ 143B-137.1. Department of Health and Human Services - duties.

It shall be the duty of the Department to provide the necessary management, development of policy, and establishment and enforcement of standards for the provisions of services in the fields of public and mental health and rehabilitation with the intent to assist all citizens - as individuals, families, and communities - to achieve and maintain an adequate level of health, social and economic well-being, and dignity. Whenever possible, the Department shall emphasize preventive measures to avoid or to reduce the need for costly emergency treatments that often result from lack of forethought. The Department shall establish priorities to eliminate those excessive expenses incurred by the State for lack of adequate funding or careful planning of preventive measures. (1997-443, s. 11A.3.)

§ 143B-138: Repealed by Session Laws 1997-443, s. 11A.2.

§ 143B-138.1. Department of Health and Human Services - functions and organization.

(a) All functions, powers, duties, and obligations previously vested in the following commissions, boards, councils, committees, or subunits of the Department of Human Resources are transferred to and vested in the Department of Health and Human Services by a Type I transfer, as defined in G.S. 143A-6:

(1) Division of Aging.

(2) Division of Services for the Blind.

(3) Division of Medical Assistance.

(4) Division of Mental Health, Developmental Disabilities, and Substance Abuse Services.

(5) Division of Social Services.

(6) Division of Health Service Regulation.

(7) Division of Vocational Rehabilitation.

(8) Repealed by Session Laws 1998-202, s. 4(v), effective January 1, 1999.

(9) Division of Services for the Deaf and the Blind.

(10) Repealed by Session Laws 2011-326, s. 19, effective June 27, 2011.

(11) Division of Child Development.

(12) Office of Rural Health.

(b) All functions, powers, duties, and obligations previously vested in the following commissions, boards, councils, committees, or subunits of the Department of Human Resources are transferred to and vested in the Department of Health and Human Services by a Type II transfer, as defined in G.S. 143A-6:

(1) Respite Care Program.

(2) Governor's Advisory Council on Aging.

(3) Commission for the Blind.

(4) Professional Advisory Committee.

(5) Consumer and Advocacy Advisory Committee for the Blind.

(6) Commission for Mental Health, Developmental Disabilities, and Substance Abuse Services.

(7) Social Services Commission.

(8) Child Day Care Commission.

(9) Medical Care Commission.

(10) Emergency Medical Services Advisory Council.

(11), (12) Repealed by Session Laws 2013-247, s. 3, effective July 3, 2013.

(13) North Carolina Council for the Hearing Impaired.

(14) Repealed by Session Laws 2002, ch. 126, s. 10.10D(c), effective October 1, 2002.

(15) Council on Developmental Disabilities.

(c) The functions, powers, duties, and obligations previously vested in the following commissions, boards, councils, committees, or subunits of the Department of Environment, Health, and Natural Resources are transferred to and vested in the Department of Health and Human Services by a Type I transfer, as defined in G.S. 143A-6:

(1) Division of Dental Health.

(2) State Center for Health Statistics.

(3) Division of Epidemiology.

(4) Division of Health Promotion.

(5) Division of Maternal and Child Health.

(6) Office of Minority Health.

(7) Office of Public Health Nursing.

(8) Division of Laboratory Services.

(9) Office of Local Health Services.

(10) Division of Postmortem Medicolegal Examinations.

(11) Office of Women's Health.

(d) All functions, powers, duties, and obligations previously vested in the following commissions, boards, councils, committees, or subunits of the Department of Environment, Health, and Natural Resources are transferred to and vested in the Department of Health and Human Services by a Type II transfer, as defined in G.S. 143A-6:

(1) Commission for Public Health.

(2) Council on Sickle Cell Syndrome.

(3) Repealed by Session Laws 2011-266, s. 1.30(b), effective July 1, 2011.

(4) Commission of Anatomy.

(5) Minority Health Advisory Council.

(6) Advisory Committee on Cancer Coordination and Control.

(e) The Department of Health and Human Services is vested with all other functions, powers, duties, and obligations as are conferred by the Constitution and laws of this State. (1997-443, s. 11A.3; 1998-202, s. 4(v); 2002-126, s. 10.10D(c); 2007-182, ss. 1, 2; 2011-266, s. 1.30(b); 2011-326, s. 19; 2013-247, s. 3.)

§ 143B-139. Department of Health and Human Services - head.

The Secretary of Health and Human Services shall be the head of the Department. (1973, c. 476, s. 120; 1997-443, s. 11A.122.)

§ 143B-139.1. Secretary of Health and Human Services to adopt rules applicable to local health and human services agencies.

The Secretary of the Department of Health and Human Services may adopt rules applicable to local health and human services agencies for the purpose of program evaluation, fiscal audits, and collection of third-party payments. The Secretary may adopt and enforce rules governing:

(1) The placement of individuals in licensable facilities located outside the individual's community and ability of the providers to return the individual to the individual's community as soon as possible without detriment to the individual or the community.

(2) The monitoring of mental health, developmental disability, and substance abuse services.

(3) The communication procedures between the area authority or county program, the local department of social services, the local education authority, and the criminal justice agency, if involved with the individual, regarding the placement of the individual outside the individual's community and the transfer of the individual's records in accordance with law.

(4) The enrollment and revocation of enrollment of Medicaid providers who have been previously sanctioned by the Department and want to provide services under this Article. (1975, c. 875, s. 45; 1997-443, s. 11A.101; 2002-164, s. 4.5.)

§ 143B-139.2. Secretary of Health and Human Services requests for grants-in-aid from non-State agencies.

It is the intent of this General Assembly that non-State health and human services agencies submit their appropriation requests for grants-in-aid through the Secretary of the Department of Health and Human Services for recommendations to the Governor and the General Assembly, and that agencies receiving these grants, at the request of the Secretary of the Department of Health and Human Services, provide a postaudit of their operations that has been done by a certified public accountant. (1975, c. 875, s. 16; 1989, c. 727, s. 173; 1997-443, s. 11A.102; 2006-203, s. 103.)

§ 143B-139.2A. Reports by non-State entities receiving direct State appropriations.

(a) The Department of Health and Human Services shall require the following non-State entities to match ten percent (10%) of the total amount of State appropriations received each fiscal year. In addition, the Department shall direct these entities to submit a written report annually, beginning December 1, 2012, of all activities funded by State appropriations to the Joint Legislative Oversight Committee on Health and Human Services, the Senate Appropriations Committee on Health and Human Services, the House of Representatives Appropriations Subcommittee on Health and Human Services, and the Fiscal Research Division:

(1) North Carolina Senior Games, Inc.

(2) ARC of North Carolina.

(3) ARC of North Carolina - Wilmington.

(4) Autism Society of North Carolina.

(5) The Mariposa School for Children with Autism.

(6) Easter Seals UCP of North Carolina.

(7) Easter Seals UCP of North Carolina and Virginia.

(8) ABC of North Carolina Child Development Center.

(9) Residential Services, Inc.

(10) Oxford House, Inc.

(11) Brain Injury Association of North Carolina.

(12) Food Bank of Central and Eastern North Carolina, Inc.

(13) Food Bank of the Albemarle.

(14) Manna Food Bank.

(15) Second Harvest Food Bank of Metrolina, Inc.

(16) Second Harvest Food Bank of Northwest North Carolina, Inc.

(17)   Second Harvest Food Bank of Southeast North Carolina.

(18)   Prevent Blindness NC.

(b)   The report required by subsection (a) of this section shall include the following information about the fiscal year preceding the year in which the report is due:

(1)   The entity's mission, purpose, and governance structure.

(2)   A description of the types of programs, services, and activities funded by State appropriations.

(3)   Statistical and demographical information on the number of persons served by these programs, services, and activities, including the counties in which services are provided.

(4)   Outcome measures that demonstrate the impact and effectiveness of the programs, services, and activities.

(5)   A detailed program budget and list of expenditures, including all positions funded and funding sources.

(6)   The source and amount of any matching funds received by the entity. (2012-142, s. 10.19(a), (b).)

§ 143B-139.3. Department of Health and Human Services - authority to contract with other entities.

(a)   The Department of Health and Human Services is authorized to contract with any governmental agency, person, association, or corporation for the accomplishment of its duties and responsibilities provided that the expenditure of funds pursuant to such contracts shall be for the purposes for which the funds were appropriated and is not otherwise prohibited by law.

(b)   The Department is authorized to enter into contracts with and to act as intermediary between any federal government agency and any county of this State for the purpose of assisting the county to recover monies expended by a county-funded financial assistance program; and, as a condition of such assistance, the county shall agree to hold and save harmless the Department against any claims, loss, or expense which the Department might incur under the contracts by reason of any erroneous, unlawful, or tortious act or omission of the county or its officials, agents, or employees. (1979, 2nd Sess., c. 1094, s. 1; 1983, c. 13; 1997-443, s. 11A.118(a).)

§ 143B-139.4. Department of Health and Human Services; authority to assist private nonprofit organizations.

(a) The Secretary of the Department of Health and Human Services may allow employees of the Department or provide other appropriate services to assist any private nonprofit organization which works directly with services or programs of the Department and whose sole purpose is to support the services and programs of the Department. Except as provided in G.S. 143B-164.18, a Department employee shall be allowed to work with an organization no more than 20 hours in any one month. These services are not subject to the provisions of Chapter 150B of the General Statutes.

(b) A private, nonprofit organization that receives employee assistance or other appropriate services in accordance with subsection (a) of this section, shall document all contributions received, including employee time, supplies, materials, equipment, and physical space. The documentation shall also provide an estimated value of all contributions received as well as any compensation paid to or bonuses received by State employees. This documentation shall be submitted annually to the Secretary of the Department of Health and Human Services in a format approved by the Secretary. Nonprofit organizations with less than five hundred thousand dollars ($500,000) in annual income shall submit an affidavit or annual audit from the chief officer of the organization providing and attesting to the financial condition of the organization and the expenditure of funds or use of State employee services or other State services, within six months from the nonprofit's fiscal year end. The board of directors of each private, nonprofit organization with an annual income of five hundred thousand dollars ($500,000) or more shall secure and pay for the services of the State Auditor's Office or employ a certified public accountant to conduct an annual audit of the financial accounts of the organization. The board of directors shall transmit to the Secretary of the Department a copy of the annual financial audit report of the private nonprofit organization. Nothing in this subsection shall be construed to relieve the private, nonprofit organization from other applicable reporting requirements established by law.

(c) Notwithstanding the limitations of subsection (a) of this section, the Secretary of the Department of Health and Human Services may assign employees of the Office of Rural Health and Resource Development to serve as in-kind match to nonprofit organizations working to establish health care programs that will improve health care access while controlling costs. (1987, c. 634, s. 1; 1997-443, s. 11A.118(a); 1999-237, s. 11.3; 2001-412, s. 3; 2006-66, s. 10.19.)

§ 143B-139.4A. Office of Rural Health and Community Care to work with organizations for expansion of mental health and substance abuse services.

The North Carolina Office of Rural Health and Community Care of the Department of Health and Human Services, in conjunction with the North Carolina Foundation for Advanced Health Programs through the Center of Excellence in Integrated Care, the Division of Mental Health, Developmental Disabilities, and Substance Abuse Services, the Governor's Institute on Substance Abuse, North Carolina Community Care Networks, Inc., the North Carolina Community Health Center Association, and other professional associations, shall work to expand the collocation in primary care practices serving the adult population of licensed health professionals trained in providing mental health and substance abuse services. (2011-185, s. 5.)

§ 143B-139.4B. Office of Rural Health and Community Care to oversee and monitor establishment and administration of statewide telepsychiatry program.

(a) The following definitions apply in this section:

(1) Consultant site. - The hospital or other site at which the consulting provider is physically located at the time the consulting provider delivers the acute mental health or substance abuse care by means of telepsychiatry.

(2) Hospital. - A facility licensed under Chapter 131E or Chapter 122C of the General Statutes, or a State facility listed in G.S. 122C-181.

(3) Referring site. - The hospital at which the patient is physically located.

(4) Telepsychiatry. - The delivery of acute mental health or substance abuse care, including diagnosis or treatment, by means of two-way real-time interactive audio and video by a consulting provider at a consultant site to an

individual patient at a referring site. The term does not include the standard use of telephones, facsimile transmissions, unsecured electronic mail, or a combination of these in the course of care.

(5) Consulting provider. - A physician or other health care provider licensed in this State to provide acute mental health or substance abuse care.

(b) The North Carolina Office of Rural Health and Community Care shall oversee the establishment and administration of a statewide telepsychiatry program that allows referring sites to utilize consulting providers at a consultant site to provide timely psychiatric assessment and rapid initiation of treatment for patients at the referring site experiencing an acute mental health or substance abuse crisis. Notwithstanding the provisions of Article 3 of Chapter 143 of the General Statutes or any other provision of law, the Office of Rural Health and Community Care shall contract with East Carolina University Center for Telepsychiatry and e-Behavioral Health to administer the telepsychiatry program. The contract shall include a provision requiring East Carolina University Center for Telepsychiatry and e-Behavioral Health to work toward implementing this program on a statewide basis by no later than January 1, 2014, and to report annually to the Office of Rural Health and Community Care on the following performance measures:

(1) Number of consultant sites and referring sites participating in the program.

(2) Number of psychiatric assessments conducted under the program, reported by site or region.

(3) Length of stay of patients receiving telepsychiatry services in the emergency departments of hospitals participating in the program, reported by disposition.

(4) Number of involuntary commitments recommended as a result of psychiatric assessments conducted by consulting providers under the program, reported by site or region and by year, and compared to the number of involuntary commitments recommended prior to implementation of this program.

(c) The Office of Rural Health and Community Care shall have all of the following powers and duties relative to the statewide telepsychiatry program:

(1) Ongoing oversight and monitoring of the program.

(2) Ongoing monitoring of the performance of East Carolina University Center for Telepsychiatry and e-Behavioral Health under its contract with the Department, including all of the following:

a. Review of the performance measures described in subsection (b) of this section.

b. Annual site visits to East Carolina University Center for Telepsychiatry and e-Behavioral Health.

(3) Facilitation of program linkages with critical access hospitals and small rural hospitals.

(4) Conducting visits to referring sites and consultant sites to monitor implementation of the program; and upon implementation, conducting these site visits at least once annually.

(5) Addressing barriers and concerns identified by consulting providers, consultant sites, and referring sites participating in the program.

(6) Encouraging participation in the program by all potential consultant sites, consulting providers, and referring sites throughout the State and promoting continued participation in the program by consultant sites, consulting providers, and referring sites throughout the State.

(7) Compiling a list of recommendations for future tele-health initiatives, based on operation of the statewide telepsychiatry program.

(8) Reviewing on a quarterly basis the financial statements of East Carolina University Center for Telepsychiatry and e-Behavioral Health related to the telepsychiatry program in order to compare and monitor projected and actual program costs.

(9) Annually reporting to the Legislative Oversight Committee on Health and Human Services and the Fiscal Research Division on or before November 1 on the operation and effectiveness of the program. The report shall include information on each of the performance measures described in subsection (b) of this section.

(d) The Department shall adopt rules necessary to ensure the health and safety of patients who receive care, diagnosis, or treatment under the telepsychiatry program authorized by this section. (2013-360, s. 12A.2B(b).)

§ 143B-139.5. Department of Health and Human Services; adult care State/county share of costs; maintenance of State/county budget allocations for State-County Special Assistance programs.

State funds available to the Department of Health and Human Services shall pay fifty percent (50%), and the counties shall pay fifty percent (50%) of the authorized rates for care in adult care homes including area mental health agency-operated or contracted-group homes. The Department shall maintain the State's appropriation to the State-County Special Assistance program at one hundred percent (100%) of the State certified budget enacted by the General Assembly for the 2012-2013 fiscal year. The Department shall use these appropriated funds for the State-County Special Assistance program, the State-County Special Assistance in-home program, and rental assistance. Each county department of social services shall maintain its allocation to the State-County Special Assistance program at one hundred percent (100%) of the county funds budgeted for this program for the 2011-2012 fiscal year. Each county shall use these funds for the State-County Special Assistance program, the State-County Special Assistance in-home program, and rental assistance. (1991, c. 689, s. 128; 1995, c. 535, s. 31; 1997-443, s. 11A.118(a); 2012-142, s. 10.23(f).)

§ 143B-139.5A. Collaboration between Division of Social Services and Commission of Indian Affairs on Indian Child Welfare Issues.

The Division of Social Services, Department of Health and Human Services, shall work in collaboration with the Commission of Indian Affairs, Department of Administration, and the North Carolina Directors of Social Services Association to develop, in a manner consistent with federal law, an effective process through which the following can be accomplished:

(1) Establishment of a relationship between the Division of Social Services and the Indian tribes set forth in G.S. 143B-407(a), either separately or through a central entity, that will enable these tribes, in general, and tribal councils or other tribal organizations, in particular, to receive reasonable notice of identified

Indian children who are being placed in foster care or adoption or who otherwise enter the child protective services system, and to be consulted on policies and other matters pertinent to placement of Indian children in foster care or adoption.

(2)   Agreement on a process by which North Carolina Indians might be identified and recruited for purposes of becoming foster care and adoptive parents.

(3)   Agreement on a process by which the cultural, social, and historical perspective and significance associated with Indian life may be taught to appropriate child welfare workers and to foster and adoptive parents.

(4)   Identification or formation of Indian child welfare advocacy, placement and training entities with which the Department of Health and Human Services might contract or otherwise form partnerships for the purpose of implementing the provisions of this act.

(5)   Development of a valid and reliable process through which Indian children within the child welfare system can be identified.

(6)   Identify the appropriate roles of the State and of Indian tribes, organizations and agencies to ensure successful means for securing the best interests of Indian children. (2001-309, s. 1.)

§ 143B-139.5B. Department of Health and Human Services - provision for joint training.

The Department of Health and Human Services shall offer joint training of Division of Health Service Regulation consultants, county DSS adult home specialists, and adult care home providers. The training shall be offered no fewer than two times per year, and subject matter of the training should be based on one or more of the 10 deficiencies cited most frequently in the State during the immediately preceding calendar year. The joint training shall be designed to reduce inconsistencies experienced by providers in the survey process, to increase objectivity by DHSR consultants and DSS specialists in conducting surveys, and to promote a higher degree of understanding between facility staff and DHSR consultants and DSS specialists in what is expected during the survey process. (2001-385, s. 1(c); 2007-182, s. 1; 2008-187, s. 25.)

§ 143B-139.5C. Internet data warehouse for provider records; annual review of accrediting body policies to avoid duplication.

(a)   The Secretary shall allow private sector development and implementation of an Internet-based, secure, and consolidated data warehouse and archive for maintaining corporate, fiscal, and administrative records of providers by September 1, 2011. This data warehouse shall not be used to store consumer records. Use of the consolidated data warehouse by the service provider agency is optional. Providers that choose to utilize the data warehouse shall ensure that the data is up to date and accessible to the regulatory body. A provider shall submit any revised, updated information to the data warehouse within 10 business days after receiving the request. The regulatory body that conducts administrative monitoring must use the data warehouse for document requests. If the information provided to the regulatory body is not current or is unavailable from the data warehouse and archive, the regulatory body may contact the provider directly. A provider that fails to comply with the regulatory body's requested documents may be subject to an on-site visit to ensure compliance. Access to the data warehouse must be provided without charge to the regulatory body under this subsection.

(b)   The Secretary shall review on an annual basis updates to policy made by the following national accrediting bodies: Council on Accreditation (COA), CARF International, Council on Quality and Leadership (CQL), the Joint Commission, NCQA, and URAC and shall take actions necessary to ensure that DHHS policy or procedural requirements do not duplicate the updated accreditation standards. (2011-253, ss. 1(c), 2.)

§ 143B-139.6. Confidentiality of records.

All privileged patient medical records in the possession of the Department of Health and Human Services shall be confidential and shall not be public records pursuant to G.S. 132-1. (1991 (Reg. Sess., 1992), c. 890, s. 20; 1997-443, s. 11A.118(a).)

§ 143B-139.6A. Secretary's responsibilities regarding availability of early intervention services.

The Secretary of the Department of Health and Human Services shall ensure, in cooperation with other appropriate agencies, that all types of early intervention services specified in the "Individuals with Disabilities Education Act" (IDEA), P.L. 102-119, the federal early intervention legislation, are available to all eligible infants and toddlers and their families to the extent funded by the General Assembly.

The Secretary shall coordinate and facilitate the development and administration of the early intervention system for eligible infants and toddlers and shall assign among the cooperating agencies the responsibility, including financial responsibility, for services. The Secretary shall be advised by the Interagency Coordinating Council for Children from Birth to Five with Disabilities and Their Families, established by G.S. 143B-179.5, and may enter into formal interagency agreements to establish the collaborative relationships with the Department of Public Instruction, other appropriate agencies, and other public and private service providers necessary to administer the system and deliver the services.

The Secretary shall adopt rules to implement the early intervention system, in consultation with all other appropriate agencies. (2001-437, s. 1.20(b).)

§ 143B-139.6B. Department of Health and Human Services; authority to deduct payroll for child care services.

Notwithstanding G.S. 143-3.3 and pursuant to rules adopted by the State Controller, an employee of the Department of Health and Human Services may, in writing, authorize the Department to periodically deduct from the employee's salary or wages paid for employment by the State, a designated lump sum to be paid to satisfy the cost of services received for child care provided by the Department. (2005-276, s. 10.8.)

Part 1A. Consolidated County Human Services.

§ 143B-139.7. Consolidated county human services funding.

(a) The Secretary of the Department of Health and Human Services shall adopt rules and policies to provide that:

(1) Any dedicated funding streams for local public health services, for social services, and for mental health, developmental disabilities, and substance abuse services may flow to a consolidated county human services agency and

the consolidated human services board in the same manner as that for funding nonconsolidated county human services, unless a different manner of allocation is otherwise required by law.

(2) The fiscal accountability and reporting requirements pertaining to local health boards, social services boards, and area mental health authority boards apply to a consolidated human services board.

(b) The Secretary of the Department of Health and Human Services may adopt any other rule or policy required to facilitate the provision of human services by a consolidated county human services agency or a consolidated human services board.

(c) For the purposes of this section, "consolidated county human services agency" means a county human services agency created pursuant to G.S. 153A-77(b). "Consolidated human services board" means a county human services board established pursuant to G.S. 153A-77(b). (1995 (Reg. Sess., 1996), c. 690, s. 1; 1997-443, s. 11A.118(a).)

§ 143B-140: Repealed by Session Laws 1989, c. 727, s. 174.

Part 2. Board of Human Resources.

§ 143B-141. Repealed by Session Laws 1983, c. 494, effective June 10, 1983.

Part 3. Commission for Public Health.

§§ 143B-142 through 143B-146: Recodified as §§ 130A-29 through 130A-33 by Session Laws 1989, c. 727, s. 175.

Part 3A. Education Programs in Residential Schools.

§ 143B-146.1. Mission of schools; definitions.

(a) It is the intent of the General Assembly that the mission of the residential school community is to challenge with high expectations each child to learn, to achieve, and to fulfill his or her potential.

(b)   The following definitions apply in this Part:

(1)   ABC's Program or Program. - The School-Based Management and Accountability Program developed by the State Board.

(2)   Department. - The Department of Health and Human Services.

(3)   Instructional personnel. - Assistant principals, teachers, instructional personnel, instructional support personnel, and teacher assistants employed in a residential school.

(4)   Participating school. - A residential school that is required to participate in the ABC's Program.

(4a)   Residential school. - A school operated by the Department of Health and Human Services that provides residential services to students. For the purposes of this Part, "residential school" does not include a school operated pursuant to Article 9C of Chapter 115C.

(5)   Residential school personnel. - The individuals included in G.S. 143B-146.16(a)(2).

(6)   Schools. - The residential schools under the control of the Secretary.

(7)   Secretary. - The Secretary of Health and Human Services.

(8)   State Board. - The State Board of Education.

(9)   Repealed by Session Laws 2013-247, s. 5, effective July 3, 2013. (1998-131, s. 5; 2005-195, s. 1; 2013-247, s. 4.)

§ 143B-146.2. ABC's Program in residential schools.

(a)   The Secretary, in consultation with the General Assembly and the State Board, may designate residential schools that must participate in the ABC's Program. The primary goal of the ABC's Program is to improve student performance. The Program is based upon an accountability, recognition, assistance, and intervention process in order to hold each participating school, its principal, and the instructional personnel accountable for improved student performance in that school.

(b)   In order to support the participating schools in the implementation of this Program, the State Board, in consultation with the Secretary, shall adopt guidelines, including guidelines to:

(1)   Assist the Secretary and the participating schools in the development and implementation of the ABC's Program.

(2)   Recognize the participating schools that meet or exceed their goals.

(3)   Identify participating schools that are low-performing and assign assistance teams to those schools. The assistance teams should include individuals with expertise in residential schools, individuals with experience in the education of children with disabilities, and others the State Board, in consultation with the Secretary, considers appropriate.

(4)   Enable assistance teams to make appropriate recommendations.

(c)   The ABC's Program shall provide increased decision making and parental involvement at the school level with the goal of improving student performance.

(d)   Consistent with improving student performance, the Secretary shall provide maximum flexibility to participating schools in the use of funds to enable those schools to accomplish their goals. (1998-131, s. 5; 2001-424, s. 21.81(c); 2005-195, s. 2; 2013-247, s. 5.)

§ 143B-146.3. Annual performance goals.

The ABC's Program shall (i) focus on student performance in the basics of reading, mathematics, and communications skills in elementary and middle schools, (ii) focus on student performance in courses required for graduation and on other measures required by the State Board in the high schools, and (iii) hold participating schools accountable for the educational growth of their students. To those ends, the State Board shall design and implement an accountability system that sets annual performance standards for each participating school in order to measure the growth in performance of the students in each individual school. (1998-131, s. 5.)

§ 143B-146.4. Performance recognition.

(a) The personnel in participating schools that achieve a level of expected growth greater than one hundred percent (100%) at a level to be determined by the State Board of Education are eligible for financial awards in amounts set by the State Board. Schools and personnel shall not be required to apply for these awards. For the purpose of this section, "personnel" includes the principal and the instructional personnel (i) serving students in one or more of the grades kindergarten through 12 or (ii) assigned to a prekindergarten program that is located within the participating school and is designed to prepare students for kindergarten at that school.

(b) The State Board shall establish a procedure to allocate the funds for these awards. Funds shall become available for expenditure July 1 of each fiscal year. Funds shall remain available until November 30 of the subsequent fiscal year for expenditure for awards to personnel.

The Secretary is encouraged to make these awards to each eligible person no later than the first regular teacher payroll following receipt of the funds, and shall make these awards to each eligible person no later than the second regular teacher payroll following the receipt of the funds. (1998-131, s. 5; 2005-195, s. 3.)

§ 143B-146.5. Identification of low-performing schools.

(a) The State Board shall design and implement a procedure to identify low-performing schools on an annual basis. Low-performing schools are those participating schools in which there is a failure to meet the minimum growth standards, as defined by the State Board, and a majority of students are performing below grade level.

(b) By July 10 of each year, the Secretary shall do a preliminary analysis of test results to determine which participating schools the State Board may identify as low-performing under this section. The Secretary then shall proceed under G.S. 143B-146.7. In addition, within 30 days of the initial identification of a school as low-performing by the Secretary or the State Board, whichever occurs first, the Secretary shall develop a preliminary plan for addressing the needs of that school. Before the Secretary adopts this plan, the Secretary shall make the plan available to the residential school personnel and the parents and guardians of the students of the school, and shall allow for written comments. Within five days of adopting the plan, the Secretary shall submit the plan to the State Board. The State Board shall review the plan expeditiously and, if appropriate, may offer recommendations to modify the plan. The Secretary shall consider any recommendations made by the State Board.

(c)   Each identified low-performing school shall provide written notification to the parents of students attending that school. The written notification shall include a statement that the State Board of Education has found that the school has "failed to meet the minimum growth standards, as defined by the State Board, and a majority of students in the school are performing below grade level." This notification also shall include a description of the steps the school is taking to improve student performance. (1998-131, s. 5.)

§ 143B-146.6. Assistance teams; review by State Board.

(a)   The State Board may assign an assistance team to any school identified as low-performing under this Part or to any other school that the State Board determines would benefit from an assistance team. The State Board shall give priority to low-performing schools in which the educational performance of the students is declining. The Department shall, with the approval of the Secretary, provide staff as needed and requested by an assistance team.

(b)   When assigned to an identified low-performing school, an assistance team shall:

(1)   Review and investigate all facets of school operations, including instructional and residential, and assist in developing recommendations for improving student performance at that school.

(2)   Evaluate at least semiannually the principal and instructional personnel assigned to the school and make findings and recommendations concerning their performance.

(3)   Collaborate with school staff, the Department, and the Secretary in the design, implementation, and monitoring of a plan that, if fully implemented, can reasonably be expected to alleviate problems and improve student performance at that school.

(4)   Make recommendations as the school develops and implements this plan.

(5) Review the school's progress.

(6) Report, as appropriate, to the Secretary, the State Board, and the parents on the school's progress. If an assistance team determines that an accepted school improvement plan developed under G.S. 143B-146.12 is impeding student performance at a school, the team may recommend to the Secretary that he vacate the relevant portions of that plan and direct the school to revise those portions.

(c) If a participating school fails to improve student performance after assistance is provided under this section, the assistance team may recommend that the assistance continue or that the Secretary take further action under G.S. 143B-146.7.

(d) The Secretary, in consultation with the State Board, shall annually review the progress made in identified low-performing schools. (1998-131, s. 5; 2005-195, s. 4; 2011-145, s. 7.13(u); 2011-391, s. 14(b).)

§ 143B-146.7. Consequences for personnel at low-performing schools.

(a) Within 30 days of the initial identification of a school as low-performing, whether by the Secretary under G.S. 143B-146.5(b) or by the State Board under G.S. 143B-146.5(a), the Secretary shall take one of the following actions concerning the school's principal: (i) decide whether the principal should be retained in the same position, (ii) decide whether the principal should be retained in the same position and a plan of remediation should be developed, (iii) decide whether the principal should be transferred, or (iv) proceed under the North Carolina Human Resources Act to dismiss or demote the principal. The principal may be retained in the same position without a plan for remediation only if the principal was in that position for no more than two years before the school is identified as low-performing. The principal shall not be transferred to another position unless (i) it is in a principal position in which the principal previously demonstrated at least two years of success, (ii) there is a plan to evaluate and provide remediation to the principal for at least one year following the transfer to assure the principal does not impede student performance at the school to which the principal is being transferred; and (iii) the parents of the students at the school to which the principal is being transferred are notified. The principal shall not be transferred to another low-performing school. The Secretary may, at any time, proceed under the North Carolina Human

Resources Act for the dismissal of any principal who is assigned to a low-performing school to which an assistance team has been assigned. The Secretary shall proceed under the North Carolina Human Resources Act for the dismissal of any principal when the Secretary receives from the assistance team assigned to that school two consecutive evaluations that include written findings and recommendations regarding the principal's inadequate performance. The Secretary shall order the dismissal of the principal if the Secretary determines from available information, including the findings of the assistance team, that the low performance of the school is due to the principal's inadequate performance. The Secretary may order the dismissal of the principal if (i) the Secretary determines that the school has not made satisfactory improvement after the State Board assigned an assistance team to that school; and (ii) the assistance team makes the recommendation to dismiss the principal. The Secretary may order the dismissal of a principal before the assistance team assigned to the principal's school has evaluated that principal if the Secretary determines from other available information that the low performance of the school is due to the principal's inadequate performance. The burden of proof is on the principal to establish that the factors leading to the school's low performance were not due to the principal's inadequate performance. The burden of proof is on the Secretary to establish that the school failed to make satisfactory improvement after an assistance team was assigned to the school. Two consecutive evaluations that include written findings and recommendations regarding that person's inadequate performance from the assistance team are substantial evidence of the inadequate performance of the principal. Within 15 days of the Secretary's decision concerning the principal, but no later than September 30, the Secretary shall submit to the State Board a written notice of the action taken and the basis for that action.

(b)   (Effective until July 1, 2014) At any time after the State Board identifies a school as low-performing under this Part, the Secretary shall proceed under G.S. 115C-325(p1) for the dismissal of certificated instructional personnel assigned to that school.

(b)   (Effective July 1, 2014 until June 30, 2018) At any time after the State Board identifies a school as low-performing under this Part, the State Board shall proceed under G.S. 115C-325(p1) or G.S. 115C-325.11 for the dismissal of licensed instructional personnel assigned to that school.

(b)   (Effective June 30, 2018) At any time after the State Board identifies a school as low-performing under this Part, the State Board shall proceed under

G.S. 115C-325.11 for the dismissal of licensed instructional personnel assigned to that school.

(c) At any time after the State Board identifies a school as low-performing under this Part, the Secretary shall proceed under the North Carolina Human Resources Act for the dismissal of instructional personnel who are not certificated when the Secretary receives two consecutive evaluations that include written findings and recommendations regarding that person's inadequate performance from the assistance team. These findings and recommendations shall be substantial evidence of the inadequate performance of the instructional personnel. The Secretary may proceed under the North Carolina Human Resources Act for the dismissal of instructional personnel who are not certificated when: (i) the Secretary determines that the school has failed to make satisfactory improvement after the State Board assigned an assistance team to that school; and (ii) that the assistance team makes the recommendation to dismiss that person for a reason that constitutes just cause for dismissal under the North Carolina Human Resources Act.

(d) The certificated instructional personnel working in a participating school at the time the school is identified by the State Board as low-performing are subject to G.S. 115C-105.38A.

(e) The Secretary may terminate the contract of a school administrator dismissed under this section. Nothing in this section shall prevent the Secretary from refusing to renew the contract of any person employed in a school identified as low-performing under this Part. (1998-131, s. 5; 2005-195, s. 5; 2013-360, s. 9.7(m), (w); 2013-382, s. 9.1(c).)

§ 143B-146.8. (Effective until July 1, 2014) Evaluation of certificated personnel and principals; action plans; State Board notification.

(a) Annual Evaluations; Low-Performing Schools. - The principal shall evaluate at least once each year all certificated personnel assigned to a participating school that has been identified as low-performing but has not received an assistance team. The evaluation shall occur early enough during the school year to provide adequate time for the development and implementation of an action plan if one is recommended under subsection (b) of this section. If the employee is a teacher as defined under G.S. 115C-325(a)(6), either the principal or an assessment team assigned under G.S. 143B-146.9 shall conduct the evaluation. If the employee is a school administrator as defined under G.S. 115C-287.1(a)(3), the Superintendent shall conduct the evaluation.

Notwithstanding this subsection or any other law, the principal shall observe at least three times annually, a teacher shall observe at least once annually, and the principal shall evaluate at least once annually, all teachers who have not attained career status. All other employees defined as teachers under G.S. 115C-325(a)(6) who are assigned to participating schools that are not designated as low-performing shall be evaluated annually unless the Secretary adopts rules that allow specified categories of teachers with career status to be evaluated more or less frequently. The Secretary also may adopt rules requiring the annual evaluation of noncertificated personnel. This section shall not be construed to limit the duties and authority of an assistance team assigned to a low-performing school.

The Secretary shall use the State Board's performance standards and criteria unless the Secretary develops an alternative evaluation that is properly validated and that includes standards and criteria similar to those adopted by the State Board. All other provisions of this section shall apply if an evaluation is used other than one adopted by the State Board.

(b) Action Plans. - If a certificated employee in a participating school that has been identified as low-performing receives an unsatisfactory or below standard rating on any function of the evaluation that is related to the employee's instructional duties, the individual or team that conducted the evaluation shall recommend to the principal that: (i) the employee receive an action plan designed to improve the employee's performance; or (ii) the principal recommend to the Secretary that the employee be dismissed or demoted. The principal shall determine whether to develop an action plan or to recommend a dismissal proceeding. The person who evaluated the employee or the employee's supervisor shall develop the action plan unless an assistance team or assessment team conducted the evaluation. If an assistance team or assessment team conducted the evaluation, that team shall develop the action plan in collaboration with the employee's supervisor. Action plans shall be designed to be completed within 90 instructional days or before the beginning of the next school year. The State Board, in consultation with the Secretary, shall develop guidelines that include strategies to assist in evaluating certificated personnel and developing effective action plans within the time allotted under this section. The Secretary may adopt policies for the development and implementation of action plans or professional development plans for personnel who do not require action plans under this section.

(c) Reevaluation. - Upon completion of an action plan under subsection (b) of this section, the principal or the assessment team shall evaluate the employee a second time. If on the second evaluation the employee receives one unsatisfactory or more than one below standard rating on any function that is related to the employee's instructional duties, the principal shall recommend that the employee be dismissed or demoted under G.S. 115C-325. The results of the second evaluation shall constitute substantial evidence of the employee's inadequate performance.

(d) State Board Notification. - If the Secretary dismisses an employee for any reason except a reduction in force under G.S. 115C-325(e)(1)l., the Secretary shall notify the State Board of the action, and the State Board annually shall provide to all local boards of education the names of those individuals. If a local board hires one of these individuals, that local board shall proceed under G.S. 115C-333(d).

(e) Civil Immunity. - There shall be no liability for negligence on the part of the Secretary or the State Board, or their employees, arising from any action taken or omission by any of them in carrying out this section. The immunity established by this subsection shall not extend to gross negligence, wanton conduct, or intentional wrongdoing that would otherwise be actionable. The immunity established by this subsection is waived to the extent of indemnification by insurance, indemnification under Articles 31A and 31B of Chapter 143 of the General Statutes, and to the extent sovereign immunity is waived under the Tort Claims Act, as set forth in Article 31 of Chapter 143 of the General Statutes.

(f) Evaluation of Principals. - Each year the Secretary or the Superintendent shall evaluate the principals. (1998-131, s. 5; 2005-195, s. 6.)

§ 143B-146.8. (Effective July 1, 2014 until June 30, 2018) Evaluation of licensed personnel and principals; action plans; State Board notification.

(a) Annual Evaluations; Low-Performing Schools. - The principal shall evaluate at least once each year all licensed personnel assigned to a participating school that has been identified as low-performing but has not received an assistance team. The evaluation shall occur early enough during the school year to provide adequate time for the development and implementation of an action plan if one is recommended under subsection (b) of this section. If the employee is a teacher as defined under G.S. 115C-325(a)(6) with career status or a teacher as defined in G.S. 115C-325.1(6) on contract, either the principal or an assessment team assigned under G.S. 143B-146.9 shall conduct the evaluation. If the employee is a school administrator as defined under G.S. 115C-287.1(a)(3), the Superintendent shall conduct the evaluation.

Notwithstanding this subsection or any other law, the principal shall observe at least three times annually, a teacher shall observe at least once annually, and the principal shall evaluate at least once annually, all teachers who have been employed for less than three consecutive years. All other employees defined as teachers under G.S. 115C-325(a)(6) with career status or teachers as defined in G.S. 115C-325.1(6) on a four-year contract who are assigned to participating schools that are not designated as low-performing shall be evaluated annually unless the State Board adopts rules that allow specified categories of teachers with career status or on four-year contracts to be evaluated more or less frequently. The State Board also may adopt rules requiring the annual evaluation of nonlicensed personnel. This section shall not be construed to limit the duties and authority of an assistance team assigned to a low-performing school.

(b)   Action Plans. - If a licensed employee in a participating school that has been identified as low-performing receives an unsatisfactory or below standard rating on any function of the evaluation that is related to the employee's instructional duties, the individual or team that conducted the evaluation shall recommend to the principal that: (i) the employee receive an action plan designed to improve the employee's performance; or (ii) the principal recommend that the employee who is a career teacher be dismissed or demoted as provided in G.S. 115C-325 or the employee who is a teacher on contract not be recommended for renewal; or (iii) if the employee who is a teacher on contract engages in inappropriate conduct or performs inadequately to such a degree that such conduct or performance causes substantial harm to the educational environment that a proceeding for immediate dismissal or demotion under G.S. 115C-325.4 be instituted. The principal shall determine whether to develop an action plan, to not recommend renewal of the employee's contract, or to recommend a dismissal proceeding. The person who evaluated the employee or the employee's supervisor shall develop the action plan unless an assistance team or assessment team conducted the evaluation. If an assistance team or assessment team conducted the evaluation, that team shall develop the action plan in collaboration with the employee's supervisor. Action plans shall be designed to be completed within 90 instructional days or before the beginning of the next school year. The State Board shall develop guidelines that include strategies to assist in evaluating licensed personnel and developing effective action plans within the time allotted under this section. The State Board may adopt policies for the development and implementation of action plans or professional development plans for personnel who do not require action plans under this section.

(c) Reevaluation. - Upon completion of an action plan under subsection (b) of this section, the principal or the assessment team shall evaluate the employee a second time. If on the second evaluation the employee receives one unsatisfactory or more than one below standard rating on any function that is related to the employee's instructional duties, the principal shall recommend that the employee with career status be dismissed or demoted under G.S. 115C-325, or that an employee's contract not be renewed or if the employee engages in inappropriate conduct or performs inadequately to such a degree that such conduct or performance causes substantial harm to the educational environment, that the employee be dismissed or demoted under G.S. 115C-325.4. The results of the second evaluation shall constitute substantial evidence of the employee's inadequate performance.

(d) State Board Notification. - If an employee is dismissed for cause or an employee's contract is not renewed as a result of a superintendent's recommendation under subsection (b) or (c) of this section, the State Board shall be notified of the action, and the State Board annually shall provide to all local boards of education the names of those individuals. If a local board hires one of these individuals, that local board shall proceed under G.S. 115C-333(d).

(e) Civil Immunity. - There shall be no liability for negligence on the part of the Secretary or the State Board, or their employees, arising from any action taken or omission by any of them in carrying out this section. The immunity established by this subsection shall not extend to gross negligence, wanton conduct, or intentional wrongdoing that would otherwise be actionable. The immunity established by this subsection is waived to the extent of indemnification by insurance, indemnification under Articles 31A and 31B of Chapter 143 of the General Statutes, and to the extent sovereign immunity is waived under the Tort Claims Act, as set forth in Article 31 of Chapter 143 of the General Statutes.

(f) Evaluation of Principals. - Each year the Secretary shall evaluate the principals. (1998-131, s. 5; 2005-195, s. 6; 2013-247, s. 6; 2013-360, s. 9.7(n).)

§ 143B-146.8. (Effective June 30, 2018) Evaluation of licensed personnel and principals; action plans; State Board notification.

(a) Annual Evaluations; Low-Performing Schools. - The principal shall evaluate at least once each year all licensed personnel assigned to a participating school that has been identified as low-performing but has not received an assistance team. The evaluation shall occur early enough during the school year to provide adequate time for the development and implementation of an action plan if one is recommended under subsection (b) of this section. If the employee is a teacher as defined in G.S. 115C-325.1(6), either the principal or an assessment team assigned under G.S. 143B-146.9 shall conduct the evaluation. If the employee is a school administrator as defined under G.S. 115C-287.1(a)(3), the Superintendent shall conduct the evaluation.

Notwithstanding this subsection or any other law, the principal shall observe at least three times annually, a teacher shall observe at least once annually, and the principal shall evaluate at least once annually, all teachers who have been employed for less than three consecutive years. All other employees who have been employed for three or more years and are defined as teachers under G.S. 115C-325.1(6) who are assigned to participating schools that are not designated as low-performing shall be evaluated annually unless the State Board adopts rules that allow specified categories of teachers with three or more years employment to be evaluated more or less frequently. The State Board also may adopt rules requiring the annual evaluation of nonlicensed personnel. This section shall not be construed to limit the duties and authority of an assistance team assigned to a low-performing school.

(b) Action Plans. - If a licensed employee in a participating school that has been identified as low-performing receives an unsatisfactory or below standard rating on any function of the evaluation that is related to the employee's instructional duties, the individual or team that conducted the evaluation shall recommend to the principal that: (i) the employee receive an action plan designed to improve the employee's performance; or (ii) the employee's contract not be recommended for renewal; or (iii) if the employee who is a teacher on contract engages in inappropriate conduct or performs inadequately to such a degree that such conduct or performance causes substantial harm to the educational environment that a proceeding for immediate dismissal or demotion under G.S. 115C-325.4 be instituted. The principal shall determine whether to develop an action plan, to not recommend renewal of the employee's contract, or to recommend a dismissal proceeding. The person who evaluated the employee or the employee's supervisor shall develop the action plan unless an assistance team or assessment team conducted the evaluation. If an assistance team or assessment team conducted the evaluation, that team shall develop the action plan in collaboration with the employee's supervisor. Action plans shall be designed to be completed within 90 instructional days or before the beginning of the next school year. The State Board shall develop guidelines that include strategies to assist in evaluating licensed personnel and developing effective action plans within the time allotted under this section. The State Board may adopt policies for the development and implementation of action plans or professional development plans for personnel who do not require action plans under this section.

(c) Reevaluation. - Upon completion of an action plan under subsection (b) of this section, the principal or the assessment team shall evaluate the employee a second time. If on the second evaluation the employee receives one unsatisfactory or more than one below standard rating on any function that is related to the employee's instructional duties, the principal shall recommend that the employee's contract not be renewed, or if the employee engages in inappropriate conduct or performs inadequately to such a degree that such conduct or performance causes substantial harm to the educational environment, that the employee be dismissed or demoted under G.S. 115C-325.4. The results of the second evaluation shall constitute substantial evidence of the employee's inadequate performance.

(d) State Board Notification. - If an employee is dismissed for cause or an employee's contract is not renewed as a result of a superintendent's recommendation under subsection (b) or (c) of this section, the State Board shall be notified of the action, and the State Board annually shall provide to all local boards of education the names of those individuals. If a local board hires one of these individuals, that local board shall proceed under G.S. 115C-333(d).

(e) Civil Immunity. - There shall be no liability for negligence on the part of the Secretary or the State Board, or their employees, arising from any action taken or omission by any of them in carrying out this section. The immunity established by this subsection shall not extend to gross negligence, wanton conduct, or intentional wrongdoing that would otherwise be actionable. The immunity established by this subsection is waived to the extent of indemnification by insurance, indemnification under Articles 31A and 31B of Chapter 143 of the General Statutes, and to the extent sovereign immunity is waived under the Tort Claims Act, as set forth in Article 31 of Chapter 143 of the General Statutes.

(f) Evaluation of Principals. - Each year the Secretary shall evaluate the principals. (1998-131, s. 5; 2005-195, s. 6; 2013-247, s. 6; 2013-360, s. 9.7(n), (x).)

§ 143B-146.9. Assessment teams.

The State Board shall develop guidelines for the Secretary to use to create assessment teams. The Secretary shall assign an assessment team to every low-performing school that has not received an assistance team. The Secretary shall ensure that assessment team members are trained in the proper administration of the employee evaluation used in the participating schools. If service on an assessment team is an additional duty for an employee of a local school administrative unit or an employee of a residential school, the Secretary may pay the employee for that additional work.

Assessment teams shall:

(1) Conduct evaluations of certificated personnel in low-performing schools;

(2) Provide technical assistance and training to principals who conduct evaluations of certificated personnel;

(3) Develop action plans for certificated personnel; and

(4) Assist principals in the development and implementation of action plans. (1998-131, s. 5; 2005-195, s. 7.)

§ 143B-146.10. Development of performance standards and criteria for certificated personnel.

The State Board, in consultation with the Secretary, shall revise and develop uniform performance standards and criteria to be used in evaluating certificated personnel, including school administrators. These standards and criteria shall include improving student achievement, employee skills, and employee knowledge. The standards and criteria for school administrators also shall include building-level gains in student learning and effectiveness in providing for school safety and enforcing student discipline. The Secretary shall develop guidelines for evaluating principals. The guidelines shall include criteria for evaluating a principal's effectiveness in providing safe schools and enforcing student discipline. (1998-131, s. 5; 2005-195, s. 8.)

§ 143B-146.11. School calendar.

Each school shall adopt a school calendar that includes a minimum of 180 days and 1,000 hours of instruction covering at least nine calendar months. In the development of its school calendar, each school shall consult with parents, the residential school personnel, and the local school administrative unit in which that school is located. (1998-131, s. 5.)

§ 143B-146.12: Repealed by Session Laws 2011-145, s. 7.13(v), effective July 1, 2011.

§ 143B-146.13. School technology plan.

(a) No later than December 15, 1998, the Secretary shall develop a school technology plan for the residential schools that meets the requirements of the State school technology plan. In developing a school technology plan, the Secretary is encouraged to coordinate its planning with other agencies of State and local government, including local school administrative units.

The Office of Information Technology Services shall assist the Secretary in developing the parts of the plan related to its technological aspects, to the extent that resources are available to do so. The Department of Public Instruction shall assist the Secretary in developing the instructional and technological aspects of the plan.

The Secretary shall submit the plan that is developed to the Office of Information Technology Services for its evaluation of the parts of the plan related to its technological aspects and to the Department of Public Instruction for its evaluation of the instructional aspects of the plan. The State Board of Education, after consideration of the evaluations of the Office of Information Technology Services and the Department of Public Instruction, shall approve all plans that comply with the requirements of the State school technology plan.

(b) After a plan is approved by the State Board of Education, all funds spent for technology in the residential schools shall be used to implement the school technology plan. (1998-131, s. 5; 2004-129, s. 45.)

§ 143B-146.14. Dispute resolution; appeals to Secretary.

The Secretary shall establish a procedure for the resolution of disputes between the residential schools and the parents or guardians of students who attend the schools.

An appeal shall lie from the decision of all residential school personnel to the Secretary or the Secretary's designee. In all of these appeals it is the duty of the Secretary to see that a proper notice is given to all parties concerned and that a record of the hearing is properly entered in the records. (1998-131, s. 5.)

§ 143B-146.15. Duty to report certain acts to law enforcement.

When the principal has personal knowledge or actual notice from residential school personnel or other reliable source that an act has occurred on school property involving assault resulting in serious personal injury, sexual assault, sexual offense, rape, kidnapping, indecent liberties with a minor, assault involving the use of a weapon, possession of a firearm in violation of the law, possession of a weapon in violation of the law, or possession of a controlled substance in violation of the law, the principal shall immediately report the act to the appropriate local law enforcement agency. Failure to report under this section is a Class 3 misdemeanor. For purposes of this section, "school property" shall include any building, bus, campus, grounds, recreational area, or athletic field, in the charge of the principal or while the student is under the supervision of school personnel. It is the intent of the General Assembly that the principal notify the Secretary of any report made to law enforcement under this section. (1998-131, s. 5; 2005-195, s. 10; 2013-247, s. 7.)

§ 143B-146.16. Residential school personnel criminal history checks.

(a) As used in this section:

(1) "Criminal history" means a county, state, or federal criminal history of conviction of a crime, whether a misdemeanor or a felony, that indicates the

employee (i) poses a threat to the physical safety of students or personnel, or (ii) has demonstrated that he or she does not have the integrity or honesty to fulfill his or her duties as school personnel. Such crimes include the following North Carolina crimes contained in any of the following Articles of Chapter 14 of the General Statutes: Article 5A, Endangering Executive and Legislative Officers; Article 6, Homicide; Article 7A, Rape and Kindred Offenses; Article 8, Assaults; Article 10, Kidnapping and Abduction; Article 13, Malicious Injury or Damage by Use of Explosive or Incendiary Device or Material; Article 14, Burglary and Other Housebreakings; Article 15, Arson and Other Burnings; Article 16, Larceny; Article 17, Robbery; Article 18, Embezzlement; Article 19, False Pretense and Cheats; Article 19A, Obtaining Property or Services by False or Fraudulent Use of Credit Device or Other Means; Article 20, Frauds; Article 21, Forgery; Article 26, Offenses Against Public Morality and Decency; Article 26A, Adult Establishments; Article 27, Prostitution; Article 28, Perjury; Article 29, Bribery; Article 31, Misconduct in Public Office; Article 35, Offenses Against the Public Peace; Article 36A, Riots, Civil Disorders, and Emergencies; Article 39, Protection of Minors; and Article 60, Computer-Related Crime. Such crimes also include possession or sale of drugs in violation of the North Carolina Controlled Substances Act, Article 5 of Chapter 90 of the General Statutes, and alcohol-related offenses such as sale to underage persons in violation of G.S. 18B-302 or driving while impaired in violation of G.S. 20-138.1 through G.S. 20-138.5. In addition to the North Carolina crimes listed in this subdivision, such crimes also include similar crimes under federal law or under the laws of other states.

(2) "Residential school personnel" means any:

a. Employee of a residential school whether full time or part time, or

b. Independent contractor or employee of an independent contractor of a residential school, if the independent contractor carries out duties customarily performed by residential school personnel,

whether paid with federal, State, local, or other funds, who has significant access to students in a residential school. Residential school personnel includes substitute teachers, driver training teachers, bus drivers, clerical staff, houseparents, and custodians.

(b) The Secretary shall require an applicant for a residential school personnel position to be checked for a criminal history before the applicant is offered an unconditional job. A residential school may employ an applicant conditionally while the Secretary is checking the person's criminal history and making a decision based on the results of the check.

The Secretary shall not require an applicant to pay for the criminal history check authorized under this subsection.

(c) The Department of Justice shall provide to the Secretary the criminal history from the State and National Repositories of Criminal Histories of any applicant for a residential school personnel position in a residential school. The Secretary shall require the person to be checked by the Department of Justice to (i) be fingerprinted and to provide any additional information required by the Department of Justice to a person designated by the Secretary, or to the local sheriff or the municipal police, whichever is more convenient for the person, and (ii) sign a form consenting to the check of the criminal record and to the use of fingerprints and other identifying information required by the repositories. The Secretary shall consider refusal to consent when making employment decisions and decisions with regard to independent contractors.

The Secretary shall not require an applicant to pay for being fingerprinted.

(d) The Secretary shall review the criminal history it receives on a person. The Secretary shall determine whether the results of the review indicate that the employee (i) poses a threat to the physical safety of students or personnel, or (ii) has demonstrated that he or she does not have the integrity or honesty to fulfill his or her duties as residential school personnel and shall use the information when making employment decisions and decisions with regard to independent contractors. The Secretary shall make written findings with regard to how it used the information when making employment decisions and decisions with regard to independent contractors.

(e) The Secretary shall provide to the State Board of Education the criminal history received on a person who is certificated, certified, or licensed by the State Board. The State Board shall review the criminal history and determine whether the person's certificate or license should be revoked in accordance with State laws and rules regarding revocation.

(f) All the information received by the Secretary through the checking of the criminal history or by the State Board in accordance with subsection (d) of this section is privileged information and is not a public record but is for the exclusive use of the Secretary or the State Board of Education. The Secretary or the State Board of Education may destroy the information after it is used for the purposes authorized by this section after one calendar year.

(g)   There shall be no liability for negligence on the part of the Secretary, the Department of Health and Human Services or its employees, a residential school or its employees, or the State Board of Education or its employees, arising from any act taken or omission by any of them in carrying out the provisions of this section. The immunity established by this subsection shall not extend to gross negligence, wanton conduct, or intentional wrongdoing that would otherwise be actionable. The immunity established by this subsection shall be deemed to have been waived to the extent of indemnification by insurance, indemnification under Articles 31A and 31B of Chapter 143 of the General Statutes, and to the extent sovereign immunity is waived under the Tort Claims Act, as set forth in Article 31 of Chapter 143 of the General Statutes. (1998-131, s. 5; 2012-12, s. 2(xx).)

§§ 143B-146.17 through 143B-146.20. Reserved for future codification purposes.

§ 143B-146.21. Policies, reports, and other miscellaneous provisions.

(a)   The Secretary of Health and Human Services shall consult with the State Board of Education in its implementation of this act as it pertains to improving the educational programs at the residential schools. The Secretary also shall fully inform and consult with the chairs of the Appropriations Subcommittees on Education and Health and Human Services of the Senate and the House of Representatives on a regular basis as the Secretary carries out his duties under this act.

(b)   Repealed by Session Laws 2013-247, s. 8, effective July 3, 2013.

(c)   The Department of Public Instruction, the Board of Governors of The University of North Carolina, and the State Board of Community Colleges shall offer and communicate the availability of professional development opportunities to the personnel assigned to the residential schools.

(d)   The Secretary of Health and Human Services shall adopt policies to ensure that students of the residential schools are given priority to residing in the independent living facilities on each school's campus.

(e) The Secretary of Health and Human Services, in consultation with the Office of State Human Resources, shall set the salary supplement paid to teachers, instructional support personnel, and school-based administrators who are employed in the programs operated by the Department of Health and Human Services and are licensed by the State Board of Education. The salary supplement shall be at least five percent (5%), but not more than the percentage supplement they would receive if they were employed in the local school administrative unit where the job site is located. These salary supplements shall not be paid to central office staff. Nothing in this subsection shall be construed to include "merit pay" under the term "salary supplement". (1998-131, ss. 3, 10, 17; 2001-424, s. 21.81(a); 2005-276, s. 29.19(a); 2013-247, s. 8; 2013-382, s. 9.1(c).)

§ 143B-146.22: Repealed by Session Laws 2001-424, s. 21.80(a).

§§ 143B-146.23 through 143B-146.27. Reserved for future codification purposes.

Part 4. Commission for Mental Health, Developmental Disabilities, and Substance Abuse Services.

§ 143B-147. Commission for Mental Health, Developmental Disabilities, and Substance Abuse Services - creation, powers and duties.

(a) There is hereby created the Commission for Mental Health, Developmental Disabilities, and Substance Abuse Services of the Department of Health and Human Services with the power and duty to adopt, amend and repeal rules to be followed in the conduct of State and local mental health, developmental disabilities, substance abuse programs including education, prevention, intervention, screening, assessment, referral, detoxification, treatment, rehabilitation, continuing care, emergency services, case management, and other related services. Such rules shall be designed to promote the amelioration or elimination of the mental illness, developmental disabilities, or substance abuse problems of the citizens of this State. Rules establishing standards for certification of child care centers providing Developmental Day programs are excluded from this section and shall be adopted by the Child Care Commission under G.S. 110-88. The Commission for

Mental Health, Developmental Disabilities, and Substance Abuse Services shall have the authority:

(1) To adopt rules regarding the

a. Admission, including the designation of regions, treatment, and professional care of individuals admitted to a facility operated under the authority of G.S. 122C-181(a), that is now or may be established;

b. Operation of education, prevention, intervention, treatment, rehabilitation and other related services as provided by area mental health, developmental disabilities, and substance abuse authorities, county programs, and all providers of public services under Part 4 of Article 4 of Chapter 122C of the General Statutes;

c. Hearings and appeals of area mental health, developmental disabilities, and substance abuse authorities as provided for in Part 4 of Article 4 of Chapter 122C of the General Statutes; and

d and e. Repealed by Session Laws 2001-437, s. 1.21(a), effective July 1, 2002.

f. Standards of public services for mental health, developmental disabilities, and substance abuse services.

(2) To adopt rules for the licensing of facilities for the mentally ill, developmentally disabled, and substance abusers, under Article 2 of Chapter 122C of the General Statutes. These rules shall include all of the following:

a. Standards for the use of electronic supervision devices during client sleep hours for facilities licensed under 10A NCAC 27G. 1700 or any related or subsequent regulations setting licensing standards for such facilities.

b. Personnel requirements for facilities licensed under 10A NCAC 27G. 1700, or any related or subsequent regulations setting licensing standards for such facilities, when continuous electronic supervision that meets the standards established under sub-subdivision a. of this of this subdivision is present.

(3) To advise the Secretary of the Department of Health and Human Services regarding the need for, provision and coordination of education,

prevention, intervention, treatment, rehabilitation and other related services in the areas of:

a. Mental illness and mental health,

b. Developmental disabilities,

c. Substance abuse.

d. Repealed by Session Laws 2001-437, s. 1.21(a), effective July 1, 2002.

(4) To review and advise the Secretary of the Department of Health and Human Services regarding all State plans required by federal or State law and to recommend to the Secretary any changes it thinks necessary in those plans; provided, however, for the purposes of meeting State plan requirements under federal or State law, the Department of Health and Human Services is designated as the single State agency responsible for administration of plans involving mental health, developmental disabilities, and substance abuse services.

(5) To adopt rules relating to the registration and control of the manufacture, distribution, security, and dispensing of controlled substances as provided by G.S. 90-100.

(6) To adopt rules to establish the professional requirements for staff of licensed facilities for the mentally ill, developmentally disabled, and substance abusers. Such rules may require that one or more, but not all staff of a facility be either licensed or certified. If a facility has only one professional staff, such rules may require that that individual be licensed or certified. Such rules may include the recognition of professional certification boards for those professions not licensed or certified under other provisions of the General Statutes provided that the professional certification board evaluates applicants on a basis which protects the public health, safety or welfare.

(7) Except where rule making authority is assigned under that Article to the Secretary of the Department of Health and Human Services, to adopt rules to implement Article 3 of Chapter 122C of the General Statutes.

(8) To adopt rules specifying procedures for waiver of rules adopted by the Commission.

(9) To adopt rules establishing a process for non-Medicaid eligible clients to appeal to the Division of Mental Health, Developmental Disabilities, and Substance Abuse Services of the Department of Health and Human Services decisions made by an area authority or county program affecting the client. The purpose of the appeal process is to ensure that mental health, developmental disabilities, and substance abuse services are delivered within available resources, to provide an additional level of review independent of the area authority or county program to ensure appropriate application of and compliance with applicable statutes and rules, and to provide additional opportunities for the area authority or county program to resolve the underlying complaint. Upon receipt of a written request by the non-Medicaid eligible client, the Division shall review the decision of the area authority or county program and shall advise the requesting client and the area authority or county program as to the Division's findings and the bases therefor. Notwithstanding Chapter 150B of the General Statutes, the Division's findings are not a final agency decision for purposes of that Chapter. Upon receipt of the Division's findings, the area authority or county program shall issue a final decision based on those findings. Nothing in this subdivision shall be construed to create an entitlement to mental health, developmental disabilities, and substance abuse services.

(10) The Commission for Mental Health, Developmental Disabilities, and Substance Abuse Services shall develop and adopt rules by December 1, 2013, to require forensic evaluators appointed pursuant to G.S. 15A-1002(b) to meet the following requirements:

a. Complete all training requirements necessary to be credentialed as a certified forensic evaluator.

b. Attend annual continuing education seminars that provide continuing education and training in conducting forensic evaluations and screening examinations of defendants to determine capacity to proceed and in preparing written reports required by law.

(b) All rules hereby adopted shall be consistent with the laws of this State and not inconsistent with the management responsibilities of the Secretary of the Department of Health and Human Services provided by this Chapter and the Executive Organization Act of 1973.

(c) All rules and regulations pertaining to the delivery of services and licensing of facilities heretofore adopted by the Commission for Mental Health and Mental Retardation Services, controlled substances rules and regulations adopted by the North Carolina Drug Commission, and all rules and regulations adopted by the Commission for Mental Health, Mental Retardation and Substance Abuse Services shall remain in full force and effect unless and until repealed or superseded by action of the Commission for Mental Health, Developmental Disabilities, and Substance Abuse Services.

(d) All rules adopted by the Commission for Mental Health, Developmental Disabilities, and Substance Abuse Services shall be enforced by the Department of Health and Human Services.

(e) The Commission for Mental Health, Developmental Disabilities, and Substance Abuse Services shall by December 1, 2013, adopt guidelines for treatment of individuals who are involuntarily committed following a determination of incapacity to proceed and a referral pursuant to G.S. 15A-1003. The guidelines shall require a treatment plan that uses best practices in an effort to restore the individual's capacity to proceed in the criminal matter. (1973, ch. 476, s. 129; 1977, c. 568, ss. 2, 3; c. 679, s. 1; 1981, c. 51, s. 1; 1983, c. 718, s. 5; 1983 (Reg. Sess., 1984), c. 1110, s. 6; 1985, c. 589, ss. 47-54; 1985 (Reg. Sess., 1986), c. 863, s. 33; 1989, c. 625, s. 23; 1991, c. 309, s. 1; 1993, c. 396, s. 6; 1997-443, s. 11A.118(a); 2001-437, s. 1.21(a); 2005-276, s. 10.35(a); 2009-187, s. 1; 2009-490, s. 6; 2013-18, ss. 9, 10.)

§ 143B-148. Commission for Mental Health, Developmental Disabilities, and Substance Abuse Services - members; selection; quorum; compensation.

(a) The Commission for Mental Health, Developmental Disabilities, and Substance Abuse Services of the Department of Health and Human Services shall consist of 32 members, as follows:

(1) Eight shall be appointed by the General Assembly, four upon the recommendation of the Speaker of the House of Representatives, and four upon the recommendation of the President Pro Tempore of the Senate in accordance with G.S. 120-121. In recommending appointments under this section, the Speaker of the House of Representatives and the President Pro Tempore of the Senate shall give consideration to ensuring a balance of appointments that represent those who may have knowledge and expertise in adult issues and those who may have knowledge and expertise in children's issues. Of the four appointments recommended by the President Pro Tempore of the Senate, one shall be an attorney licensed in this State with preference given to an attorney with experience in the practice of administrative law, one shall be a physician

licensed to practice medicine in North Carolina, with preference given to a psychiatrist, and two shall be members of the public. Of the four appointments recommended by the Speaker of the House of Representatives, one shall be an attorney licensed in this State with preference given to an attorney with experience in the practice of mental health law, one shall be a physician licensed to practice medicine in North Carolina who has expertise and experience in the field of developmental disabilities, or a professional holding a Ph.D. with experience in the field of developmental disabilities, and two shall be members of the public. Vacancies in appointments made by the General Assembly shall be filled in accordance with G.S. 120-122.

(2)   Twenty-four shall be appointed by the Governor, one from each congressional district in the State in accordance with G.S. 147-12(3)b, and the remainder at-large members.

The Governor's appointees shall represent the following categories of appointment:

a.   Three professionals licensed or certified under Chapter 90 or Chapter 90B of the General Statutes who are practicing, teaching, or conducting research in the field of mental health.

b.   Four consumers or immediate family members of consumers of mental health services. Of these four, at least one shall be a consumer and at least one shall be an immediate family member of a consumer. No more than two of the consumers or immediate family members shall be selected from nominations submitted by the Coalition 2001 or its successor organization.

c.   Two professionals licensed or certified under Chapter 90 or Chapter 90B of the General Statutes who are practicing, teaching, or conducting research in the field of developmental disabilities, and one individual who is a "qualified professional" as that term is defined in G.S. 122C-3(31) who has experience in the field of developmental disabilities.

d.   Four consumers or immediate family members of consumers of developmental disabilities services. Of these four, at least one shall be a consumer and at least one shall be an immediate family member of a consumer. No more than two of the consumers or immediate family members shall be selected from nominations submitted by the Coalition 2001 or its successor organization.

e. Two professionals licensed or certified under Chapter 90 of the General Statutes who are practicing, teaching, or conducting research in the field of substance abuse, and one professional who is a certified prevention specialist or who specializes in the area of addiction education.

f. An individual knowledgeable and experienced in the field of controlled substances regulation and enforcement. The controlled substances appointee shall be selected from recommendations made by the Attorney General of North Carolina.

g. A physician licensed to practice medicine in North Carolina who has expertise and experience in the field of substance abuse with preference given to a physician that is certified by the American Society of Addiction Medicine (ASAM).

h. Four consumers or immediate family members of consumers of substance abuse services. Of these four, at least one shall be a consumer and at least one shall be an immediate family member of a consumer. No more than two of the consumers or immediate family members shall be selected from nominations submitted by the Coalition 2001 or its successor organization.

i. An attorney licensed in this State. The appointments of professionals licensed or certified under Chapter 90 or Chapter 90B of the General Statutes made in accordance with this subdivision, and physicians appointed in accordance with subdivision (1) of this subsection shall be selected from nominations submitted to the appointing authority by the respective professional associations.

(2a) The terms of all Commission members shall be three years. All Commission members shall serve their designated terms and until their successors are duly appointed and qualified. All Commission members may succeed themselves. A member appointed on and after July 1, 2002, shall not serve more than two consecutive terms.

(3) All appointments shall be made pursuant to current federal rules and regulations, when not inconsistent with State law, which prescribe the selection process and demographic characteristics as a necessary condition to the receipt of federal aid.

(b) Except as otherwise provided in this section, the provisions of G.S. 143B-13 through 143B-20 relating to appointment, qualifications, terms and removal of members shall apply to all members of the Commission for Mental Health, Developmental Disabilities, and Substance Abuse Services.

(c)   Commission members shall receive per diem, travel and subsistence allowances in accordance with G.S. 138-5 and G.S. 138-6, as appropriate.

(d)   A majority of the Commission shall constitute a quorum for the transaction of business.

(e)   All clerical and other services required by the Commission shall be supplied by the Secretary of the Department of Health and Human Services. To ensure effective and efficient coordination of rules and policies adopted by the Commission and the Secretary, the Secretary shall assign an individual who is knowledgeable about and experienced in the rule-making processes of the Commission and the Secretary and in the fields of mental health, developmental disabilities, and substance abuse to assist the Commission in carrying out its duties and responsibilities. (1973, c. 476, s. 130; 1977, c. 679, s. 2; 1981, c. 51, s. 1; 1981 (Reg. Sess., 1982), c. 1191, ss. 55.1 through 57; 1989, c. 625, s. 23; 1991 (Reg. Sess., 1992), c. 1038, s. 17; 1995, c. 490, s. 34; 1997-443, s. 11A.118(a); 2001-437, s. 1.21(b); 2001-486, s. 2.13; 2001-487, s. 90.5; 2002-61, s. 1; 2007-504, s. 2.5(a).)

§ 143B-149. Commission for Mental Health, Developmental Disabilities, and Substance Abuse Services - officers.

The Commission for Mental Health, Developmental Disabilities, and Substance Abuse Services shall have a chairman and a vice-chairman. The chairman shall be designated by the Governor from among the members and shall serve as chairman at his pleasure. The vice-chairman shall be elected by and from the members of the Commission and shall serve for a term of two years or until the expiration of his regularly appointed term. (1973, c. 476, s. 131; 1977, c. 679, s. 3; 1981, c. 51, s. 1; 1989, c. 625, s. 23.)

§ 143B-150. Commission for Mental Health, Developmental Disabilities, and Substance Abuse Services - regular and special meetings.

The Commission for Mental Health, Developmental Disabilities, and Substance Abuse Services shall meet at least once in each quarter and may hold special meetings at any time and place within the State at the call of the chairman or upon the written request of at least eight members. (1973, c. 476, s. 132; 1977, c. 679, s. 4; 1981, c. 51, s. 1; 1989, c. 625, s. 23.)

§§ 143B-150.1 through 143B-150.4. Reserved for future codification purposes.

Part 4A. Family Preservation Act.

§ 143B-150.5. Family Preservation Services Program established; purpose.

(a) There is established the Family Preservation Services Program of the Department of Health and Human Services. To the extent that funds are made available, locally-based family preservation services shall be available to all 100 counties. The Secretary of the Department of Health and Human Services shall be responsible for the development and implementation of the Family Preservation Services Program as established in this Part.

(b) The purpose of the Family Preservation Services Program is, where feasible and in the best interests of the child and the family, to keep the family unit intact by providing intensive family-centered services that help create, within the family, positive, long-term changes in the home environment.

(c) Family preservation services shall be financed in part through grants to local agencies for the development and implementation of locally-based family preservation services. Grants to local agencies shall be made in accordance with the provisions of G.S. 143B-150.6.

(d) The Secretary of the Department of Health and Human Services shall ensure the cooperation of the Division of Social Services, the Division of Mental Health, Developmental Disabilities, and Substance Abuse Services, and the Division of Medical Assistance, in carrying out the provisions of this Part. (1991, c. 743, s. 1; 1997-443, s. 11A.118(a); 2000-137, s. 4(z); 2001-424, s. 21.50(f).)

§ 143B-150.6. Program services; eligibility; grants for local projects; fund transfers.

(a) Services: Services to be provided under the Family Preservation Services Program shall include but are not limited to: family assessment, intensive family and individual counseling, client advocacy, case management, development and enhancement of parenting skills, and referral for other services as appropriate.

(b) Eligibility: Families eligible for services under the Family Preservation Services Program are those with children ages 0-17 years who are at risk of imminent separation through placement in public welfare, mental health, or juvenile justice systems.

(c) Service Delivery: Services delivered to eligible families under the Family Preservation Services Program shall be provided in accordance with the following requirements:

(1) Each eligible family shall receive intensive family preservation services, beginning with identification of an imminent risk of out-of-home placement for an average of four weeks but not more than six weeks;

(2) At least one-half of a caseworker's time spent providing family preservation services to each eligible family shall be provided in the family's home and community;

(3) Family preservation caseworkers shall be available to each eligible family by telephone and on call for visits 24 hours a day, seven days a week.

(4) Each family preservation caseworker shall provide services to a maximum of four families at any given time.

(d) Grants for local projects: The Secretary of the Department of Health and Human Services shall award grants to local agencies for the development and implementation of locally-based family preservation services projects. The number of grants awarded and the level of funding of each grant for each fiscal year shall be contingent upon and determined by funds appropriated for that purpose by the General Assembly.

(e) Inter-agency fund transfers: The Department may allow the Division of Social Services and the Division of Mental Health, Developmental Disabilities, and Substance Abuse Services, to use funds available to each Division to support family preservation services provided by the Division under the Program; provided that such use does not violate federal regulations pertaining to, or otherwise jeopardize the availability of federal funds. (1991, c. 743, s. 1; 1997-443, s. 11A.118(a); 1999-423, s. 9; 2001-424, s. 21.50(g).)

§§ 143B-150.7 through 143B-150.9: Repealed by Session Laws 2001-424, ss. 21.50(h) to (j).

§§ 143B-150.10 through 143B-150.19. Reserved for future codification purposes.

Part 4B. State Child Fatality Review Team.

§ 143B-150.20. State Child Fatality Review Team; establishment; purpose; powers; duties; report by Division of Social Services.

(a) There is established in the Department of Health and Human Services, Division of Social Services, a State Child Fatality Review Team to conduct in-depth reviews of any child fatalities which have occurred involving children and families involved with local departments of social services child protective services in the 12 months preceding the fatality. Steps in this in-depth review shall include interviews with any individuals determined to have pertinent information as well as examination of any written materials containing pertinent information.

(b) The purpose of these reviews shall be to implement a team approach to identifying factors which may have contributed to conditions leading to the fatality and to develop recommendations for improving coordination between local and State entities which might have avoided the threat of injury or fatality and to identify appropriate remedies. The Division of Social Services shall make public the findings and recommendations developed for each fatality reviewed relating to improving coordination between local and State entities. These findings shall not be admissible as evidence in any civil or administrative proceedings against individuals or entities that participate in child fatality reviews conducted pursuant to this section. The State Child Fatality Review Team shall consult with the appropriate district attorney in accordance with G.S. 7B-2902(d) prior to the public release of the findings and recommendations.

(c) The State Child Fatality Review Team shall include representatives of the local departments of social services and the Division of Social Services, a member of the local Community Child Protection Team, a member of the local child fatality prevention team, a representative from local law enforcement, a prevention specialist, and a medical professional.

(d)   The State Child Fatality Review Team shall have access to all medical records, hospital records, and records maintained by this State, any county, or any local agency as necessary to carry out the purposes of this subsection, including police investigative data, medical examiner investigative data, health records, mental health records, and social services records. The State Child Fatality Review Team may receive a copy of any reviewed materials necessary to the conduct of the fatality review. Any member of the State Child Fatality Review Team may share, only in an official meeting of the State Child Fatality Review Team, any information available to that member that the State Child Fatality Review Team needs to carry out its duties.

If the State Child Fatality Review Team does not receive information requested under this subsection within 30 days after making the request, the State Child Fatality Review Team may apply for an order compelling disclosure. The application shall state the factors supporting the need for an order compelling disclosure. The State Child Fatality Review Team shall file the application in the district court of the county where the investigation is being conducted, and the court shall have jurisdiction to issue any orders compelling disclosure. Actions brought under this section shall be scheduled for immediate hearing, and subsequent proceedings in these actions shall be given priority by the appellate courts.

(e)   Meetings of the State Child Fatality Review Team are not subject to the provisions of Article 33C of Chapter 143 of the General Statutes. However, the State Child Fatality Review Team may hold periodic public meetings to discuss, in a general manner not revealing confidential information about children and families, the findings of their reviews and their recommendations for preventive actions. Minutes of all public meetings, excluding those of closed sessions, shall be kept in compliance with Article 33C of Chapter 143 of the General Statutes. Any minutes or any other information generated during any executive session shall be sealed from public inspection.

(f)   All otherwise confidential information and records acquired by the State Child Fatality Review Team, in the exercise of its duties are confidential; are not subject to discovery or introduction into evidence in any proceedings except pursuant to an order of the court; and may only be disclosed as necessary to carry out the purposes of the State Child Fatality Review Team. In addition, all otherwise confidential information and records created by the State Child Fatality Review Team in the exercise of its duties are confidential; are not subject to discovery or introduction into evidence in any proceedings; and may only be disclosed as necessary to carry out the purposes of the State Child

Fatality Review Team. No member of the State Child Fatality Review Team, nor any person who attends a meeting of the State Child Fatality Review Team, may testify in any proceeding about what transpired at the meeting, about information presented at the meeting, or about opinions formed by the person as a result of the meetings. This subsection shall not, however, prohibit a person from testifying in a civil or criminal action about matters within that person's independent knowledge.

(g)   Each member of the State Child Fatality Review Team and invited participant shall sign a statement indicating an understanding of and adherence to confidentiality requirements, including the possible civil or criminal consequences of any breach of confidentiality.

(h)   Repealed by Session Laws 2013-360, s. 12A.8(f), effective July 1, 2013. (1998-202, s. 13(oo); 1998-212, s. 12.22(e); 1999-190, s. 4; 2000-67, s. 11.14(a); 2003-304, s. 6; 2013-360, s. 12A.8(f).)

Part 5. Eugenics Commission.

§§ 143B-151 through 143B-152: Repealed by Session Laws 1977, c. 497.

Part 5A. S.O.S. Program.

§ 143B-152.1: Repealed by Session Laws 2009-451, s. 18.6, as amended by Session Laws 2010-123, s. 6.2, effective July 1, 2009.

§ 143B-152.2: Repealed by Session Laws 2009-451, s. 18.6, as amended by Session Laws 2010-123, s. 6.2, effective July 1, 2009.

§ 143B-152.3: Repealed by Session Laws 2009-451, s. 18.6, as amended by Session Laws 2010-123, s. 6.2, effective July 1, 2009.

§ 143B-152.4: Repealed by Session Laws 2009-451, s. 18.6, as amended by Session Laws 2010-123, s. 6.2, effective July 1, 2009.

§ 143B-152.5: Repealed by Session Laws 2009-451, s. 18.6, as amended by Session Laws 2010-123, s. 6.2, effective July 1, 2009.

§ 143B-152.6: Repealed by Session Laws 2009-451, s. 18.6, as amended by Session Laws 2010-123, s. 6.2, effective July 1, 2009.

§ 143B-152.7: Repealed by Session Laws 2009-451, s. 18.6, as amended by Session Laws 2010-123, s. 6.2, effective July 1, 2009.

§ 143B-152.8. Reserved for future codification purposes.

§ 143B-152.9. Reserved for future codification purposes.

Part 5B. Family Resource Center Grant Program.

§ 143B-152.10. Family Resource Center Grant Program; creation; purpose; intent.

(a)   There is created in the Department of Health and Human Services the Family Resource Center Grant Program. The purpose of the program is to provide grants to implement family support programs that are research-based and have been evaluated for effectiveness that provide services to children from birth through 17 years of age and to their families that:

(1)   Enhance the children's development and ability to attain academic and social success;

(1a)   Prevent child abuse and neglect by implementing program models that have been evaluated and found to improve outcomes for children and families;

(2)   Ensure a successful transition from early childhood education programs and child care to the public schools;

(3)   Assist families in achieving economic independence and self-sufficiency; and

(4)   Mobilize public and private community resources to help children and families in need.

(b)   It is the intent of the General Assembly to encourage and support broad-based collaboration among public and private agencies and among people who reflect the racial and socioeconomic diversity in communities to develop initiatives that (i) improve outcomes for children by preventing child abuse and neglect, (ii) enhance and strengthen the ability of families to ensure the safety, health, and well-being of their children, (iii) enhance the ability of families to become advocates for and supporters of the children in their families, and (iv) enhance the ability of families to function as nurturing and effective family units.

(c)   It is further the intent of the General Assembly that this program shall be targeted to those neighborhoods that have disproportionately high levels of (i) children who would be less likely to attain educational or social success, (ii) families with low incomes, and (iii) crime and juvenile delinquency. (1994, Ex. Sess., c. 24, s. 31(a); 1997-443, s. 11A.118(a); 2007-130, s. 1.)

§ 143B-152.11. Administration of program.

The Department of Health and Human Services shall develop and implement the Family Resource Center Grant Program. The Department shall:

(1)   Sponsor a statewide conference for teams of interested representatives to provide background information and assistance regarding all aspects of the program;

(2)   Disseminate information regarding the program to interested local community groups;

(3)   Provide initial technical assistance and ongoing technical assistance to grant recipients;

(4)   Administer funds appropriated by the General Assembly;

(5)   Monitor the grants funded and the ongoing operations of family resource centers;

(6)   Revoke a grant if necessary or appropriate;

(7)   Report to the General Assembly and the Joint Legislative Commission on Governmental Operations, in accordance with G.S. 143B-152.15; and

(8)   Adopt rules to implement this Part. (1994, Ex. Sess., c. 24, s. 31(a); 1997-443, s. 11A.118(a).)

§ 143B-152.12. Eligible applicants: applications for grants.

(a) A community-or neighborhood-based 501(c)(3) entity or a consortium consisting of one or more local 501(c)(3) entities and one or more local school administrative units may apply for a grant.

(b) Applicants for grants shall identify the neighborhood or neighborhoods whose children and families will be served by a family resource center. The decision-making process for identifying and establishing family resource centers shall reflect the racial and socioeconomic diversity of the neighborhood or neighborhoods to be served.

(c) A grant application shall include a process for assessing on an annual basis the success of the local plan in addressing problems. (1994, Ex. Sess., c. 24, s. 31(a).)

§ 143B-152.13. Grants review and selection.

(a) The Department shall develop and disseminate a request for applications and establish procedures to be followed in developing and submitting applications to establish local family resource centers and administering grants to establish local family resource centers.

(b) The Secretary of Health and Human Services shall appoint a State task force to assist the Secretary in reviewing grant applications. The State task force shall include representatives of the Department of Health and Human Services, the Department of Public Instruction, local school administrative units, educators, parents, the juvenile justice system, social services, and governmental agencies providing services to children, and other members the Secretary considers appropriate. In appointing the State task force, the Secretary shall consult with the Superintendent of Public Instruction in an effort to coordinate the membership of this State task force, the State task force appointed by the Secretary pursuant to G.S. 143B-152.5, and the State task force appointed by the Superintendent pursuant to G.S. 115C-238.42.

In reviewing grant applications, the Secretary and the State task force may consider (i) the severity of the local problems as determined by the needs assessment data, (ii) the likelihood that the locally designed plan will result in high quality services for children and their families, (iii) evidence of local collaboration and coordination of services, (iv) any innovative or experimental aspects of the plan that will make it a useful model for replication in other counties, (v) the availability of other resources or funds, (vi) the incidence of crime and juvenile delinquency, (vii) the amount needed to implement the proposal, and (viii) any other factors consistent with the intent of this Part.

(c)   In determining the amount of funds an applicant receives, the Secretary and the State task force may consider (i) the number of children to be served, (ii) the number and percentage of children to be served who participate in the subsidized lunch program, (iii) the number and percentage of school-aged children to be served with two working parents or one single parent, (iv) the availability of other resources or funds, and (v) the amount needed to implement the proposal.

(d)   The Secretary shall award the grants. (1994, Ex. Sess., c. 24, s. 31(a); 1997-443, s. 11A.118(a).)

§ 143B-152.14. Cooperation of State and local agencies.

All agencies of the State and local government, including the Division of Juvenile Justice of the Department of Public Safety, departments of social services, health departments, local mental health, mental retardation, and substance abuse authorities, court personnel, law enforcement agencies, The University of North Carolina, the community college system, and cities and counties, shall cooperate with the Department of Health and Human Services, and local nonprofit corporations that receive grants in coordinating the program at the State level and in implementing the program at the local level. The Secretary of Health and Human Services, after consultation with the Superintendent of Public Instruction, shall develop a plan for ensuring the cooperation of State agencies and local agencies and encouraging the cooperation of private entities, especially those receiving State funds, in the coordination and implementation of the program. (1994, Ex. Sess., c. 24, s. 31(a); 1997-443, s. 11A.118(a); 1998-202, s. 4(y); 2000-137, s. 4(cc); 2011-145, s. 19.1(l).)

§ 143B-152.15. Program evaluation; reporting requirements.

(a)   The Department of Health and Human Services shall develop and implement an evaluation system that will assess the efficiency and effectiveness of the Family Resource Center Grant Program. The department shall design this system to:

(1) Provide information to the Department and to the General Assembly on how to improve and refine the programs;

(2) Enable the Department and the General Assembly to assess the overall quality, efficiency, and impact of the existing programs;

(3) Enable the Department and the General Assembly to determine whether to modify the Family Resource Center Grant Program; and

(4) Provide a detailed fiscal analysis of how State funds for these programs were used.

(b) Repealed by Session Laws 2013-360, s. 12A.8(b), effective July 1, 2013.

(c) A local 501(c)(3) entity or consortium that receives a grant under this Part shall report by August 1 of each year to the Department on the implementation of the program. This report shall demonstrate the extent to which the local family resource center has met the local needs, goals, and anticipated outcomes as set forth in the grant application. (1994, Ex. Sess., c. 24, s. 31(a); 1997-443, s. 11A.118(a); 2001-424, s. 21.48(f); 2013-360, s. 12A.8(b).)

Part 6. Social Services Commission.

§ 143B-153. Social Services Commission - creation, powers and duties.

There is hereby created the Social Services Commission of the Department of Health and Human Services with the power and duty to adopt rules and regulations to be followed in the conduct of the State's social service programs with the power and duty to adopt, amend, and rescind rules and regulations under and not inconsistent with the laws of the State necessary to carry out the provisions and purposes of this Article. Provided, however, the Department of Health and Human Services shall have the power and duty to adopt rules and regulations to be followed in the conduct of the State's medical assistance program.

(1) The Social Services Commission is authorized and empowered to adopt such rules and regulations that may be necessary and desirable for the programs administered by the Department of Health and Human Services as provided in Chapter 108A of the General Statutes of the State of North Carolina.

(2) The Social Services Commission shall have the power and duty to establish standards and adopt rules and regulations:

a. For the programs of public assistance established by federal legislation and by Article 2 of Chapter 108A of the General Statutes of the State of North Carolina with the exception of the program of medical assistance established by G.S. 108A-25(b);

b. To achieve maximum cooperation with other agencies of the State and with agencies of other states and of the federal government in rendering services to strengthen and maintain family life and to help recipients of public assistance obtain self-support and self-care;

c. For the placement and supervision of dependent juveniles and of delinquent juveniles who are placed in the custody of the Division of Juvenile Justice of the Department of Public Safety, and payment of necessary costs of foster home care for needy and homeless children as provided by G.S. 108A-48;

d. For the payment of State funds to private child-placing agencies as defined in G.S. 131D-10.2(4) and residential child care facilities as defined in G.S. 131D-10.2(13) for care and services provided to children who are in the custody or placement responsibility of a county department of social services. The Commission shall establish standardized rates for child caring institutions. In establishing standardized rates, the Commission shall consider the rate-setting recommendations provided by the Office of the State Auditor; and

e. For client assessment and independent case management pertaining to the functions of county departments of social services for public assistance programs authorized under paragraph a. of this subdivision.

(2a) The Social Services Commission shall have the power and duty to establish standards and adopt rules and regulations:

a. For social services programs established by federal legislation and by Article 3 of G.S. Chapter 108A;

b. For implementation of Title XX of the Social Security Act, except for Title XX services provided solely through the Division of Mental Health, Developmental Disabilities, and Substance Abuse Services, by promulgating rules and regulations in the following areas:

1. Eligibility for all services established under a Comprehensive Annual Services Plan, as required by federal law;

2. Standards to implement all services established under the Comprehensive Annual Services Plan;

3. Maximum rates of payment for provision of social services;

4. Fees for services to be paid by recipients of social services;

5. Designation of certain mandated services, from among the services established by the Secretary below, which shall be provided in each county of the State; and

6. Title XX services for the blind, after consultation with the Commission for the Blind.

Provided, that the Secretary is authorized to promulgate all other rules in at least the following areas:

1. Establishment, identification, and definition of all services offered under the Comprehensive Annual Services Plan;

2. Policies governing the allocation, budgeting, and expenditures of funds administered by the Department;

3. Contracting for and purchasing services; and

4. Monitoring for effectiveness and compliance with State and federal law and regulations.

(3) The Social Services Commission shall have the power and duty to establish and adopt standards:

a. For the inspection and licensing of maternity homes as provided by G.S. 131D-1;

b. Repealed by Session Laws 1999-334, s. 3.5, effective October 1, 1999.

c. For the inspection and licensing of child-care institutions as provided by G.S. 131D-10.5;

d. For the inspection and operation of jails or local confinement facilities as provided by G.S. 153A-220 and Article 2 of Chapter 131D of the General Statutes of the State of North Carolina;

e. Repealed by Session Laws 1981, c. 562, s. 7.

f. For the regulation and licensing of charitable organizations, professional fund-raising counsel and professional solicitors as provided by Chapter 131D of the General Statutes of the State of North Carolina.

(4) The Social Services Commission shall have the power and duty to authorize investigations of social problems, with authority to subpoena witnesses, administer oaths, and compel the production of necessary documents.

(5) The Social Services Commission shall have the power and duty to ratify reciprocal agreements with agencies in other states that are responsible for the administration of public assistance and child welfare programs to provide assistance and service to the residents and nonresidents of the State.

(6) The Commission is authorized and empowered to adopt such rules and regulations, not inconsistent with the laws of this State, as may be required by the federal government of grants-in-aid for social services purposes which may be made available for the State by the federal government. This section is to be liberally construed in order that the State and its citizens may benefit from such grants-in-aid.

(7) The Commission shall adopt rules and regulations consistent with the provisions of this Chapter. All rules and regulations not inconsistent with the provisions of this Chapter heretofore adopted by the Board of Social Services shall remain in full force and effect unless and until repealed or superseded by action of the Social Services Commission. All rules and regulations adopted by the Commission shall be enforced by the Department of Health and Human Services.

(8) The Commission may establish by regulation, except for Title XX services provided solely through the Division of Mental Health, Developmental Disabilities, and Substance Abuse Services, rates or fees for:

a. A fee schedule for the payment of the costs of necessary child care in licensed facilities and registered plans for minor children of needy families.

b. A fee schedule for the payment by recipients for services which are established in accordance with Title XX of the Social Security Act and implementing regulations; and

c. The payment of an administrative fee not to exceed two hundred dollars ($200.00) to be paid by public or nonprofit agencies which employ students under the Plan Assuring College Education (PACE) program.

d. Child support enforcement services as defined by G.S. 110-130.1. (1973, c. 476, s. 134; 1975, c. 747, s. 2; 1977, c. 674, s. 7; 1977, 2nd Sess., c. 1219, ss. 26, 27; 1981, c. 275, s. 5; c. 562, s. 7; c. 961, ss. 1-3; 1983, c. 278, ss. 1, 2; c. 527, s. 2; 1985, c. 206; c. 479, s. 96; c. 689, s. 29f; 1991, c. 462, s. 1; c. 636, s. 19(d); c. 689, s. 105; c. 761, s. 28; 1993, c. 553, s. 46; 1995, c. 449, s. 4; c. 535, s. 32; 1997-443, s. 11A.118(a); 1997-456, s. 22; 1997-506, s. 55; 1998-202, s. 4(z); 1999-334, s. 3.5; 2000-111, s. 4; 2000-137, s. 4(dd); 2000-140, s. 99(a); 2006-66, s. 10.2(c); 2011-145, s. 19.1(l).)

§ 143B-153.1. Repealed by Session Laws 1983, c. 883, s. 2, effective July 20, 1983.

§ 143B-154. Social Services Commission - members; selection; quorum; compensation.

The Social Services Commission of the Department of Health and Human Services shall consist of one member from each congressional district in the State, all of whom shall be appointed by the Governor for four-year terms.

The initial members of the Commission shall be the appointed members of the current Social Services Commission who shall serve for the remainder of their current terms and four additional members appointed by the Governor for terms expiring April 1, 1981. Any appointment to fill a vacancy on the Commission created by the resignation, dismissal, death, removal or disability of a member shall be for the balance of the unexpired term.

In the event that more than 11 congressional districts are established in the State, the Governor shall on July 1 following the establishment of such additional congressional districts appoint a member of the Commission from that congressional district.

The Governor shall have the power to remove any member of the Commission from office for misfeasance, malfeasance, or nonfeasance in accordance with the provisions of G.S. 143B-13 of the Executive Organization Act of 1973.

The members of the Commission shall receive per diem and necessary travel and subsistence expenses in accordance with the provisions of G.S. 138-5.

A majority of the Commission shall constitute a quorum for the transaction of business.

All clerical and other services required by the Commission shall be supplied by the Secretary of Health and Human Services. (1973, c. 476, s. 135; 1977, c. 516; 1981 (Reg. Sess., 1982), c. 1191, s. 77; 1997-443, s. 11A.118(a).)

§ 143B-155. Social Services Commission - regular and special meetings.

The Social Services Commission shall meet at least once in each quarter and may hold special meetings at any time and place within the State at the call of the chairman or upon the written request of at least four members. (1973, c. 476, s. 136.)

§ 143B-156. Social Services Commission - officers.

The Commission for Social Services shall have a chairman and a vice-chairman. The chairman shall be designated by the Governor from among the members of the Commission to serve as chairman at his pleasure. The vice-chairman shall be elected by and from the members of the Commission and shall serve for a term of two years or until the expiration of his regularly appointed term. (1973, c. 476, s. 137.)

Part 7. Commission for the Blind.

§ 143B-157. Commission for the Blind - creation, powers and duties.

There is recreated the Commission for the Blind of the Department of Health and Human Services with the power and duty to adopt rules governing the conduct of the State's rehabilitative programs for the blind that are necessary to carry out the provisions and purposes of this Article.

(1)   The Commission shall adopt rules that are necessary and desirable for the programs administered by the Department of Health and Human Services as provided in Chapter 111 of the General Statutes of North Carolina.

(2)   Repealed by Session Laws 1993, c. 561, s. 89(a).

(3)   The Commission shall adopt rules, not inconsistent with the laws of this State, that are required by the federal government for grants-in-aid for rehabilitative purposes for the blind that may be made available to the State from the federal government. This section is to be liberally construed in order that the State and its citizens may benefit from such grants-in-aid.

(3a)   The Commission shall review, analyze, and advise the Department regarding the performance of its responsibilities under the federal rehabilitation program in which the State participates, as it relates to the provision of services to the blind, particularly its responsibilities relating to the following:

a.   Eligibility for the program;

b.   The extent, scope, and effectiveness of the services provided; and

c.   The functions performed by the Department that affect, or that have the potential to affect, the ability of individuals who are blind or visually impaired to achieve rehabilitative goals and objectives under the federal rehabilitation program;

(3b)   The Commission shall advise the Department regarding preparation of applications, the State Plan, amendments to this plan, the State needs assessments, and the evaluations required by the federal rehabilitation program; and in partnership with the Department develop, agree to, and review State goals and priorities;

(3c) The Commission shall, to the extent feasible, conduct a review and analysis (i) of the effectiveness of, and consumer satisfaction with, the functions performed by the Department and other public and private entities responsible for performing functions for individuals who are blind or visually impaired, and (ii) of vocational rehabilitation services provided or paid for from funds made available through other public or private sources and provided by State agencies and other public and private entities responsible for providing vocational rehabilitation services to individuals who are blind or visually impaired;

(3d) The Commission shall prepare and submit an annual report to the Governor, the Secretary, and the federal rehabilitation program, and make the report available to the public;

(3e) The Commission shall coordinate with other councils within the State, including the statewide Independent Living Council established under section 705 of the federal Rehabilitation Act, 29 U.S.C. § 720, et seq., the advisory panel established under section 612(a)(21) of the Individuals with Disabilities Education Act, 20 U.S.C. § 1413(A)(12), the Council on Developmental Disabilities described in section 124 of the Developmental Disabilities Assistance and Bill of Rights Act, 42 U.S.C. § 6024, the State Mental Health Planning Council established pursuant to section 1916(e) of the Public Health Service Act, 42 U.S.C. § 300x-4(e), and the Commission on Workforce Development;

(3f) The Commission shall advise the Department and provide for coordination with, and establishment of working relationships between, the Department and the Independent Living Council;

(3g) The Commission shall prepare, in conjunction with the Department, a plan for the provision of those resources, including staff and other personnel, that are necessary to carry out the Commission's function under this Part. The resource plan shall, to the maximum extent possible, rely on the use of resources in existence during the period of implementation of the plan. The agreed-upon resources shall be provided pursuant to G.S. 143B-14. To the extent that there is a disagreement between the Commission and the Department with regard to the resources necessary to carry out the functions of the Commission required by this Part, the Governor shall resolve the disagreement. The Department or other State agency shall not assign any other duties to the staff and other personnel who are assisting the Commission in carrying out its duties that would create a conflict of interest;

(4)   The Commission shall adopt rules consistent with the provisions of this Chapter. All rules not inconsistent with the provisions of this Chapter heretofore adopted by the North Carolina State Commission for the Blind shall remain in full force and effect unless and until repealed or superseded by action of the recreated Commission for the Blind. All rules adopted by the Commission shall be enforced by the Department of Health and Human Services. (1973, c. 476, s. 139; 1993, c. 561, s. 89(a); 1997-443, s. 11A.118(a); 2000-121, ss. 29, 30.)

§ 143B-158. Commission for the Blind.

(a)   The Commission for the Blind of the Department of Health and Human Services shall consist of 19 members as follows:

(1)   One representative of the Statewide Independent Living Council.

(2)   One representative of a parent training and information center established pursuant to section 631(c) of the Individuals with Disabilities Education Act, 20 U.S.C. § 1431(c).

(3)   One representative of the State's Client Assistance Program.

(4)   One vocational rehabilitation counselor who has knowledge of and experience in vocational rehabilitation services for the blind. A vocational rehabilitation counselor appointed pursuant to this subdivision shall serve as a nonvoting member of the Commission if the counselor is an employee of the Department of Health and Human Services.

(5)   One representative of community rehabilitation program services providers.

(6)   One current or former applicant for, or recipient of, vocational rehabilitation services.

(7)   One representative of a disability advocacy group representing individuals who are blind.

(8)   One parent, family member, guardian, advocate, or authorized representative of an individual who is blind, has multiple disabilities, and either has difficulty representing himself or herself or who is unable, due to disabilities, to represent himself or herself.

(9)   One representative of business, industry, and labor.

(10)   One representative of the directors of projects carried out under section 121 of the Rehabilitation Act of 1973, 29 U.S.C. § 741, as amended, if there are any of these projects in the State.

(11)   One representative of the Department of Public Instruction.

(12)   One representative of the Commission on Workforce Development.

(12a)   Two licensed physicians nominated by the North Carolina Medical Society whose practice is limited to ophthalmology.

(12b)   Two optometrists nominated by the North Carolina State Optometric Society.

(12c)   Two opticians nominated by the North Carolina Opticians Association.

(13)   The Director of the Division of Services for the Blind shall serve as an ex officio, nonvoting member.

(b)   The members of the Commission for the Blind shall be appointed by the Governor. The Governor shall appoint members after soliciting recommendations from representatives of organizations representing a broad range of individuals who have disabilities and organizations interested in those individuals. In making appointments to the Commission, the Governor shall consider, to the greatest extent practicable, the extent to which minority populations are represented on the Commission.

(c)   Except for individuals appointed to the Commission under subdivisions (12a), (12b), and (12c) of subsection (a) of this section, a majority of Commission members shall be persons who are blind, as defined in G.S. 111-11 and who are not employed by the Division of Services for the Blind.

(d)   The Commission for the Blind shall select a Chairperson from among its members.

(e)   The term of office of members of the Commission is three years. The term of members appointed under subdivisions (1), (2), (3), (4), and (12a) of subsection (a) of this section shall expire on June 30 of years evenly divisible by three. The term of members appointed under subdivisions (5), (6), (7), (8), and

(12b) of subsection (a) of this section shall expire on June 30 of years that follow by one year those years that are evenly divisible by three. The term of members appointed under subdivisions (9), (10), (11), (12), and (12c) of subsection (a) of this section shall expire on June 30 of years that precede by one year those years that are evenly divisible by three.

(f)   No individual may be appointed to more than two consecutive three-year terms. Upon the expiration of a term, a member shall continue to serve until a successor is appointed, as provided by G.S. 128-7. An appointment to fill a vacancy shall be for the unexpired balance of the term.

(g)   A member of the Commission shall not vote on any issue before the Commission that would have a significant and predictable effect on the member's financial interest. The Governor shall have the power to remove any member of the Commission from office for misfeasance, malfeasance, or nonfeasance in accordance with the provisions of G.S. 143B-13 of the Executive Organization Act of 1973.

(h)   The members of the Commission shall receive per diem and necessary travel and subsistence expenses in accordance with the provisions of G.S. 138-5.

(i)   A majority of the Commission shall constitute a quorum for the transaction of business.

(j)   All clerical and other services required by the Commission shall be supplied by the Secretary of Health and Human Services. (1973, c. 476, s. 140; 1977, c. 581; 1993, c. 561, s. 89(b); 1997-443, s. 11A.118(a); 2000-121, s. 31; 2013-360, s. 12A.14(b).)

§ 143B-159. Commission for the Blind - regular and special meetings.

The Commission for the Blind shall meet at least once in each quarter and may hold special meetings at any time and place within the State at the call of the chairman or upon the written request of at least five members. (1973, c. 476, s. 141.)

§ 143B-160. Commission for the Blind - officers.

The Commission for the Blind shall have a chairman and a vice-chairman. The chairman shall be designated by the Governor from among the members of the Commission to serve as chairman at his pleasure. The vice-chairman shall be elected by and from the members of the Commission and shall serve for a term of two years or until the expiration of his regularly appointed term. (1973, c. 476, s. 142.)

Part 8. Professional Advisory Committee.

§§ 143B-161, 143B-162: Repealed by Session Laws 2013-360, s. 12A.14(a), effective July 1, 2013.

Part 9. Consumer and Advocacy Advisory Committee for the Blind.

§ 143B-163. Consumer and Advocacy Advisory Committee for the Blind - creation, powers and duties.

(a) There is hereby created the Consumer and Advocacy Advisory Committee for the Blind of the Department of Health and Human Services. This Committee shall make a continuing study of the entire range of problems and needs of the blind and visually impaired population of this State and make specific recommendations to the Secretary of Health and Human Services as to how these may be solved or alleviated through legislative action. The Committee shall examine national trends and programs of other states, as well as programs and priorities in North Carolina. Because of the cost of treating persons who lose their vision, the Committee's role shall also include studying and making recommendations to the Secretary of Health and Human Services concerning methods of preventing blindness and restoring vision.

(b) The Consumer and Advocacy Advisory Committee for the Blind shall advise all State boards, commissions, agencies, divisions, departments, schools, corporations, or other State-administered associations or entities, including the secretary, director and members of said boards, commissions, agencies, divisions, departments, schools, et cetera, on the needs of the citizens of the State of North Carolina who are now or will become visually impaired.

(c) The Consumer and Advocacy Advisory Committee for the Blind shall also advise every State board, commission, agency, division, department, school, corporation, or other State-administered associations or entity concerning sight conservation programs that it supervises, administers or controls.

(d) All State boards, commissions, agencies, divisions, departments, schools, corporations, or other State-administered associations or entities including the secretary, director and members of said State boards, agencies, departments, et cetera, which supervise, administer or control any program for or affecting the citizens of the State of North Carolina who are now or will become visually impaired shall inform the Consumer and Advocacy Advisory Committee for the Blind of any proposed change in policy, program, budget, rule, or regulation which will affect the citizens of North Carolina who are now or will become visually impaired. Said board, commission, et cetera, shall allow the Consumer and Advocacy Advisory Committee for the Blind, prior to passage, unless such change is made pursuant to G.S. 150B-21.1, an opportunity to object to the change and present information and proposals on behalf of the citizens of North Carolina who are now or will become visually impaired. This subsection shall also apply to all sight conservation programs of the State of North Carolina.

(e) Nothing in this statute shall prohibit a board, commission, agency, division, department, et cetera, from implementing any change after allowing the Consumer and Advocacy Advisory Committee for the Blind an opportunity to object and propose alternatives. Shifts in budget items within a program or administrative changes in a program required in the day-to-day operation of an agency, department, or school, et cetera, shall be allowed without prior consultation with said Committee. (1977, c. 842, s. 1; c. 1050; 1979, c. 973, s. 1; 1987, c. 827, s. 1; 1991 (Reg. Sess., 1992), c. 1030, s. 44; 1997-443, s. 11A.118(a); 2000-121, s. 32.)

§ 143B-164. Consumer and Advocacy Advisory Committee for the Blind - members; selection; quorum; compensation.

(a) The Consumer and Advocacy Advisory Committee for the Blind of the Department of Health and Human Services shall consist of the following members:

(1) One member of the North Carolina Senate to be appointed by the President Pro Tempore of the Senate;

(2) One member of the North Carolina House of Representatives to be appointed by the Speaker of the House of Representatives;

(3) President and Vice-President of the National Federation of the Blind of North Carolina;

(4) President and Vice-President of the North Carolina Council of the Blind;

(5) President and Vice-President of the North Carolina Association of Workers for the Blind;

(6) President and Vice-President of the North Carolina Chapter of the American Association of Workers for the Blind;

(7) Chairman of the State Council of the North Carolina Lions and Executive Director of the North Carolina Lions Association for the Blind, Inc.;

(8) Chairman of the Concession Stand Committee of the Division of Services for the Blind of the Department of Health and Human Services; and

(9) Executive Director of the North Carolina Society for the Prevention of Blindness, Inc.

With respect to members appointed from the General Assembly, these appointments shall be made in the odd-numbered years, and the appointments shall be made for two-year terms beginning on the first day of July and continuing through the 30th day of June two years thereafter; provided, such appointments shall be made within two weeks after ratification of this act, and the first members which may be so appointed prior to July 1 of the year of ratification shall serve through the 30th day of June of the second year thereafter. If any Committee member appointed from the General Assembly ceases to be a member of the General Assembly, for whatever reason, his position on the Committee shall be deemed vacant. In the event that either Committee position which is designated herein to be filled by a member of the General Assembly becomes vacant during a term, for whatever reason, a successor to fill that position shall be appointed for the remainder of the unexpired term by the person who made the original appointment or his successor. Provided members appointed by the President Pro Tempore of the Senate and the Speaker of the House shall not serve more than two complete consecutive terms.

With respect to the remaining Committee members, each officeholder shall serve on the Committee only so long as he holds the named position in the specified organization. Upon completion of his term, failure to secure reelection or appointment, or resignation, the individual shall be deemed to have resigned from the Committee and his successor in office shall immediately become a member of the Committee. Further, if any of the above-named organizations dissolve or if any of the above-stated positions no longer exist, then the successor organization or position shall be deemed to be substituted in the place of the former one and the officeholder in the new organization or of the new position shall become a member of the Committee.

(b)   A chairman shall be elected by a majority vote of the Committee members for a one-year term to coincide with the fiscal year of the State. Provided, the first chairman shall be elected for a term to end June 30, 1978.

Provided, further, if any chairman does not desire or is unable to continue to perform as chairman for any reason, including his becoming ineligible to be a member of the Committee as specified in subsection (a), the remaining members shall elect a chairman to fulfill the remainder of his term.

(c)   A majority of the members shall constitute a quorum for the transaction of business.

(d)   The Committee shall meet once a quarter to act upon any information provided them by any board, commission, agency, division, department, school, et cetera. Special meetings may be held at any time and place within the State at the call of the chairman or upon written request of at least a majority of the members. Provided, a majority of the members shall be allowed to waive any meeting.

(e)   All clerical and other services required by the Committee shall be supplied by the Secretary of Health and Human Services.

(f)   Members of the Committee shall receive per diem and necessary travel and subsistence expenses in accordance with the provisions of G.S. 138-5. (1977, c. 842, s. 1; c. 1050; 1979, c. 973, s. 2; 1991, c. 739, s. 27; 1997-443, s. 11A.118(a).)

§§ 143B-164.1 through 143B-164.9. Reserved for future codification purposes.

Part 9A. State School for Sight-Impaired Children.

§§ 143B-164.10 through 143B-164.18: Repealed by Session Laws 2013-247, s. 1(b), effective July 3, 2013.

Part 10. North Carolina Medical Care Commission.

§ 143B-165. North Carolina Medical Care Commission - creation, powers and duties.

There is hereby created the North Carolina Medical Care Commission of the Department of Health and Human Services with the power and duty to promulgate rules and regulations to be followed in the construction and maintenance of public and private hospitals, medical centers, and related facilities with the power and duty to adopt, amend and rescind rules and regulations under and not inconsistent with the laws of the State necessary to carry out the provisions and purposes of this Article.

(1) The North Carolina Medical Care Commission has the duty to adopt statewide plans for the construction and maintenance of hospitals, medical centers, and related facilities, or such other as may be found desirable and necessary in order to meet the requirements and receive the benefits of any federal legislation with regard thereto.

(2) The Commission is authorized to adopt such rules and regulations as may be necessary to carry out the intent and purposes of Article 13 of Chapter 131 of the General Statutes of North Carolina.

(3) The Commission may adopt such reasonable and necessary standards with reference thereto as may be proper to cooperate fully with the Surgeon General or other agencies or departments of the United States and the use of funds provided by the federal government as contained and referenced in Article 13 of Chapter 131 of the General Statutes of North Carolina.

(4)   The Commission shall have the power and duty to approve projects in the amounts of grants-in-aid from funds supplied by the federal and State governments for the planning and construction of hospitals and other related medical facilities according to the provisions of Article 13 of Chapter 131 of the General Statutes of North Carolina.

(5)   Repealed by Session Laws 1981 (Regular Session, 1982), c. 1388, s. 3.

(6)   The Commission has the duty to adopt rules and regulations and standards with respect to the different types of hospitals to be licensed under the provisions of Article 13A of Chapter 131 of the General Statutes of North Carolina.

(7)   The Commission is authorized and empowered to adopt such rules and regulations, not inconsistent with the laws of this State, as may be required by the federal government for grants-in-aid for medical facility services and licensure which may be made available to the State by the federal government. This section is to be liberally construed in order that the State and its citizens may benefit from such grants-in-aid.

(8)   The Commission shall adopt such rules and regulations, consistent with the provisions of this Chapter. All rules and regulations not inconsistent with the provisions of this Chapter heretofore adopted by the North Carolina Medical Care Commission shall remain in full force and effect unless and until repealed or superseded by action of the North Carolina Medical Care Commission. All rules and regulations adopted by the Commission shall be enforced by the Department of Health and Human Services.

(9)   The Commission shall have the power and duty to adopt rules and regulations with regard to emergency medical services in accordance with the provisions of Article 26 of Chapter 130 and Article 56 of Chapter 143 of the General Statutes of North Carolina.

(10)   The Commission shall have the power and duty to adopt rules for the operation of nursing homes, as defined by Article 6 of Chapter 131E of the General Statutes.

(11)   The Commission is authorized to adopt such rules as may be necessary to carry out the provisions of Part C of Article 6, and Article 10, of Chapter 131E of the General Statutes of North Carolina.

(12) The Commission shall adopt rules, including temporary rules pursuant to G.S. 150B-13, providing for the accreditation of facilities that perform mammography procedures and for laboratories evaluating screening pap smears. Mammography accreditation standards shall address, but are not limited to, the quality of mammography equipment used and the skill levels and other qualifications of personnel who administer mammographies and personnel who interpret mammogram results. The Commission's standards shall be no less stringent than those established by the United States Department of Health and Human Services for Medicare/Medicaid coverage of screening mammography. These rules shall also specify procedures for waiver of these accreditation standards on an individual basis for any facility providing screening mammography to a significant number of patients, but only if there is no accredited facility located nearby. The Commission may grant a waiver subject to any conditions it deems necessary to protect the health and safety of patients, including requiring the facility to submit a plan to meet accreditation standards.

(13) The Commission shall have the power and duty to adopt rules for the inspection and licensure of adult care homes and operation of adult care homes, as defined by Article 1 of Chapter 131D of the General Statutes, and for personnel requirements of staff employed in adult care homes, except where rule-making authority is assigned to the Secretary. (1973, c. 476, s. 148; c. 1090, s. 2; c. 1224, s. 3; 1981, c. 614, s. 10; 1981 (Reg. Sess.,1982), c. 1388, s. 3; 1983 (Reg. Sess., 1984), c. 1022, s. 6; 1987, c. 34; 1991, c. 490, s.4; 1997-443, s. 11A.118(a); 1999-334, ss. 3.6, 3.7).

§ 143B-166. North Carolina Medical Care Commission - members; selection; quorum; compensation.

The North Carolina Medical Care Commission of the Department of Health and Human Services shall consist of 17 members appointed by the Governor. Three of the members appointed by the Governor shall be nominated by the North Carolina Medical Society, one member shall be nominated by the North Carolina Nurses Association, one member shall be nominated by the North Carolina Pharmaceutical Association, one member nominated by the Duke Foundation and one member nominated by the North Carolina Hospital Association. The remaining 10 members of the North Carolina Medical Care Commission shall be appointed by the Governor and selected so as to fairly represent agriculture, industry, labor, and other interest groups in North

Carolina. One such member appointed by the Governor shall be a dentist licensed to practice in North Carolina. The initial members of the Commission shall be 18 members of the North Carolina Medical Care Commission who shall serve for a period equal to the remainder of their current terms on the North Carolina Medical Care Commission, six of whose appointments expire June 30, 1973, four of whose appointments expire June 30, 1974, four of whose appointments expire June 30, 1975, and four of whose appointments expire June 30, 1976. To achieve the required 17 members the Governor shall appoint three members to the Commission upon the expiration of four members' initial terms on June 30, 1973. At the end of the respective terms of office of the initial members of the Commission, their successors shall be appointed for terms of four years and until their successors are appointed and qualify. Any appointment to fill a vacancy on the Commission created by the resignation, dismissal, death, or disability of a member shall be for the balance of the unexpired term.

The Governor shall have the power to remove any member of the Commission from office for misfeasance, malfeasance or nonfeasance in accordance with the provisions of G.S. 143B-13 of the Executive Organization Act of 1973.

Vacancies on said Commission among the membership nominated by a society, association, or foundation as hereinabove provided shall be filled by the Executive Committee or other authorized agent of said society, association or foundation until the next meeting of the society, association or foundation at which time the society, association or foundation shall nominate a member to fill the vacancy for the unexpired term.

The members of the Commission shall receive per diem and necessary travel and subsistence expenses in accordance with the provisions of G.S. 138-5.

A majority of the Commission shall constitute a quorum for the transaction of business.

All clerical and other services required by the Commission shall be supplied by the Secretary of Health and Human Services. (1973, c. 476, s. 149; c. 1090, s. 2; 1997-443, s. 11A.118(a).)

§ 143B-167. North Carolina Medical Care Commission - regular and special meetings.

The North Carolina Medical Care Commission shall meet at least once in each quarter and may hold special meetings at any time and place within the State at the call of the chairman or upon the written request of at least nine members. (1973, c. 476, s. 150; c. 1090, s. 2.)

§ 143B-168. North Carolina Medical Care Commission - officers.

The North Carolina Medical Care Commission shall have a chairman and vice-chairman. The chairman shall be designated by the Governor from among the members of the Commission to serve as chairman at his pleasure. The vice-chairman shall be elected by and from the members of the Commission and shall serve for a term of two years or until the expiration of his regularly appointed term. (1973, c. 476, s. 151; c. 1090, s. 2.)

Part 10A. Child Day-Care Commission.

§ 143B-168.1. Repealed by Session Laws 1987, c. 788, s. 23.

§ 143B-168.2. Repealed by Session Laws 1987, c. 788, s. 24.

§ 143B-168.3. Child Care Commission - powers and duties.

(a)   The Child Day-Care Licensing Commission of the Department of Administration is transferred, recodified, and renamed the Child Care Commission of the Department of Health and Human Services with the power and duty to adopt rules to be followed in the licensing and operation of child care facilities as provided by Article 7 of Chapter 110 of the General Statutes.

(a1)   The Child Care Commission shall adopt rules:

(1)   For the issuance of licenses to any child care facility; and

(2)   To adopt rules as provided by Article 7 of Chapter 110 of the General Statutes of the State of North Carolina, and to establish standards for enhanced program licenses, as authorized by G.S. 110-88(7).

(b)   The Commission shall adopt rules consistent with the provisions of this Chapter. All rules not inconsistent with the provisions of this Chapter heretofore adopted by the Child Day-Care Licensing Commission shall remain in full force and effect unless and until repealed or superseded by action of the Child Care Commission. All rules and regulations adopted by the Commission shall be enforced by the Department of Health and Human Services. (1985, c. 757, s. 155(a); 1987, c. 788, ss. 25, 26; 1997-443, s. 11A.118(a); 1997-456, s. 27; 1997-506, s. 56.)

§ 143B-168.4. Child Care Commission - members; selection; quorum.

(a)   The Child Care Commission of the Department of Health and Human Services shall consist of 17 members. Seven of the members shall be appointed by the Governor and 10 by the General Assembly, five upon the recommendation of the President Pro Tempore of the Senate, and five upon the recommendation of the Speaker of the House of Representatives. Four of the members appointed by the Governor, two by the General Assembly on the recommendation of the President Pro Tempore of the Senate, and two by the General Assembly on the recommendation of the Speaker of the House of Representatives, shall be members of the public who are not employed in, or providing, child care and who have no financial interest in a child care facility. Two of the foregoing public members appointed by the Governor, one of the foregoing public members recommended by the President Pro Tempore of the Senate, and one of the foregoing public members recommended by the Speaker of the House of Representatives shall be parents of children receiving child care services. Of the remaining two public members appointed by the Governor, one shall be a pediatrician currently licensed to practice in North Carolina. Three of the members appointed by the Governor shall be child care providers, one of whom shall be affiliated with a for profit child care center, one of whom shall be affiliated with a for profit family child care home, and one of whom shall be affiliated with a nonprofit facility. Two of the members appointed by the General Assembly on the recommendation of the President Pro Tempore of the Senate, and two by the General Assembly on recommendation of the Speaker of the House of Representatives, shall be child care providers, one affiliated with a for profit child care facility, and one affiliated with a nonprofit child care facility. The General Assembly, upon the recommendation of the President Pro Tempore of the Senate, and the General Assembly, upon the recommendation of the Speaker of the House of Representatives, shall appoint two early childhood education specialists. None may be employees of the State.

(b)   Members shall be appointed as follows:

(1)   Of the Governor's initial appointees, four shall be appointed for terms expiring June 30, 2015, and three shall be appointed for terms expiring June 30, 2016;

(2)   Of the General Assembly's initial appointees appointed upon recommendation of the President Pro Tempore of the Senate, three shall be appointed for terms expiring June 30, 2015, and two shall be appointed for terms expiring June 30, 2016;

(3)   Of the General Assembly's initial appointees appointed upon recommendation of the Speaker of the House of Representatives, two shall be appointed for terms expiring June 30, 2015, and three shall be appointed for terms expiring June 30, 2016.

Appointments by the General Assembly shall be made in accordance with G.S. 120-121. After the initial appointees' terms have expired, all members shall be appointed to serve two-year terms. Any appointment to fill a vacancy on the Commission created by the resignation, dismissal, death, or disability of a member shall be for the balance of the unexpired term.'

(c)   A vacancy occurring during a term of office is filled:

(1)   By the Governor, if the Governor made the initial appointment;

(2)   By the General Assembly, if the General Assembly made the initial appointment in accordance with G.S. 120-122.

At its first meeting the Commission members shall elect a chairman to serve a two-year term. Chairmen shall be elected for two-year terms thereafter. The same member may serve as chairman for two consecutive terms.

Commission members may be reappointed and may succeed themselves for a maximum of four consecutive terms.

The Commission shall meet quarterly, and at other times at the call of the chairman or upon written request of at least six members.

The members of the Commission shall receive per diem and necessary travel and subsistence expenses in accordance with the provisions of G.S. 138-5. A majority of the Commission shall constitute a quorum for the transaction of business.

All clerical and other services required by the Commission shall be supplied by the Secretary of Health and Human Services. (1985, c. 757, s. 155(a); 1987 (Reg. Sess., 1988), c. 896; 1989, c. 342; 1995, c. 490, s. 10; 1997-443, s. 11A.118(a); 1997-506, s. 57; 2011-145, s. 10.7(c); 2013-360, s. 12B.1(h); 2013-363, s. 4.2.)

§ 143B-168.5. Child Care - special unit.

There is established within the Department of Health and Human Services a special unit to deal primarily with violations involving child abuse and neglect in child care arrangements. The Child Care Commission shall make rules for the investigation of reports of child abuse or neglect and for administrative action when child abuse or neglect is substantiated, pursuant to G.S. 110-88(6a), 110-105, and 110-105.2. (1985, c. 757, s. 156(r); 1991, c. 273, s. 12; 1997-443, s. 11A.118(a); 1997-506, s. 58.)

§§ 143B-168.6 through 143B-168.9. Reserved for future codification purposes.

Part 10B. Early Childhood Initiatives.

§ 143B-168.10. Early childhood initiatives; findings.

The General Assembly finds, upon consultation with the Governor, that every child can benefit from, and should have access to, high-quality early childhood education and development services. The economic future and well-being of the State depend upon it. To ensure that all children have access to high-quality early childhood education and development services, the General Assembly further finds that:

(1)   Parents have the primary duty to raise, educate, and transmit values to young preschool children;

(2)   The State can assist parents in their role as the primary caregivers and educators of young preschool children; and

(3)   There is a need to explore innovative approaches and strategies for aiding parents and families in the education and development of young preschool children. (1993, c. 321, s. 254(a); 1998-212, s. 12.37B(a).)

§ 143B-168.10A. NC Pre-K Reports.

The Division of Child Development and Early Education shall submit an annual report no later than March 15 of each year to the Joint Legislative Commission on Governmental Operations, the Joint Legislative Oversight Committee on Health and Human Services, the Senate Appropriations Committee on Health and Human Services, the House of Representatives Appropriations Subcommittee on Health and Human Services, the Office of State Budget and Management, and the Fiscal Research Division. The report shall include the following:

(1)   The number of children participating in the NC Pre-K program.

(2)   The number of children participating in the NC Pre-K program who have never been served in other early education programs, such as child care, public or private preschool, Head Start, Early Head Start, or early intervention programs.

(3)   The expected NC Pre-K expenditures for the programs and the source of the local contributions.

(4)   The results of an annual evaluation of the NC Pre-K program. (2012-142, s. 10.1(g).)

§ 143B-168.11. Early childhood initiatives; purpose; definitions.

(a) The purpose of this Part is to establish a framework whereby the General Assembly, upon consultation with the Governor, may support through financial and other means, the North Carolina Partnership for Children, Inc. and comparable local partnerships, which have as their missions the development of a comprehensive, long-range strategic plan for early childhood development and the provision, through public and private means, of high-quality early childhood education and development services for children and families. It is the intent of the General Assembly that communities be given the maximum flexibility and discretion practicable in developing their plans while remaining subject to the approval of the North Carolina Partnership and accountable to the North Carolina Partnership and to the General Assembly for their plans and for the programmatic and fiscal integrity of the programs and services provided to implement them.

(b) The following definitions apply in this Part:

(1) Board of Directors. - The Board of Directors of the North Carolina Partnership for Children, Inc.

(2) Department. - The Department of Health and Human Services.

(2a) Early Childhood. - Birth through five years of age.

(3) Local Partnership. - A county or regional private, nonprofit 501(c)(3) organization established to coordinate a local demonstration project, to provide ongoing analyses of their local needs that must be met to ensure that the developmental needs of children are met in order to prepare them to begin school healthy and ready to succeed, and, in consultation with the North Carolina Partnership and subject to the approval of the North Carolina Partnership, to provide programs and services to meet these needs under this Part, while remaining accountable for the programmatic and fiscal integrity of their programs and services to the North Carolina Partnership.

(4) North Carolina Partnership. - The North Carolina Partnership for Children, Inc.

(5) Secretary. - The Secretary of Health and Human Services. (1993, c. 321, s. 254(a); 1993 (Reg. Sess., 1994), c. 766, s. 1; 1997-443, s. 11A.118(a); 1998-212, s. 12.37B(a).)

§ 143B-168.12. North Carolina Partnership for Children, Inc.; conditions.

(a) In order to receive State funds, the following conditions shall be met:

(1) The North Carolina Partnership shall have a Board of Directors consisting of the following 26 members:

a. The Secretary of Health and Human Services, ex officio, or the Secretary's designee;

b. Repealed by Session Laws 1997, c. 443, s. 11A.105.

c. The Superintendent of Public Instruction, ex officio, or the Superintendent's designee;

d. The President of the Community Colleges System, ex officio, or the President's designee;

e. Three members of the public, including one child care provider, one other who is a parent, and one other who is a board chair of a local partnership serving on the North Carolina Partnership local partnership advisory committee, appointed by the General Assembly upon recommendation of the President Pro Tempore of the Senate;

f. Three members of the public, including one who is a parent, one other who is a representative of the faith community, and one other who is a board chair of a local partnership serving on the North Carolina Partnership local partnership advisory committee, appointed by the General Assembly upon recommendation of the Speaker of the House of Representatives;

g. Twelve members, appointed by the Governor. Three of these 12 members shall be members of the party other than the Governor's party, appointed by the Governor. Seven of these 12 members shall be appointed as follows: one who is a child care provider, one other who is a pediatrician, one other who is a health care provider, one other who is a parent, one other who is a member of the business community, one other who is a member representing a philanthropic agency, and one other who is an early childhood educator;

h. Repealed by Session Laws 1998-212, s. 12.37B(a), effective October 30, 1998.

h1. The Chair of the North Carolina Partnership Board shall be appointed by the Governor;

i. Repealed by Session Laws 1998-212, s. 12.37B(a), effective October 30, 1998.

j. One member of the public appointed by the General Assembly upon recommendation of the Majority Leader of the Senate;

k. One member of the public appointed by the General Assembly upon recommendation of the Majority Leader of the House of Representatives;

l. One member of the public appointed by the General Assembly upon recommendation of the Minority Leader of the Senate;

m. One member of the public appointed by the General Assembly upon recommendation of the Minority Leader of the House of Representatives; and

n. The Director of the More at Four Pre-Kindergarten Program, or the Director's designee.

All members appointed to succeed the initial members and members appointed thereafter shall be appointed for three-year terms. Members may succeed themselves.

All appointed board members shall avoid conflicts of interests and the appearance of impropriety. Should instances arise when a conflict may be perceived, any individual who may benefit directly or indirectly from the North Carolina Partnership's disbursement of funds shall abstain from participating in any decision or deliberations by the North Carolina Partnership regarding the disbursement of funds.

All ex officio members are voting members. Each ex officio member may be represented by a designee. These designees shall be voting members. No members of the General Assembly shall serve as members.

The North Carolina Partnership may establish a nominating committee and, in making their recommendations of members to be appointed by the General

Assembly or by the Governor, the President Pro Tempore of the Senate, the Speaker of the House of Representatives, the Majority Leader of the Senate, the Majority Leader of the House of Representatives, the Minority Leader of the Senate, the Minority Leader of the House of Representatives, and the Governor shall consult with and consider the recommendations of this nominating committee.

The North Carolina Partnership may establish a policy on members' attendance, which policy shall include provisions for reporting absences of at least three meetings immediately to the appropriate appointing authority.

Members who miss more than three consecutive meetings without excuse or members who vacate their membership shall be replaced by the appropriate appointing authority, and the replacing member shall serve either until the General Assembly and the Governor can appoint a successor or until the replaced member's term expires, whichever is earlier.

The North Carolina Partnership shall establish a policy on membership of the local boards. No member of the General Assembly shall serve as a member of a local board. Within these requirements for local board membership, the North Carolina Partnership shall allow local partnerships that are regional to have flexibility in the composition of their boards so that all counties in the region have adequate representation.

All appointed local board members shall avoid conflicts of interests and the appearance of impropriety. Should instances arise when a conflict may be perceived, any individual who may benefit directly or indirectly from the partnership's disbursement of funds shall abstain from participating in any decision or deliberations by the partnership regarding the disbursement of funds.

(2)   The North Carolina Partnership and the local partnerships shall agree to adopt procedures for its operations that are comparable to those of Article 33C of Chapter 143 of the General Statutes, the Open Meetings Law, and Chapter 132 of the General Statutes, the Public Records Law, and provide for enforcement by the Department. The procedures may provide for the confidentiality of personnel files comparable to Article 7 of Chapter 126 of the General Statutes.

(3)   The North Carolina Partnership shall oversee the development and implementation of the local demonstration projects as they are selected and

shall approve the ongoing plans, programs, and services developed and implemented by the local partnerships and hold the local partnerships accountable for the financial and programmatic integrity of the programs and services. The North Carolina Partnership may contract at the State level to obtain services or resources when the North Carolina Partnership determines it would be more efficient to do so.

In the event that the North Carolina Partnership determines that a local partnership is not fulfilling its mandate to provide programs and services designed to meet the developmental needs of children in order to prepare them to begin school healthy and ready to succeed and is not being accountable for the programmatic and fiscal integrity of its programs and services, the North Carolina Partnership may suspend all funds to the partnership until the partnership demonstrates that these defects are corrected. Further, at its discretion, the North Carolina Partnership may assume the managerial responsibilities for the partnership's programs and services until the North Carolina Partnership determines that it is appropriate to return the programs and services to the local partnership.

(4) The North Carolina Partnership shall develop and implement a comprehensive standard fiscal accountability plan to ensure the fiscal integrity and accountability of State funds appropriated to it and to the local partnerships. The standard fiscal accountability plan shall, at a minimum, include a uniform, standardized system of accounting, internal controls, payroll, fidelity bonding, chart of accounts, and contract management and monitoring. The North Carolina Partnership may contract with outside firms to develop and implement the standard fiscal accountability plan. All local partnerships shall be required to participate in the standard fiscal accountability plan developed and adopted by the North Carolina Partnership pursuant to this subdivision.

(5) Repealed by Session Laws 2011-145, s. 10.5(b), effective July 1, 2011.

(6) The North Carolina Partnership shall develop a formula for allocating direct services funds appropriated for this purpose to local partnerships.

(7) The North Carolina Partnership may adjust its allocations by up to ten percent (10%) on the basis of local partnerships' performance assessments. In determining whether to adjust its allocations to local partnerships, the North Carolina Partnership shall consider whether the local partnerships are meeting the outcome goals and objectives of the North Carolina Partnership and the

goals and objectives set forth by the local partnerships in their approved annual program plans.

The North Carolina Partnership may use additional factors to determine whether to adjust the local partnerships' allocations. These additional factors shall be developed with input from the local partnerships and shall be communicated to the local partnerships when the additional factors are selected. These additional factors may include board involvement, family and community outreach, collaboration among public and private service agencies, and family involvement.

On the basis of performance assessments, local partnerships annually shall be rated "superior", "satisfactory", or "needs improvement".

The North Carolina Partnership may contract with outside firms to conduct the performance assessments of local partnerships.

(8) The North Carolina Partnership shall establish a local partnership advisory committee comprised of 15 members. Eight of the members shall be chosen from past board chairs or duly elected officers currently serving on local partnerships' board of directors at the time of appointment and shall serve three-year terms. Seven of the members shall be staff of local partnerships. Members shall be chosen by the Chair of the North Carolina Partnership from a pool of candidates nominated by their respective boards of directors. The local partnership advisory committee shall serve in an advisory capacity to the North Carolina Partnership and shall establish a schedule of regular meetings. Members shall be chosen from local partnerships on a rotating basis. The advisory committee shall annually elect a chair from among its members.

(9) Repealed by Session Laws 2001-424, s. 21.75(h), effective July 1, 2001.

(b) The North Carolina Partnership shall be subject to audit and review by the State Auditor under Article 5A of Chapter 147 of the General Statutes. The State Auditor shall conduct annual financial and compliance audits of the North Carolina Partnership.

(c) The North Carolina Partnership shall require each local partnership to place in each of its contracts a statement that the contract is subject to monitoring by the local partnership and North Carolina Partnership, that contractors and subcontractors shall be fidelity bonded, unless the contractors or subcontractors receive less than one hundred thousand dollars ($100,000) or unless the contract is for child care subsidy services, that contractors and subcontractors are subject to audit oversight by the State Auditor, and that contractors and subcontractors shall be subject to the requirements of G.S. 143C-6-22. Organizations subject to G.S. 159-34 shall be exempt from this requirement.

(d) The North Carolina Partnership for Children, Inc., shall make a report no later than December 1 of each year to the General Assembly that shall include the following:

(1) A description of the program and significant services and initiatives.

(2) A history of Smart Start funding and the previous fiscal year's expenditures.

(3) The number of children served by type of service.

(4) The type and quantity of services provided.

(5) The results of the previous year's evaluations of the Initiatives or related programs and services.

(6) A description of significant policy and program changes.

(7) Any recommendations for legislative action.

(e) The North Carolina Partnership shall develop guidelines for local partnerships to follow in selecting capital projects to fund. The guidelines shall include assessing the community needs in relation to the quantity of child care centers, assessing the cost of purchasing or constructing new facilities as opposed to renovating existing facilities, and prioritizing capital needs such as construction, renovations, and playground equipment and other amenities.

(f) The North Carolina Partnership for Children, Inc., shall establish uniform guidelines and a reporting format for local partnerships to document the qualifying expenses occurring at the contractor level. Local partnerships shall monitor qualifying expenses to ensure they have occurred and meet the requirements prescribed in this subsection. (1993, c. 321, s. 254(a); 1993 (Reg. Sess., 1994), c. 766, s. 1; 1995, c. 324, s. 27A.1; 1996, 2nd Ex. Sess., c. 18, s. 24.29(b); 1997-443, ss. 11.55(l), 11A.105; 1998-212, s. 12.37B(a), (b); 1999-84,

s. 24; 1999-237, s. 11.48(a); 2000-67, s. 11.28(a); 2001-424, ss. 21.75(h), 21.75(i); 2002-126, s. 10.55(d); 2003-284, ss. 10.38(l), 10.38(m), 10.38(n); 2004-124, s. 10.37; 2006-203, s. 104; 2006-264, s. 1(b); 2007-323, s. 10.19B(a); 2009-451, s. 20C.1(a); 2011-145, s. 10.5(b).)

§ 143B-168.13. Implementation of program; duties of Department and Secretary.

(a) The Department shall:

(1) Repealed by Session Laws 1998-212, s. 12.37B(a), effective October 30, 1998.

(1a) Develop and conduct a statewide needs and resource assessment every third year, beginning in the 1997-98 fiscal year. This needs assessment shall be conducted in cooperation with the North Carolina Partnership and with the local partnerships. This needs assessment shall include a statewide assessment of capital needs. The data and findings of this needs assessment shall form the basis for annual program plans developed by local partnerships and approved by the North Carolina Partnership.

(2) Recodified as (a)(1a) by Session Laws 1998-212, s. 12.37B(a).

(2a) Repealed by Session Laws 1998-212, s. 12.37B(l), effective October 30, 1998.

(3) Provide technical and administrative assitance to local partnerships, particularly during the first year after they are selected under this Part to receive State funds. The Department, at any time, may authorize the North Carolina Partnership or a governmental or public entity to do the contracting for one or more local partnerships. After a local partnership's first year, the Department may allow the partnership to contract for itself.

(4) Adopt, in cooperation with the North Carolina Partnership, any rules necessary to implement this Part, including rules to ensure that State leave policy is not applied to the North Carolina Partnership and the local partnerships. In order to allow local partnerships to focus on the development of long-range plans in their initial year of funding, the Department may adopt rules

that limit the categories of direct services for young children and their families for which funds are made available during the initial year.

(5)   Repealed by Session Laws 1996, Second Extra Session, c. 18, s. 24.29(c).

(6)   Annually update its funding formula, in collaboration with the North Carolina Partnership for Children, Inc., using the most recent data available. These amounts shall serve as the basis for determining "full funding" amounts for each local partnership.

(b)   Repealed by Session Laws 1998-212, s. 12.37B(a), effective October 30, 1998. (1993 (Reg. Sess., 1994), c. 766, s. 1; 1996, 2nd Ex. Sess., c. 18, s. 24.29(c); 1997-443, s. 11.55(m); 1998-212, s. 12.37B(a), (b); 2000-67, s. 11.28(b); 2002-126, s. 10.55(e).)

§ 143B-168.14. Local partnerships; conditions.

(a)   In order to receive State funds, the following conditions shall be met:

(1)   Each local partnership shall develop a comprehensive, collaborative, long-range plan of services to children and families in the service-delivery area. No existing local, private, nonprofit 501(c)(3) organization, other than one established on or after July 1, 1993, and that meets the guidelines for local partnerships as established under this Part, shall be eligible to apply to serve as the local partnership for the purpose of this Part. The Board of the North Carolina Partnership may authorize exceptions to this eligibility requirement.

(2)   Each local partnership shall agree to adopt procedures for its operations that are comparable to those of Article 33C of Chapter 143 of the General Statutes, the Open Meetings Law, and Chapter 132 of the General Statutes, the Public Records Law, and provide for enforcement by the Department. The procedures may provide for the confidentiality of personnel files comparable to Article 7 of Chapter 126 of the General Statutes.

(3)   Each local partnership shall adopt procedures to ensure that all personnel who provide services to young children and their families under this Part know and understand their responsibility to report suspected child abuse, neglect, or dependency, as defined in G.S. 7B-101.

(4) Each local partnership shall participate in the uniform, standard fiscal accountability plan developed and adopted by the North Carolina Partnership.

(b) Each local partnership shall be subject to audit and review by the North Carolina Partnership. The North Carolina Partnership shall contract for annual financial and compliance audits of local partnerships that are rated "needs improvement" in performance assessments authorized in G.S. 143B-168.12(a)(7). Local partnerships that are rated "superior" or "satisfactory" in performance assessments authorized in G.S. 143B-168.12(a)(7) shall undergo biennial financial and compliance audits as contracted for by the North Carolina Partnership. The North Carolina Partnership shall provide the State Auditor with a copy of each audit conducted pursuant to this subsection. (1993 (Reg. Sess., 1994), c. 766, s. 1; 1996, 2nd Ex. Sess., c. 18, s. 24.29(d)(1); 1997-506, s. 59; 1998-202, s. 13(II); 1998-212, s. 12.37B(a); 2003-284, s. 19.1; 2007-323, s. 10.19B(b); 2009-451, s. 20C.1(b).)

§ 143B-168.15. Use of State funds.

(a) State funds allocated to local projects for services to children and families shall be used to meet assessed needs, expand coverage, and improve the quality of these services. The local plan shall address the assessed needs of all children to the extent feasible. It is the intent of the General Assembly that the needs of both young children below poverty who remain in the home, as well as the needs of young children below poverty who require services beyond those offered in child care settings, be addressed. Therefore, as local partnerships address the assessed needs of all children, they should devote an appropriate amount of their State allocations, considering these needs and other available resources, to meet the needs of children below poverty and their families.

(b) Depending on local, regional, or statewide needs, funds may be used to support activities and services that shall be made available and accessible to providers, children, and families on a voluntary basis. Of the funds allocated to local partnerships for direct services, seventy percent (70%) of the funds spent in each year shall be used in child care related activities and early childhood education programs that improve access to child care and early childhood education services, develop new child care and early childhood education services, and improve the quality of child care and early childhood education services in all settings.

(c) Long-term plans for local projects that do not receive their full allocation in the first year, other than those selected in 1993, should consider how to meet the assessed needs of low-income children and families within their neighborhoods or communities. These plans also should reflect a process to meet these needs as additional allocations and other resources are received.

(d) State funds designated for start-up and related activities may be used for capital expenses or to support activities and services for children, families, and providers. State funds designated to support direct services for children, families, and providers shall not be used for major capital expenses unless the North Carolina Partnership approves this use of State funds based upon a finding that a local partnership has demonstrated that (i) this use is a clear priority need for the local plan, (ii) it is necessary to enable the local partnership to provide services and activities to underserved children and families, and (iii) the local partnership will not otherwise be able to meet this priority need by using State or federal funds available to that local partnership. The funds approved for capital projects in any two consecutive fiscal years may not exceed ten percent (10%) of the total funds for direct services allocated to a local partnership in those two consecutive fiscal years.

(e) State funds allocated to local partnerships shall not supplant current expenditures by counties on behalf of young children and their families, and maintenance of current efforts on behalf of these children and families shall be sustained. State funds shall not be applied without the Secretary's approval where State or federal funding sources, such as Head Start, are available or could be made available to that county.

(f) Repealed by Session Laws 2001-424, s. 21.75(g), effective July 1, 2001.

(g) Not less than thirty percent (30%) of the funds spent in each year of each local partnership's direct services allocation shall be used to expand child care subsidies. To the extent practicable, these funds shall be used to enhance the affordability, availability, and quality of child care services as described in this section. The North Carolina Partnership may increase this percentage requirement up to a maximum of fifty percent (50%) when, based upon a significant local waiting list for subsidized child care, the North Carolina Partnership determines a higher percentage is justified.

(h) State funds allocated to local partnerships that are unexpended at the end of a fiscal year shall remain available to the North Carolina Partnership for Children, Inc., to reallocate to local partnerships. (1993 (Reg. Sess., 1994), c. 766, s. 1; 1995, c. 509, s. 97; 1996, 2nd Ex. Sess., c. 18, s. 24.29(e); 1997-443, s. 11.55(n); 1997-506, s. 60; 1998-212, s. 12.37B(a), (b); 1999-237, s. 11.48(o); 2000-67, ss. 11.28(c), 11.28(d); 2001-424, s. 21.75(g); 2008-123, s. 2.)

§ 143B-168.16. Home-centered services; consent.

No home-centered services including home visits or in-home parenting training shall be allowed under this Part unless the written, informed consent of the participating parents authorizing the home-centered services is first obtained by the local partnership, educational institution, local school administrative unit, private school, not-for-profit organization, governmental agency, or other entity that is conducting the parenting program. The participating parents may revoke at any time their consent for the home-centered services.

The consent form shall contain a clear description of the program including (i) the activities and information to be provided by the program during the home visits, (ii) the number of expected home visits, (iii) any responsibilities of the parents, (iv) the fact, if applicable, that a record will be made and maintained on the home visits, (v) the fact that the parents may revoke at any time the consent, and (vi) any other information as may be necessary to convey to the parents a clear understanding of the program.

Parents at all times shall have access to any record maintained on home-centered services provided to their family and may place in that record a written response to any information with which they disagree that is in the record. (1993 (Reg. Sess., 1994), c. 766, s. 1.)

Part 11. Council for Institutional Boards.

§§ 143B-169 through 143B-172: Repealed by Session Laws 1979, c. 504, s. 9.

Part 12. Boards of Directors of Institutions.

§§ 143B-173 through 143B-176: Repealed by Session Laws 1989, c. 533, s. 3.

Part 12A. Board of Directors of the Governor Morehead School.

§§ 143B-176.1 through 143B-176.2: Recodified as §§ 143B-164.11 and 143B-164.12 by Session Laws 1997-18, ss. 13(b) and (c).

Part 13. Council on Developmental Disabilities.

§ 143B-177. Council on Developmental Disabilities - creation, powers and duties.

There is hereby created the Council on Developmental Disabilities of the Department of Health and Human Services. The Council on Developmental Disabilities shall have the following functions and duties:

(1) To advise the Secretary of Health and Human Services regarding the development and implementation of the State plan as required by Public Law 98-527, the Developmental Disabilities Act of 1984, by:

a. Identifying ways and means of promoting public understanding of developmental disabilities;

b. Examining the federally assisted State programs of all State agencies which provide services for persons with developmental disabilities;

c. Describing the quality, extent and scope of services being provided, or to be provided, to persons with developmental disabilities in North Carolina;

d. Recommending ways and means for coordination of programs to prevent duplication and overlapping of such services;

e. Considering the need for new State programs and laws in the field of developmental disabilities; and

f. Conducting activities which will increase and support the independence, productivity, and integration into the community of persons with developmental disabilities.

(2) To advise the Secretary of Health and Human Services regarding the coordination of planning and service delivery of all State-funded programs which provide service to persons with developmental disabilities by:

a. Gathering, analyzing and interpreting individual and aggregate needs assessment data from all State agencies that provide services to developmentally disabled;

b. Conducting special needs assessment studies as may be necessary;

c. Specifying and supporting activities that will enhance the services delivered by individual agencies by reducing barriers between agencies;

d. Identifying service development priorities that require cooperative interagency planning and development;

e. Providing coordinative and technical assistance in interagency planning and development efforts; and

f. Coordinating interagency training efforts that will promote more effective service delivery to persons with developmental disabilities.

(3) To advise the Secretary of Health and Human Services regarding other matters relating to developmental disabilities and upon any matter the Secretary may refer to it. (1973, c. 476, s. 167; 1987, c. 780; 1997-443, s. 11A.118(a).)

§ 143B-178. Council on Developmental Disabilities - definitions.

The following definitions apply to this Chapter:

(1) The term "developmental disability" means a severe, chronic disability of a person which:

a. Is attributable to a mental or physical impairment or combination of mental and physical impairments;

b. Is manifested before the person attains age 22, unless the disability is caused by a traumatic head injury and is manifested after age 22;

c. Is likely to continue indefinitely;

d. Results in substantial functional limitations in three or more of the following areas of major life activity: (i) self-care, (ii) receptive and expressive language, (iii) learning, (iv) mobility, (v) self-direction, (vi) capacity for independent living, and (vii) economic self-sufficiency; and

e. Reflects the person's need for a combination and sequence of special, interdisciplinary, or generic care, treatment, or other services which are of lifelong or extended duration and are individually planned and coordinated.

(2) The term "services for persons with developmental disabilities," as it is used in this Article, means:

a. Alternative community living arrangement services, employment related activities, child development services, and case management services; and

b. Any other specialized services or special adaptations of generic services including diagnosis, evaluation, treatment, personal care, child care, adult care, special living arrangements, training, education, sheltered employment, recreation and socialization, counseling of the individual with such a disability and of his family, protective and other social and sociolegal services, information and referral services, follow-along services, nonvocational social-developmental services, and transportation services necessary to assure delivery of services to persons with developmental disabilities, and services to promote and coordinate activities to prevent developmental disabilities. (1973, c. 476, s. 168; 1977, c. 881, ss. 1, 2; 1979, c. 752, s. 1 1987, c. 780; 1995, c. 535, s. 33; 1997-506, s. 61.)

§ 143B-179. Council on Developmental Disabilities - members; selection; quorum; compensation.

(a) The Council on Developmental Disabilities of the Department of Health and Human Services shall consist of 32 members appointed by the Governor. The composition of the Council shall be as follows:

(1) Eleven members from the General Assembly and State government agencies as follows: One person who is a member of the Senate, one person who is a member of the House of Representatives, one representative of the Department of Public Instruction, one representative of the Division of Adult

Correction of the Department of Public Safety, and seven representatives of the Department of Health and Human Services to include the Secretary or his designee.

(2) Sixteen members designated as consumers of service for the developmentally disabled. A consumer of services for the developmentally disabled is a person who (i) has a developmental disability or is the parent or guardian of such a person, or (ii) is an immediate relative or guardian of a person with mentally impairing developmental disability, and (iii) is not an employee of a State agency that receives funds or provides services under the provisions of Part B, Title 1, P.L. 98-527, as amended, the Developmental Disabilities Act of 1984, is not a managing employee (as defined in Section 1126(b) of the Social Security Act) of any other entity that receives funds or provides services under such Part, and is not a person with an ownership or control interest (within the meaning of Section 1124(a)(3) of the Social Security Act) with respect to such an entity. Of these 16 members, at least one third shall be persons with developmental disabilities and at least another one third shall be the immediate relatives or guardians of persons with mentally impairing developmental disabilities, of whom at least one shall be an immediate relative or guardian of an institutionalized developmentally disabled person.

(3) Five members at large as follows: One representative of the university affiliated facility, one representative of the State protection and advocacy system, one representative of a local agency, one representative of a nongovernmental agency or nonprofit group concerned with services to persons with developmental disabilities, and one representative from the public at large.

The appointments of all members, with the exception of those from the General Assembly and State agencies shall be for terms of four years and until their successors are appointed and qualify. Any appointment to fill a vacancy on the Council created by the resignation, dismissal, death, or disability of a member shall be for the balance of the unexpired term.

The Governor shall make appropriate provisions for the rotation of membership on the Council.

(b) The Governor shall have the power to remove any member of the Council from office in accordance with the provisions of G.S. 143B-16.

The Governor shall designate one member of the Council to serve as chairman at his pleasure.

Members of the Council shall receive per diem and necessary travel and subsistence expenses in accordance with the provisions of G.S. 138-5.

A majority of the Council shall constitute a quorum for the transaction of business.

All clerical and other services required by the council shall be supplied by the Secretary of Health and Human Services. (1973, c. 476, s. 169; c. 1117; 1977, c. 881, s. 3; 1979, c. 752, s. 2; 1987, c. 780; 1997-443, s. 11A.118(a); 1997-456, s. 27; 2011-145, s. 19.1(h).)

§ 143B-179.1 through 143B-179.4. Reserved for future codification purposes.

Part 13A. Interagency Coordinating Council for Children with Disabilities from Birth to Five Years of Age.

§ 143B-179.5. Interagency Coordinating Council for Children from Birth to Five with Disabilities and Their Families; establishment, composition, organization; duties, compensation, reporting.

(a)   There is established an Interagency Coordinating Council for Children from Birth to Five with Disabilities and Their Families in the Department of Health and Human Services.

(b)   The Interagency Coordinating Council shall have 26 members, appointed by the Governor. Effective July 1, 1994, the Governor shall designate 13 appointees to serve for two years and 13 appointees to serve for one year. Thereafter, the terms of all Council members shall be two years. The Governor shall have the power to remove any member of the Council from office in accordance with the provisions of G.S. 143B-16. Any appointment to fill a vacancy on the Council created by the resignation, dismissal, death, or disability of a member shall be for the balance of the unexpired term. Members may be appointed to succeed themselves for one term and may be appointed again, after being off the Council for one term.

The composition of the Council and the designation of the Council's chair shall be as specified in the "Individuals with Disabilities Education Act" (IDEA), P.L. 102-119, the federal early intervention legislation, except that two members shall be members of the Senate, appointed from recommendations of the President Pro Tempore of the Senate and two members shall be members of the House of Representatives, appointed from recommendations of the Speaker of the House of Representatives.

(c) The chair may establish those standing and ad hoc committees and task forces as may be necessary to carry out the functions of the Council and appoint Council members or other individuals to serve on these committees and task forces. The Council shall meet at least quarterly. A majority of the Council shall constitute a quorum for the transaction of business.

(d) The Council shall advise the Department of Health and Human Services and other appropriate agencies in carrying out their early intervention services, and the Department of Public Instruction, and other appropriate agencies, in their activities related to the provision of special education services for preschoolers. The Council shall specifically address in its studies and evaluations that it considers necessary to its advising:

(1) The identification of sources of fiscal and other support for the early intervention system;

(2) The development of policies related to the early intervention services;

(3) The preparation of applications for available federal funds;

(4) The resolution of interagency disputes; and

(5) The promotion of interagency agreements.

(e) Members of the Council and parents on ad hoc committees and task forces of the Council shall receive travel and subsistence expenses in accordance with the provisions of G.S. 138-5.

(f) The Council shall prepare and submit an annual report to the Governor and to the General Assembly on the status of the early intervention system for eligible infants and toddlers and on the status of special education services for preschoolers.

All clerical and other services required by the Council shall be supplied by the Secretary of Health and Human Services and the Superintendent of Public Instruction, as specified by the interagency agreement authorized by G.S. 122C-

112(a)(13). (1989 (Reg. Sess., 1990), c. 1003, s. 1; 1993, c. 487, s. 1; 1997-443, s. 11A.106; 2006-69, s. 3(o); 2006-259, s. 34.)

§ 143B-179.5A: Repealed by Session Laws 2008-85, s. 1, effective July 11, 2008.

§ 143B-179.6. Interagency Coordinating Council for Children with Disabilities from Birth to Five Years of Age; agency cooperation.

All appropriate agencies, including the Department of Health and Human Services and the Department of Public Instruction, and other public and private service providers shall cooperate with the Council in carrying out its mandate. (1989 (Reg. Sess., 1990), c. 1003, s. 1; 1997-443, s. 11A.107; 2006-69, s. 3(p).)

Part 14. Governor's Advisory Council on Aging; Division of Aging.

§ 143B-180. Governor's Advisory Council on Aging - creation, powers and duties.

There is hereby created the Governor's Advisory Council on Aging of the Department of Health and Human Services. The Advisory Council on Aging shall have the following functions and duties:

(1) To make recommendations to the Governor and the Secretary of Health and Human Services aimed at improving human services to the elderly;

(2) To study ways and means of promoting public understanding of the problems of the aging, to consider the need for new State programs in the field of aging, and to make recommendations to and advise the Governor and the Secretary on these matters;

(3) To advise the Department of Health and Human Services in the preparation of a plan describing the quality, extent and scope of services being provided, or to be provided, to elderly persons in North Carolina;

(4) To study the programs of all State agencies which provide services for elderly persons and to advise the Governor and the Secretary of Health and Human Services on the coordination of programs to prevent duplication and overlapping of such services;

(5) To advise the Governor and the Secretary of Health and Human Services upon any matter which the Governor and the Secretary may refer to it. (1973, c. 476, s. 171; 1977, c. 242, s. 1; 1983, c. 40, s. 1; 1997-443, s. 11A.118(a).)

§ 143B-181. Governor's Advisory Council on Aging - members; selection; quorum; compensation.

The Governor's Advisory Council on Aging of the Department of Health and Human Services shall consist of 33 members, 29 members to be appointed by the Governor, two members to be appointed by the President Pro Tempore of the Senate, and two members to be appointed by the Speaker of the House of Representatives. The composition of the Council shall be as follows: one representative of the Department of Administration; one representative of the Department of Cultural Resources; one representative of the Division of Employment Security; one representative of the Teachers' and State Employees' Retirement System; one representative of the Commissioner of Labor; one representative of the Department of Public Instruction; one representative of the Department of Environment and Natural Resources; one representative of the Department of Insurance; one representative of the Department of Public Safety; one representative of the Department of Community Colleges; one representative of the School of Public Health of The University of North Carolina; one representative of the School of Social Work of The University of North Carolina; one representative of the Agricultural Extension Service of North Carolina State University; one representative of the collective body of the Medical Society of North Carolina; and 19 members at large. The at large members shall be citizens who are knowledgeable about services supported through the Older Americans Act of 1965, as amended, and shall include persons with greatest economic or social need, minority older persons, and participants in programs under the Older Americans Act of 1965, as amended. The Governor shall appoint 15 members at large who meet these qualifications and are 60 years of age or older. The four remaining members at large, two of whom shall be appointed by the President Pro Tempore of the Senate and two of whom shall be appointed by the Speaker of the House of Representatives, shall be broadly representative of the major private agencies and organizations in the State who are experienced in or have demonstrated particular interest in the special concerns of older persons. At least one of each of the at-large appointments of the President Pro Tempore of the Senate and the Speaker of the House of Representatives shall be persons 60 years of age or older. The Council shall meet at least quarterly.

Members at large shall be appointed for four-year terms and until their successors are appointed and qualify. Ad interim appointments shall be for the balance of the unexpired term.

The Governor shall have the power to remove any member of the Council from office in accordance with the provisions of G.S. 143B-16 of the Executive Organization Act of 1973.

The Governor shall designate one member of the Council as chair to serve in such capacity at his pleasure.

Members of the Council shall receive per diem and necessary travel and subsistence expenses in accordance with the provisions of G.S. 138-5.

A majority of the Council shall constitute a quorum for the transaction of business.

All clerical and other services required by the Council shall be supplied by the Secretary of Health and Human Services. (1973, c. 476, s. 172; 1975, c. 128, ss. 1, 2; 1977, c. 242, s. 2; c. 771, s. 4; 1983, c. 40, s. 2; 1989, c. 727, s. 218(127); 1993, c. 522, s. 16; 1995, c. 490, s. 3; 1997-443, s. 11A.108; 2011-145, s. 19.1(g); 2011-401, s. 3.19.)

§ 143B-181.1. Division of Aging - creation, powers and duties.

(a)   There is hereby created within the office of the Secretary of the Department of Health and Human Services a Division of Aging, which shall have the following functions and duties:

(1)   To maintain a continuing review of existing programs for the aging in the State of North Carolina, and periodically make recommendations to the Secretary of Health and Human Services for transmittal to the Governor and the General Assembly as appropriate for improvements in and additions to such programs;

(2)   To study, collect, maintain, publish and disseminate factual data and pertinent information relative to all aspects of aging. These include the societal, economic, educational, recreational and health needs and opportunities of the aging;

(3) To stimulate, inform, educate and assist local organizations, the community at large, and older people themselves about aging, including needs, resources and opportunities for the aging, and about the role they can play in improving conditions for the aging;

(4) To serve as the agency through which various public and nonpublic organizations concerned with the aged can exchange information, coordinate programs, and be helped to engage in joint endeavors;

(5) To provide advice, information and technical assistance to North Carolina State government departments and agencies and to nongovernmental organizations which may be considering the inauguration of services, programs, or facilities for the aging, or which can be stimulated to take such action;

(6) To coordinate governmental programs with private agency programs for aging in order that such efforts be effective and that duplication and wasted effort be prevented or eliminated;

(7) To promote employment opportunities as well as proper and adequate recreational use of leisure for older people, including opportunities for uncompensated but satisfying volunteer work;

(8) To identify research needs, encourage research, and assist in obtaining funds for research and demonstration projects;

(9) To establish or help to establish demonstration programs of services to the aging;

(10) To establish a fee schedule to cover the cost of providing in-home and community-based services funded by the Division. The fees may vary on the basis of the type of service provided and the ability of the recipient to pay for the service. The fees may be imposed on the recipient of a service unless prohibited by federal law. The local agency shall retain the fee and use it to extend the availability of in-home and community-based services provided by the Division in support of functionally impaired older adults and family caregivers of functionally impaired older adults;

(11) To administer a Home and Community Care Block Grant for older adults, effective July 1, 1992. The Home and Community Care Block Grant shall be comprised of applicable Older Americans Act funds, Social Services Block Grant funding in support of the Respite Care Program (G.S. 143B-181.10),

State funds for home and community care services administered by the Division of Aging, portions of the State In-Home and Adult Day Care funds (Chapter 1048, 1981 Session Laws) administered by the Division of Social Services which support services to older adults, and other funds appropriated by the General Assembly as part of the Home and Community Care Block Grant. Funding currently administered by the Division of Social Services to be included in the block grant will be based on the expenditures for older adults at a point in time to be mutually determined by the Divisions of Social Services and Aging. The total amount of Older Americans Act funds to be included in the Home and Community Care Block Grant and the matching rates for the block grant shall be established by the Department of Health and Human Services, Division of Aging. Allocations made to counties in support of older adults shall not be less than resources made available for the period July 1, 1990, through June 30, 1991, contingent upon availability of current State and federal funding; and

(12) To organize, coordinate, and provide staff support to the North Carolina Senior Tar Heel Legislature.

(b) The Division shall function under the authority of the Department of Health and Human Services and the Secretary of Health and Human Services as provided in the Executive Organization Act of 1973 and shall perform such other duties as are assigned by the Secretary.

(c) The Secretary of Health and Human Services shall adopt rules to implement this Part and Title 42, Chapter 35, of the United States Code, entitled Programs for Older Americans. (1977, c. 242, s. 4; 1981, c. 614, s. 19; 1987, c. 827, s. 244; 1991, c. 52, s. 1; c. 241, s. 1; 1993, c. 503, s. 2; 1997-443, s. 11A.118(a).)

§ 143B-181.1A. Plan for serving older adults; inventory of existing data; cooperation by State agencies.

(a) The Division of Aging, Department of Health and Human Services shall submit a regularly updated plan to the General Assembly by March 1 of every other odd-numbered year, beginning March 1, 1995. This plan shall include:

(1) A detailed analysis of the needs of older adults in North Carolina, based on existing available data, including demographic, geographic, health, social, economical, and other pertinent indicators;

(2) A clear statement of the goals of the State's long-term public policy on aging;

(3) An analysis of services currently provided and an analysis of additional services needed; and

(4) Specific implementation recommendations on expansion and funding of current and additional services and services levels.

(b) The Division of Aging, Department of Health and Human Services, shall maintain an inventory of existing data sets regarding the elderly in North Carolina, in order to ensure that adequate demographic, geographic, health, social, economic, and other pertinent indicators are available to generate its regularly updated Plan for Serving Older Adults.

Upon request, the Division shall make information on these data sets available within a reasonable time.

All State agencies and entities that possess data relating to the elderly, including the Department of Health and Human Services' Division of Health Services, the Division of Health Service Regulation, and the Division of Social Services, and the Department of Administration, shall cooperate, upon request, with the Division of Aging in implementing this subsection. (1989, c. 52, s. 1; c. 695, s. 1; 1995, c. 253, s. 1; 1997-443, s. 11A.118(a); 2007-182, s. 1.)

§ 143B-181.1B. Division as clearinghouse for information; agencies to provide information.

(a) The Division of Aging, Department of Health and Human Services, shall be the central clearinghouse for information regarding all State education and training programs available and being provided about and for the elderly in North Carolina.

(b) The Division of Aging, Department of Health and Human Services, shall produce and distribute annually an updated calendar of conferences, training events, and educational programs about and for the elderly in North Carolina.

(c) All State agencies and entities administering State or federal funding for education and training programs about and for the elderly shall provide to the

Division of Aging by September 1 of each year all information required by the Division regarding conferences, training events, and educational programs provided about and for the elderly. (1989, c. 696, ss. 1-3; 1997-443, s. 11A.118(a).)

§ 143B-181.2. Assistant Secretary for Aging - appointment and duties.

(a) The Secretary of Health and Human Services shall appoint an assistant secretary in the Department of Health and Human Services, whose title shall be the Assistant Secretary for Aging. The Assistant Secretary for Aging shall monitor all aging programs in the Department of Health and Human Services and shall have such powers and duties as are conferred on him by this Part and delegated to him by the Secretary of Health and Human Services.

(b) The Assistant Secretary for Aging, through the appropriate subunits of the Department of Health and Human Services, shall, at the request of the Secretary, identify program needs for the aging, recommend program changes, coordinate intra-departmental program efforts, represent the Secretary in aging matters before boards and commissions, the General Assembly and the public, coordinate program contacts between the Department of Health and Human Services and private, State and federal agencies, initiate special studies on aging matters, and have the responsibility of assuring that services are delivered to the elderly of the State. (1977, c. 242, s. 4; 1997-443, s. 11A.118(a).)

Part 14A. Older Adults.

§ 143B-181.3. Older adults - findings; policy.

(a) The North Carolina General Assembly finds the following:

(1) Older adults should be able to live as independently as possible, and to live free from abuse, neglect, and exploitation.

(2) Older adults should have opportunities to be involved in their communities in ways they desire.

(3)   Preventive and primary health care are necessary to assure optimal health and to enable active social and civic engagement by older adults.

(4)   Sufficient opportunities for training in gerontology and geriatrics should be developed and readily available for individuals serving older adults.

(5)   Older adults should have access to a broad range of services, supports, and opportunities, and they should have transportation options available to allow access to these services and to meet their daily needs and interests.

(6)   Services for older adults should be person-centered and coordinated so that an individual's needs can be met efficiently, effectively, and in the least restrictive environment.

(7)   Information should be readily available in each county on all programs and services for older adults.

(8)   Older adults should have adequate opportunities for employment.

(9)   Each county should have available a variety of housing options, including retirement housing, accessible affordable rental housing, and opportunities for residential home modifications, in order to allow older adults to remain in their communities.

(10)   Older adults and their caregivers should have input in the planning and evaluation of programs and services for older adults, and they should have opportunities to advocate for these programs and services.

(11)   The State should assist older adults who desire to remain as independent as possible and should encourage and support families in caring for their older members.

(b)   It is the policy of the State to effectively utilize its resources to support and enhance the quality of life for older adults in North Carolina. (1979, c. 983, s. 1; 2010-66, s. 1.)

§ 143B-181.4. Responsibility for policy.

Responsibility for developing policy to carry out the purpose of this Part is vested in the Secretary of the Department of Health and Human Services as provided in G.S. 143B-181.1 who may assign responsibility to the Assistant Secretary for Aging. The Assistant Secretary for Aging shall, at the request of the Secretary, be the bridge between the federal and local level and shall review policies that affect the well being of older people with the goal of providing a balance in State programs to meet the social welfare and health needs of the total population. Responsibilities may include:

(1)   Serving as chief advocate for older adults;

(2)   Developing the State plan which will aid in the coordination of all programs for older people;

(3)   Providing information and research to identify gaps in existing services;

(4)   Promoting the development and expansion of services;

(5)   Evaluation of programs;

(6)   Bringing together the public and private sectors to provide services for older people. (1979, c. 983, s. 1; 1997-443, s. 11A.118(a).)

Part 14B. Long-Term Services and Supports.

§ 143B-181.5. Long-term services and supports - findings.

The North Carolina General Assembly finds that the aging of the population and advanced medical technology have resulted in a growing number of persons who require long-term services and supports. The primary resources for long-term assistance continues to be family and friends. However, these traditional caregivers are increasingly employed outside the home. There is growing demand for improvement and expansion of home and community-based long-term services and supports to complement the care provided by these informal caregivers.

The North Carolina General Assembly further finds that the public interest would best be served by a broad array of long-term services and supports that enable persons who need such services to remain in the home or in the community whenever practicable and that promote individual autonomy and dignity as these individuals exercise choice and control over their lives.

The North Carolina General Assembly finds that as other long-term service and support options become more readily available, the need for institutional care will stabilize or decline relative to the growing population of older adults and people living with disabilities. The General Assembly recognizes, however, that institutional care will continue to be a critical part of the State's long-term service and support options and that such care should promote individual dignity, autonomy, and a home like environment. (1981, c. 675, s. 1; 1995 (Reg. Sess., 1996), c. 583, s. 2; 2010-66, s. 2.)

§ 143B-181.6. Purpose and intent.

The development and implementation of policies for long-term services and supports should reflect the intent of the North Carolina General Assembly as follows:

(1)   Long-term services and supports administered by the Department of Health and Human Services and other State and local agencies shall include a balanced array of health, social, and supportive services that are well coordinated to promote individual choice, dignity, and the highest practicable level of independence.

(2)   Home and community-based services shall be developed, expanded, or maintained in order to meet the needs of consumers in the least confusing and least restrictive manner. Services should be based on the desires of older adults, persons with disabilities, their families, and others that support them.

(3)   All services shall be responsive and appropriate to individual need and shall be delivered through a uniform and seamless system that is flexible and responsive regardless of funding source. Information and services shall be available through the effective use of Community Resource Connections for Aging and Disabilities as they are developed throughout the State.

(4)   Services shall be available to all persons who need them, but shall be targeted primarily to those citizens who are the most frail and those with the greatest need.

(5) State and local agencies shall maximize the use of limited resources by establishing a fee system for persons who have the ability to pay.

(6) Care provided in facilities shall be offered in such a manner and in such an environment as to promote for each resident, maintenance of health, enhancement of the quality of life, and timely discharge to a less restrictive care setting when appropriate.

(7) State health planning for institutional bed supply shall take into account increased availability of home and community-based services options.

(8) In an effort to maximize the use of limited resources, State and local agencies shall invest in supports for families and other informal caregivers of persons requiring assistance.

(9) Emphasis shall be placed on offering evidence-based activities to promote healthy aging, prevent injuries, and manage chronic diseases and conditions.

(10) Individuals and families shall be encouraged and supported in planning for and financing their own future needs for long-term services and supports. (1981, c. 675, ss. 1, 2; 1995 (Reg. Sess., 1996), c. 583, s. 2; 1997-443, s. 11A.118(a); 2010-66, s. 2.)

§§ 143B-181.7 through 143B-181.9: Repealed by Session Laws 1995 (Regular Session, 1996), c. 583, s. 2.

§ 143B-181.9A: Repealed by Session Laws 1995, c. 179, s. 1.

Part 14C. Respite Care Program.

§ 143B-181.10. Respite care program established; eligibility; services; administration; payment rates.

(a) A respite care program is established to provide needed relief to caregivers of impaired adults who cannot be left alone because of mental or physical problems.

(b) Those eligible for respite care under the program established by this section are limited to those unpaid primary caregivers who are caring for people 60 years of age or older and their spouses, or those unpaid primary caregivers 60 years of age or older who are caring for persons 18 years of age or older, who require constant supervision and who cannot be left alone either because of memory impairment, physical immobility, or other problems that renders them unsafe alone.

(c) Respite care services provided by the programs established by this section may include:

(1) Counseling and training in the caregiving role, including coping mechanisms and behavior modification techniques;

(2) Counseling and accessing available local, regional, and State services;

(3) Support group development and facilitation;

(4) Assessment and care planning for the patient of the caregiver;

(5) Attendance and companion services for the patient in order to provide release time to the caregiver;

(6) Personal care services, including meal preparation, for the patient of the caregiver;

(7) Temporarily placing the person out of his home to provide the caregiver total respite when the mental or physical stress on the caregiver necessitates this type of respite.

Program funds may provide no more than the current adult care. An out of home placement is defined as placement in a hospital, skilled or intermediate nursing facility, adult care home, adult day health center, or adult day care center. Duration of the service period may extend beyond a year.

(d) The respite care program established by this section shall be administered by the Division of Aging consistent with the policies and procedures of the Older Americans Act. The programs shall be coordinated with other appropriate Divisions in the Department of Health and Human Services, and with agencies and organizations concerned with the delivery of services to frail older adults and their unpaid caregivers. The Division shall choose respite care provider agencies in accordance with procedures outlined under the Older Americans Act and shall include the following criteria: documented capacity to provide care, adequacy of quality assurance, training, supervision, abuse prevention, complaint mechanisms, and cost. All funds allocated by the Division pursuant to this section shall be allocated on the same basis as funding under the Older Americans Act.

(e)   Funding for the Division of Aging to administer this program shall not exceed the percentage allowed for administration as provided in the Older Americans Act but shall not be less than that budgeted for administration in fiscal year 1988-89.

(f)   Unless prohibited by federal law, caregivers receiving respite care services through the program established by this section shall pay for some of the services on a sliding scale depending on their ability to pay. The Division of Aging, in consultation with the Councils of Governments in each region, shall specify rates of payment for the services. (1985 (Reg. Sess., 1986), c. 1014, s. 7.1; 1989, c. 500, s. 96(a); c. 770, s. 63; 1991, c. 332, s. 1; 1995, c. 535, s. 34; 1997-443, s. 11A.118(a); 1998-97, s. 1; 2000-50, s. 1.)

§§ 143B-181.11 through 143B-181.14. Reserved for future codification purposes.

Part 14D. Long-Term Care Ombudsman Program.

§ 143B-181.15. Long-Term Care Ombudsman Program/Office; policy.

The General Assembly finds that a significant number of older citizens of this State reside in long-term care facilities and are dependent on others to provide their care. It is the intent of the General Assembly to protect and improve the quality of care and life for residents through the establishment of a program to assist residents and providers in the resolution of complaints or common concerns, to promote community involvement and volunteerism in long-term care facilities, and to educate the public about the long-term care system. It is the further intent of the General Assembly that the Department of Health and Human Services, within available resources and pursuant to its duties under the Older Americans Act of 1965, as amended, 42 U.S.C. § 3001 et seq., ensure that the quality of care and life for these residents is maintained, that necessary reports are made, and that, when necessary, corrective action is taken at the

Department level. (1989, c. 403, s. 1; 1995, c. 254, s. 1; 1997-443, s. 11A.118(a).)

§ 143B-181.16. Long-Term Care Ombudsman Program/Office; definition.

Unless the content clearly requires otherwise, as used in this Article:

(1)   "Long-term care facility" means any skilled nursing facility and intermediate care facility as defined in G.S. 131A-3(4) or any adult care home as defined in G.S. 131D-20(2).

(2)   "Resident" means any person who is receiving treatment or care in any long-term care facility.

(3)   "State Ombudsman" means the State Ombudsman as defined by the Older Americans Act of 1965, as amended, 42 U.S.C. § 3001 et seq., who carries out the duties and functions established by this Article.

(4)   "Regional Ombudsman" means a person employed by an Area Agency on Aging to carry out the functions of the Regional Ombudsman Office established by this Article. (1989, c. 403, s. 1; 1995, c. 254, s. 2; c. 535, s. 35.)

§ 143B-181.17. Office of State Long-Term Care Ombudsman Program/Office; establishment.

The Secretary of Department of Health and Human Services shall establish and maintain the Office of State Long-Term Ombudsman in the Division of Aging. The Office shall carry out the functions and duties required by the Older Americans Act of 1965, as amended. This Office shall be headed by a State Ombudsman who is a person qualified by training and with experience in geriatrics and long-term care. The Attorney General shall provide legal staff and advice to this Office. (1989, c. 403, s. 1; 1997-443, s. 11A.118(a).)

§ 143B-181.18. Office of State Long-Term Care Ombudsman Program/State Ombudsman duties.

The State Ombudsman shall:

(1) Promote community involvement with long-term care providers and residents of long-term care facilities and serve as liaison between residents, residents' families, facility personnel, and facility administration;

(2) Supervise the Long-Term Care Program pursuant to rules adopted by the Secretary of the Department of Health and Human Services pursuant to G.S. 143B-10;

(3) Certify regional ombudsmen. Certification requirements shall include an internship, training in the aging process, complaint resolution, long-term care issues, mediation techniques, recruitment and training of volunteers, and relevant federal, State, and local laws, policies, and standards;

(4) Attempt to resolve complaints made by or on behalf of individuals who are residents of long-term care facilities, which complaints relate to administrative action that may adversely affect the health, safety, or welfare of residents;

(5) Provide training and technical assistance to regional ombudsmen;

(6) Establish procedures for appropriate access by regional ombudsmen to long-term care facilities and residents' records including procedures to protect the confidentiality of these records and to ensure that the identity of any complainant or resident will not be disclosed except as permitted under the Older Americans Act of 1965, as amended, 42 U.S.C. § 3001 et seq.;

(7) Analyze data relating to complaints and conditions in long-term care facilities to identify significant problems and recommend solutions;

(8) Prepare an annual report containing data and findings regarding the types of problems experienced and complaints reported by residents as well as recommendations for resolutions of identified long-term care issues;

(9) Prepare findings regarding public education and community involvement efforts and innovative programs being provided in long-term care facilities; and

(10) Provide information to public agencies, and through the State Ombudsman, to legislators, and others regarding problems encountered by residents or providers as well as recommendations for resolution. (1989, c. 403, s. 1; 1995, c. 254, s. 3; 1997-443, s. 11A.118(a).)

§ 143B-181.19. Office of Regional Long-Term Care Ombudsman; Regional Ombudsman; duties.

(a) An Office of Regional Ombudsman Program shall be established in each of the Area Agencies on Aging, and shall be headed by a Regional Ombudsman who shall carry out the functions and duties of the Office. The Area Agency on Aging administration shall provide administrative supervision to each Regional Ombudsman.

(b) Pursuant to policies and procedures established by the State Office of Long-Term Care Ombudsman, the Regional Ombudsman shall:

(1) Promote community involvement with long-term care facilities and residents of long-term care facilities and serve as a liaison between residents, residents' families, facility personnel, and facility administration;

(2) Receive and attempt to resolve complaints made by or on behalf of residents in long-term care facilities;

(3) Collect data about the number and types of complaints handled;

(4) Work with long-term care providers to resolve issues of common concern;

(5) Work with long-term care providers to promote increased community involvement;

(6) Offer assistance to long-term care providers in staff training regarding residents' rights;

(7) Report regularly to the office of State Ombudsman about the data collected and about the activities of the Regional Ombudsman;

(8) Provide training and technical assistance to the community advisory committees; and

(9) Provide information to the general public on long-term care issues. (1989, c. 403.)

§ 143B-181.20. State/Regional Long-Term Care Ombudsman; authority to enter; cooperation of government agencies; communication with residents.

(a) The State and Regional Ombudsman may enter any long-term care facility and may have reasonable access to any resident in the reasonable pursuit of his function. The Ombudsman may communicate privately and confidentially with residents of the facility individually or in groups. The Ombudsman shall have access to the patient records as permitted under the Older Americans Act of 1965, as amended, 42 U.S.C. § 3001 et seq., and under procedures established by the State Ombudsman pursuant to G.S. 143B-181.18(6). Entry shall be conducted in a manner that will not significantly disrupt the provision of nursing or other care to residents and if the long-term care facility requires registration of all visitors entering the facility, then the State or Regional Ombudsman must also register. Any State or Regional Ombudsman who discloses any information obtained from the patient's records except as permitted under the Older Americans Act of 1965, as amended, 42 U.S.C. § 3001 et seq., is guilty of a Class 1 misdemeanor.

(b) The State or Regional Ombudsman shall identify himself as such to the resident, and the resident has the right to refuse to communicate with the Ombudsman.

(c) The resident has the right to participate in planning any course of action to be taken on his behalf by the State or Regional Ombudsman, and the resident has the right to approve or disapprove any proposed action to be taken on his behalf by the Ombudsman.

(d) The State or Regional Ombudsman shall meet with the facility administrator or person in charge before any action is taken to allow the facility the opportunity to respond, provide additional information, or take appropriate action to resolve the concern.

(e) The State and Regional Ombudsman may obtain from any government agency, and this agency shall provide, that cooperation, assistance, services, data, and access to files and records that will enable the Ombudsman to properly perform his duties and exercise his powers, provided this information is not privileged by law.

(f) If the subject of the complaint involves suspected abuse, neglect, or exploitation, the State or Regional Ombudsman shall notify the county department of social services' Adult Protection Services section of the county department of social services, pursuant to Article 6 of Chapter 108A of the General Statutes. (1989, c. 403, s. 1; 1993, c. 539, s. 1038; 1994, Ex. Sess., c. 24, s. 14(c); 1995, c. 254, s. 4.)

§ 143B-181.21. State/Regional Long-Term Care Ombudsman; resolution of complaints.

(a) Following receipt of a complaint, the State or Regional Ombudsman shall attempt to resolve the complaint using, whenever possible, informal technique of mediation, conciliation, and persuasion.

(b) Complaints or conditions adversely affecting residents of long-term care facilities that cannot be resolved in the manner described in subsection (a) of this section shall be referred by the State or Regional Ombudsman to the appropriate licensure agency pursuant to G.S. 131E-100 through 110 and Part 1 of Article 1 of Chapter 131D of the General Statutes. (1989, c. 403, s. 1; 2009-462, s. 4(n).)

§ 143B-181.22. State/Regional Long-Term Care Ombudsman; confidentiality.

The identity of any complainant, resident on whose behalf a complaint is made, or any individual providing information on behalf of the resident or complainant relevant to the attempted resolution of the complaint along with the information produced by the process of complaint resolution is confidential and shall be disclosed only as permitted under the Older Americans Act of 1965, as amended, 42 U.S.C. § 3001 et seq. (1989, c. 403, s. 1; 1995, c. 254, s. 5.)

§ 143B-181.23. State/Regional Long-Term Care Ombudsman; prohibition of retaliation.

No person shall discriminate or retaliate in any manner against any resident or relative or guardian of a resident, any employee of a long-term care facility, or any other person because of the making of a complaint or providing of information in good faith to the State Ombudsman or Regional Ombudsman. (1989, c. 403.)

§ 143B-181.24. Office of State/Regional Long-Term Care Ombudsman; immunity from liability.

No representative of the Office shall be liable for good faith performance of official duties. (1989, c. 403.)

§ 143B-181.25. Office of State/Regional Long-Term Care Ombudsman; penalty for willful interference.

Willful or unnecessary obstruction with the State or Regional Long-Term Care Ombudsman in the performance of his official duties is a Class 1 misdemeanor. (1989, c. 403; 1993, c. 539, s. 1039; 1994, Ex. Sess., c. 24, s. 14(c).)

§§ 143B-181.26 through 143B-181.49. Reserved for future codification purposes.

Part 14E. Standards for Alzheimer's Special Care Units.

§§ 143B-181.50 through 143B-181.54. Repealed by Session Laws 1999-334, s. 3.11.

Part 14F. Senior Tar Heel Legislature.

§ 143B-181.55. Creation, membership, meetings, organization, and adoption of measures.

(a)   There is created the North Carolina Senior Tar Heel Legislature. It shall:

(1)   Provide information and education to senior citizens on the legislative process and matters being considered by the General Assembly;

(2)   Promote citizen involvement and advocacy concerning aging issues before the General Assembly; and

(3)   Assess the legislative needs of older citizens by convening a forum modeled after the General Assembly.

(b) The delegates to the Senior Tar Heel Legislature shall be age 60 or over and shall be duly selected pursuant to procedures developed by the Department of Health and Human Services, Division of Aging, and approved by the Secretary of the Department in consultation with senior citizens advocacy groups who have given written notice to the Division of Aging that they desire to be consulted. The Senior Tar Heel Legislative Session shall be organized and coordinated by the Division with Area Agencies on Aging organizing the local election procedures and other related matters. At the conclusion of each session, the Senior Tar Heel Legislature shall make a report of that session's proceedings and recommendations to the General Assembly. Delegates to the Senior Tar Heel Legislature shall be from each county.

(c) The Senior Tar Heel Legislature is authorized to meet one day in March of every year beginning in 1994 but shall hold its first session no later than August 1993. The sessions shall be held in the State Capitol or in a building to be selected by the Governor or the Governor's designee. The Senior Tar Heel Legislature is authorized to adopt bylaws to govern its internal procedures and is authorized to adopt such recommendations as it deems appropriate to present to the General Assembly for consideration.

(d) A report of the proceedings of each session of the Senior Tar Heel Legislature shall be presented to the next Regular Session of the North Carolina General Assembly. (1993, c. 503, s. 1; 1997-443, s. 11A.118(a).)

Part 15. Mental Health Advisory Council.

§§ 143B-182 through 143B-183: Repealed by Session Laws 1981, c. 51, s. 13.

Part 16. Governor's Council on Employment of the Handicapped [Transferred.]

Part 16A. North Carolina Arthritis Program Committee.

§§ 143B-184 through 143B-185: Repealed by Session Laws 1985 (Reg. Sess., 1986), c. 1028, s. 28.

Part 17. Governor's Advocacy Council on Children and Youth.

§§ 143B-186 through 143B-187: Transferred to §§ 143B-414, 143B-415 by Session Laws 1977, c. 872, s. 6.

Part 18. Council on Sickle Cell Syndrome.

§§ 143B-188 through 143B-190: Recodified as §§ 130A-131 through 130A-131.2 by Session Laws 1989, c. 727, s. 179.

§§ 143B-191 through 143B-196: Repealed by Session Laws 1987, c. 822, s. 1.

Part 19. Commission for Human Skills and Resource Development.

§§ 143B-197 through 143B-201. Repealed by Session Laws 1979, c. 504, s. 10.

§§ 143B-202 through 143B-203: Repealed by Session Laws 1989, c. 727, s. 181.

Part 20. Commission of Anatomy.

§§ 143B-204 through 143B-206: Recodified as §§ 130A-33.30 through 130A-33.32 by Session Laws 1989, c. 727, s. 182(a).

Part 21. Youth Services Advisory Committee.

§§ 143B-207 through 143B-208: Repealed by Session Laws 1981, c. 50, s. 7.

Part 22. Human Tissue Advisory Council.

§ 143B-209. Repealed by Session Laws 1983, c. 891, s. 10, effective January 1, 1984.

Part 23. North Carolina Drug Commission.

§§ 143B-210 through 143B-212. Repealed by Session Laws 1981, c. 51, s. 7, effective July 1, 1981.

Part 24. North Carolina Council for the Hearing Impaired.

§§ 143B-213 through 143B-216.5B: Repealed by Session Laws 1989, c. 533, s. 1.

Part 25. Nutrition Advisory Committee.

§§ 143B-216.6 through 143B-216.7: Repealed by Session Laws 1979, c. 504, s. 13.

Part 26. Governor's Council on Physical Fitness and Health.

§§ 143B-216.8 through 143B-216.9: Recodified as §§ 130A-33.40, 130A-33.41 by Session Laws 1989, c. 727, s. 186.

Part 27. Governor's Waste Management Board.

§§ 143B-216.10 through 143B-216.15: Recodified as §§ 143B-285.10 through 143B-285.15 by Session Laws 1989, c. 727, s. 189.

§§ 143B-216.16 through 143B-216.19. Reserved for future codification purposes.

Part 28. North Carolina Council on the Holocaust.

§ 143B-216.20: Recodified as G.S. 143A-48.1(a) by Session Laws 2002-126, s. 10.10D(a), effective October 1, 2002.

§ 143B-216.21: Recodified as G.S. 143A-48.1(b) by Session Laws 2002-126, s. 10.10D(a), effective October 1, 2002.

§ 143B-216.22: Recodified as G.S. 143A-48.1(c) by Session Laws 2002-126, s. 10.10D(a), effective October 1, 2002.

§ 143B-216.23: Recodified as G.S. 143A-48.1(d) by Session Laws 2002-126, s. 10.10D(a), effective October 1, 2002.

§§ 143B-216.24 through 143B-216.29. Reserved for future codification purposes.

Part 29. Council for the Deaf and the Hard of Hearing; Division of Services for the Deaf and the Hard of Hearing.

§ 143B-216.30. Definitions.

The following definitions shall apply throughout this Part unless otherwise specified:

(1) "Council" means the Council for the Deaf and the Hard of Hearing of the Department of Health and Human Services.

(2) "Deaf" means the inability to hear and/or understand oral communication, with or without assistance of amplification devices.

(3) "Division" means the Division of Services for the Deaf and the Hard of Hearing of the Department of Health and Human Services.

(4) "Hard of hearing" means permanent hearing loss which is severe enough to necessitate the use of amplification devices to hear oral communication.

(5) "Ring signaling device" means a mechanism such as a flashing light which visually indicates that a communication is being received through a telephone line. This phrase also means mechanisms such as adjustable volume ringers and buzzers which audibly and loudly indicate an incoming telephone communication.

(6) "Speech impaired" means permanent loss of oral communication ability.

(7) "Telecommunications device" or "TDD" means a keyboard mechanism attached to or in place of a standard telephone by some coupling device, used to transmit or receive signals through telephone lines.

(8) "Volume control handset" means a telephone handset or other telephone listening device which has an adjustable control for increasing the volume of the sound being produced by the telephone receiving unit. (1989, c. 533, s. 2; 1997-443, s. 11A.118(a).)

§ 143B-216.31. Council for the Deaf and the Hard of Hearing - creation and duties.

There is hereby created the Council for the Deaf and the Hard of Hearing of the Department of Health and Human Services. The Council shall have duties including the following:

(1) To make recommendations to the Secretary of the Department of Health and Human Services for cost-effective provision, coordination, and improvement of services;

(2) To create public awareness of the specific needs and abilities of people who are deaf, hard of hearing, or deaf-blind and to consider the need for new State programs concerning the deaf, hard of hearing, and deaf-blind;

(3) To advise the Secretary of the Department of Health and Human Services during planning and implementation of services being provided to North Carolina citizens who are deaf, hard of hearing, or deaf-blind with respect to the quality, extent, and scope of those services;

(4) To advise the Secretary of the Department of Health and Human Services and the Superintendent of the Department of Public Instruction regarding planning, implementation, and cost-effective coordination of State programs providing educational services for persons who are deaf, hard of hearing, or deaf-blind; and

(5) To respond to the request of the Secretary of the Department of Health and Human Services for advice or recommendations pertaining to any matter affecting deaf, hard of hearing, or deaf-blind citizens of North Carolina. (1989, c. 533, s. 2; 1997-443, s. 11A.118(a); 2003-343, s. 1.)

§ 143B-216.32. Council for the Deaf and the Hard of Hearing - membership; quorum; compensation.

(a) The Council for the Deaf and the Hard of Hearing shall consist of 28 members. Twenty members shall be members appointed by the Governor. Three members appointed by the Governor shall be persons who are deaf and three members shall be persons who are hard of hearing. One appointment shall be an educator who trains deaf education teachers and one appointment shall be an audiologist licensed under Article 22 of Chapter 90 of the General Statutes. Three appointments shall be parents of deaf or hard of hearing children including one parent of a student in a residential school; one parent of a student in a preschool program; and one parent of a student in a mainstream education program, with at least one parent coming from each region of the North Carolina schools for the deaf regions. One member appointed by the Governor shall be recommended by the President of the North Carolina Association of the Deaf; one member shall be recommended by the President of the North Carolina Deaf-Blind Associates; one member shall be recommended by the North Carolina Chapter of Self Help for the Hard of Hearing (SHHH); one member shall be recommended by the North Carolina Black Deaf Advocates (NCBDA); one member shall be a representative from a facility that performs cochlear implants; one member shall be recommended by the President of the North Carolina Pediatric Society; one member shall be recommended by the President of the North Carolina Registry of Interpreters for the Deaf; one member shall be recommended by a local education agency; and one member shall be recommended by the Superintendent of Public Instruction. Two members shall be appointed from the House of Representatives by the Speaker of the House of Representatives and two members shall be appointed from the Senate by the President Pro Tempore of the Senate. The Secretary of Health and Human Services shall appoint four members as follows: one from the Division of Vocational Rehabilitation, one from the Division of Aging, one from the Division of Mental Health, Developmental Disabilities, and Substance Abuse Services, and one from the Division of Social Services.

(b) The terms of the initial members of the Council shall commence July 1, 1989. In his initial appointments, the Governor shall designate four members who shall serve terms of five years, four who shall serve terms of four years, four who shall serve terms of three years, and three who shall serve terms of two years. After the initial appointees' terms have expired, all members shall be appointed for a term of four years. No member shall serve more than two successive terms unless the member is an employee of the Department of

Health and Human Services or the Department of Public Instruction representing his or her agency as a specialist in the field of service.

Any appointment to fill a vacancy on the Council created by the resignation, dismissal, death, or disability of a member shall be for the balance of the unexpired term.

(c)   The chairman of the Council shall be designated by the Secretary of the Department of Health and Human Services from the Council members. The chairman shall hold this office for not more than four years.

(d)   The Council shall meet quarterly and at other times at the call of the chairman. A majority of the Council shall constitute a quorum.

(e)   Council members shall be reimbursed for expenses incurred in the performance of their duties in accordance with G.S. 138-5.

(f)   The Secretary of the Department of Health and Human Services shall provide clerical and other assistance as needed. (1989, c. 533, s. 2; 1993, c. 551, s. 1; 1997-443, s. 11A.118(a); 2001-424, s. 21.81(d); 2001-486, s. 2.14; 2003-343, s. 2.)

§ 143B-216.33. Division of Services for the Deaf and the Hard of Hearing - creation, powers and duties.

(a)   There is hereby created within the Department of Health and Human Services, the Division of Services for the Deaf and the Hard of Hearing. The Division shall have the powers and duties including the following:

(1)   To review existing programs for persons who are deaf or hard of hearing in the State, and make recommendations to the Secretary of the Department of Health and Human Services and to the Superintendent of the Department of Public Instruction for improvements to such programs;

(2)   Repealed by Session Laws 1999-237, s. 11.4(b).

(3)   To provide a network of resource centers for local access to services such as interpreters, information and referral, telephone relay, and advocacy for persons who are deaf or hard of hearing;

(4) To collect, study, maintain, publish and disseminate information relative to all aspects of deafness;

(5) To promote public awareness of the needs of, resources and opportunities available to persons who are deaf or hard of hearing;

(6) To provide technical assistance to agencies and organizations in the development of services to persons who are deaf or hard of hearing;

(7) To administer the Telecommunications Program for the Deaf pursuant to G.S. 143B-216.34; and

(8) To provide training and skill development programming to enhance the competence of individuals who aspire to be licensed or who are currently licensed as interpreters or transliterators under Chapter 90D of the General Statutes.

(b) The Division shall function under the authority of the Department of Health and Human Services and the Secretary of the Department of Health and Human Services as provided in the Executive Organization Act of 1973 and shall perform such other duties as are assigned by the Secretary.

(c) The Department of Health and Human Services may receive monies from any source, including federal funds, gifts, grants and devises which shall be expended for the purposes designated in this Part. Gifts and devises received shall be deposited in a trust fund with the State Treasurer who shall hold them in trust in a separate account in the name of the Division. The cash balance of this account may be pooled for investment purposes, but investment earnings shall be credited pro rata to this participating account. Monies deposited with the State Treasurer in the trust fund account pursuant to this subsection, and investment earnings thereon, are available for expenditure without further authorization from the General Assembly. Such funds shall be administered by the Division under the direction of the director and fiscal officer of the Division and will be subject to audits normally conducted with the agency.

(d) The Secretary of the Department of Health and Human Services shall adopt rules to implement this Part. (1989, c. 533, s. 2; 1997-443, s. 11A.118(a); 1999-237, s. 11.4(b); 2002-182, s. 5; 2003-56, s. 3; 2011-284, s. 100.)

§ 143B-216.34. Division of Services for the Deaf and the Hard of Hearing - temporary loan program established.

(a) There is established an assistive equipment loan program for the deaf, hard of hearing, and speech impaired to be developed, administered, and implemented by the Division of Services for the Deaf and the Hard of Hearing. The assistive equipment loan program supplements the telecommunications equipment distribution program established pursuant to G.S. 62-157.

(b) The Division shall develop rules for the distribution of the communications and alerting equipment and shall determine performance standards. The Division shall select equipment for distribution to qualifying recipients. The equipment discussed in this section shall be leased at no cost to qualifying recipients for a period of time up to and not exceeding two years. Nothing herein shall be construed to prevent the renewal of any lease previously executed with a qualified recipient. In addition, the Division shall provide consultative services and training to those individuals and organizations utilizing communications and alerting equipment pursuant to this section.

(c) The central communications office of each county sheriff's department shall purchase and continually operate at least one telecommunications device that is functionally equivalent in providing equal access to services for individuals who are deaf, hard of hearing, deaf-blind, and speech impaired.

The central communications office of each police department and firefighting agency in municipalities with a population of 25,000 to 250,000 shall purchase and continually operate at least one such device.

The central communications office of each police department and firefighting agency in municipalities with a population exceeding 250,000 persons shall purchase and continually operate at least two such devices.

(d) Each public safety office, health care facility (including hospitals and urgent care facilities), and the 911 emergency number system is required to obtain a telecommunications device that is functionally equivalent in providing equal access to services for individuals who are deaf, hard of hearing, and speech impaired pursuant to this section and shall continually operate and staff the equipment during hours of operation, including up to 24 hours. (1989, c. 533, s. 2; 2007-149, s. 1.)

§§ 143B-216.35 through 143B-216.39. Reserved for future codification purposes.

Part 30. State Schools for Hearing-impaired Children.

§§ 143B-216.40 through 143B-216.44: Repealed by Session Laws 2013-247, s. 1(c), effective July 3, 2013.

§§ 143B-216.45 through 143B-216.49. Reserved for future codification purposes.

Part 31. Office of the Internal Auditor.

§ 143B-216.50. Department of Health and Human Services; office of the Internal Auditor.

(a) The office of Internal Auditor is established in the Department of Health and Human Services. The office of the Internal Auditor shall provide independent reviews and analyses of various functions and programs within the Department that will provide management information to promote accountability, integrity, and efficiency within the Department.

(b) It shall be the duty and responsibility of the Internal Auditor to:

(1) Advise in the development of performance measure, standards, and procedures for the evaluation of the Department;

(2) Assess the reliability and validity of performance measures and the information provided by the Department on performance measures and standards and make recommendations for improvement, if necessary;

(3) Review the actions taken by the Department of Health and Human Services to improve program performance and meet program standards and make recommendations for improvement, if necessary;

(4) Provide direction for, supervise, and coordinate audits, investigations, and management reviews relating to programs and operations of the Department;

(5) Conduct independent analysis of programs carried out or financed by the Department of Health and Human Services for the purpose of promoting economy and efficiency in the administration of, or preventing and detecting waste, management, misconduct, fraud and abuse in its programs and operations;

(6) Keep the Secretary of the Department of Health and Human Services informed concerning fraud, abuses, and deficiencies relating to programs and operations administered or financed by the Department of Health and Human Services, recommend corrective action concerning fraud, abuses, and deficiencies, and report on the progress made in implementing corrective action;

(7) Ensure effective coordination and cooperation between the State Auditor, federal auditors, and other governmental bodies with a view toward avoiding duplication; and

(8) Ensure that an appropriate balance is maintained between audit, investigative, and other accountability activities.

(c) The Internal Auditor shall be appointed by the Secretary. The Internal Auditor shall be appointed without regard to political affiliation.

(d) The Internal Auditor shall report to an official designated by the Secretary.

(e) The Internal Auditor shall have access to any records, data, or other information of the Department the Internal Auditor believes necessary to carry out the Internal Auditor's duties. (1997-443, s. 12.21(c).)

§ 143B-216.51. Department of Health and Human Services office of the Internal Auditor; Department audits.

(a) To ensure that Department audits are performed in accordance with applicable auditing standards, the Internal Auditor shall possess the following qualifications:

(1) A bachelors degree from an accredited college or university with a major in accounting, or with a major in business which includes five courses in accounting, and five years' experience as an internal auditor or independent

postauditor, electronic data processing auditor, accountant, or any combination thereof. The experience shall, at a minimum, consist of audits of units of government or private business enterprises operating for profit or not for profit;

(2) A masters degree in accounting, business administration, or public administration from an accredited college or university and four years of experience as required in subdivision (1) of this subsection; or

(3) A certified public accountant license issued pursuant to law or a certified internal audit certificate issued by the Institute of Internal Auditors or earned by examination, and four years' experience as required in subdivision (1) of this subsection.

The Internal Auditor shall, to the extent both necessary and practicable, include on the Internal Auditor's staff individuals with electronic data processing auditing experience.

(b) In carrying out the auditing duties and responsibilities of this Part, the Internal Auditor shall review and evaluate internal controls necessary to ensure the fiscal accountability of the Department. The Internal Auditor shall conduct financial, compliance, electronic data processing, and performance audits of the Department and prepare audit reports of findings. The scope and assignment of the audits shall be determined by the Internal Auditor; however, the Secretary may at any time direct the Internal Auditor to perform an audit of a special program, function, or organizational unit. The performance of the audit shall be under the direction of the Internal Audit.

(c) Audits undertaken pursuant to this Part shall be conducted in accordance with auditing standards prescribed by the State Auditor. All audit reports issued by internal audit staff shall include a statement that the audit was conducted pursuant to these standards.

(d) The Internal Auditor shall maintain, for 10 years, a complete file of all audit reports and reports of other examinations, investigations, surveys, and reviews issued under the Internal Auditor's authority. Audit work papers and other evidence and related supportive material directly pertaining to the work of his office shall be retained according to an agreement between the Internal Auditor and State Archives. To promote cooperation and avoid unnecessary duplication of audit effort, audit work papers related to issued audit reports shall be, unless otherwise prohibited by law, made available for inspection by duly authorized representatives of the State and federal governments in connection with some matter officially before them. Except as otherwise provided in this subsection, or upon subpoena issued by a duly authorized court or court official, audit work papers shall be kept confidential. Audit reports shall be public records to the extent that they do not include information which, under State laws, is confidential and exempt from Chapter 132 of the General Statutes or would compromise the security systems of the Department.

(e) The Internal Auditor shall submit the final report to the Secretary.

(f) The State Auditor shall review a sample of the Department's internal audit reports and related work papers when determined by the State Auditor that, when conducting audits, it would be efficient to consider the work of the Internal Auditor. If the State Auditor finds deficiencies in the work of the Internal Auditor, the State Auditor shall include a statement of these findings in the audit report of the Department. The office of the Internal Auditor will cause to be made an external quality control review at least once every three years by a qualified organization not affiliated with the office of the Internal Auditor. The external quality review should determine whether the Department's internal quality control system is in place and operating effectively to provide reasonable assurance that established policies and procedures and applicable audit standards are being followed.

(g) The Internal Auditor shall monitor the implementation of the Department's response to any audit of the Department conducted by the State Auditor pursuant to law. No later than six months after the State Auditor publishes a report of the audit of the Department, the Internal Auditor shall report to the Secretary on the status of corrective actions taken. A copy of the report shall be filed with the Joint Legislative Commission on Governmental Operations.

(h) The Internal Auditor shall develop long-term and annual audit plans based on the findings of periodic risk assessments. The plan, where appropriate, should include postaudit samplings of payments and accounts. The plan shall show the individual audits to be conducted during each year and related resources to be devoted to the respective audits. The State Controller may utilize audits performed by the Internal Auditor. The plan shall be submitted to the Secretary for approval. A copy of the approved plan shall be submitted to the State Auditor. (1997-443, s. 12.21(c).)

§§ 143B-216.52 through 143B-216.59. Reserved for future codification purposes.

Part 32. Heart Disease and Stroke Prevention Task Force.

§ 143B-216.60. The Justus-Warren Heart Disease and Stroke Prevention Task Force.

(a) The Justus-Warren Heart Disease and Stroke Prevention Task Force is created in the Department of Health and Human Services.

(b) The Task Force shall have 27 members. The Governor shall appoint the Chair, and the Vice-Chair shall be elected by the Task Force. The Director of the Department of Health and Human Services, the Director of the Division of Medical Assistance in the Department of Health and Human Services, and the Director of the Division of Aging in the Department of Health and Human Services, or their designees, shall be members of the Task Force. Appointments to the Task Force shall be made as follows:

(1) By the General Assembly upon the recommendation of the President Pro Tempore of the Senate, as follows:

a. Three members of the Senate;

b. A heart attack survivor;

c. A local health director;

d. A certified health educator;

e. A hospital administrator; and

f. A representative of the North Carolina Association of Area Agencies on Aging.

(2) By the General Assembly upon the recommendation of the Speaker of the House of Representatives, as follows:

a. Three members of the House of Representatives;

b. A stroke survivor;

c. A county commissioner;

d. A licensed dietitian/nutritionist;

e. A pharmacist; and

f. A registered nurse.

(3) By the Governor, as follows:

a. A practicing family physician, pediatrician, or internist;

b. A president or chief executive officer of a business upon recommendation of a North Carolina wellness council which is a member of the Wellness Councils of America;

c. A news director of a newspaper or television or radio station;

d. A volunteer of the North Carolina Affiliate of the American Heart Association;

e. A representative from the North Carolina Cooperative Extension Service;

f. A representative of the Governor's Council on Physical Fitness and Health; and

g. Two members at large.

(c) Each appointing authority shall assure insofar as possible that its appointees to the Task Force reflect the composition of the North Carolina population with regard to ethnic, racial, age, gender, and religious composition.

(d) The General Assembly and the Governor shall make their appointments to the Task Force not later than 30 days after the adjournment of the 1995 General Assembly, Regular Session 1995. A vacancy on the Task Force shall be filled by the original appointing authority, using the criteria set out in this section for the original appointment.

(e)   The Task Force shall meet not more than twice annually at the call of the Chair.

(f)   Repealed by Session Laws 2013-360, s. 12A.13, effective July 1, 2013.

(g)   Members of the Task Force shall receive per diem and necessary travel and subsistence expenses in accordance with G.S. 120-3.1, 138-5 and 138-6, as applicable.

(h)   A majority of the Task Force shall constitute a quorum for the transaction of its business.

(i)   The Task Force may use funds allocated to it to establish two positions and for other expenditures needed to assist the Task Force in carrying out its duties.

(j)   The Task Force has the following duties:

(1)   To undertake a statistical and qualitative examination of the incidence of and causes of heart disease and stroke deaths and risks, including identification of subpopulations at highest risk for developing heart disease and stroke, and establish a profile of the heart disease and stroke burden in North Carolina.

(2)   To publicize the profile of the heart disease and stroke burden and its preventability in North Carolina.

(3)   To identify priority strategies which are effective in preventing and controlling risks for heart disease and stroke.

(4)   To identify, examine limitations of, and recommend to the Governor and the General Assembly changes to existing laws, regulations, programs, services, and policies to enhance heart disease and stroke prevention by and for the people of North Carolina.

(5)   To determine and recommend to the Governor and the General Assembly the funding and strategies needed to enact new or to modify existing laws, regulations, programs, services, and policies to enhance heart disease and stroke prevention by and for the people of North Carolina.

(6)   To adopt and promote a statewide comprehensive Heart Disease and Stroke Prevention Plan to the general public, State and local elected officials,

various public and private organizations and associations, businesses and industries, agencies, potential funders, and other community resources.

(7) To identify and facilitate specific commitments to help implement the Plan from the entities listed in subdivision (6) above.

(8) To facilitate coordination of and communication among State and local agencies and organizations regarding current or future involvement in achieving the aims of the Heart Disease and Stroke Prevention Plan.

(9) To receive and consider reports and testimony from individuals, local health departments, community-based organizations, voluntary health organizations, and other public and private organizations statewide, to learn more about their contributions to heart disease and stroke prevention, and their ideas for improving heart disease and stroke prevention in North Carolina.

(10) Establish and maintain a Stroke Advisory Council, which shall advise the Task Force regarding the development of a statewide system of stroke care that shall include, among other items, a system for identifying and disseminating information about the location of primary stroke centers.

(k) Notwithstanding Section 11.57 of S.L. 1999-237, the Task Force shall submit a final report to the Governor and the General Assembly by June 30, 2003, and a report to each subsequent regular legislative session within one week of its convening. (1995-507, s. 26.9; 1997-443, ss. 11A-122, 11A-123; 2001-424, s. 21.95; 2002-126, s. 10.45; 2003-284, s. 10.33B; 2006-197, s. 1; 2013-360, s. 12A.13.)

§§ 143B-216.61 through 143B-216.64: Reserved for future codification purposes.

Part 33. North Carolina Brain Injury Advisory Council.

§ 143B-216.65. North Carolina Brain Injury Advisory Council - creation and duties.

There is established the North Carolina Brain Injury Advisory Council in the Department of Health and Human Services to review traumatic and other acquired brain injuries in North Carolina. The Council shall have duties including the following:

(1)   Review how the term "traumatic brain injury" is defined by State and federal regulations and to determine whether changes should be made to the State definition to include "acquired brain injury" or other appropriate conditions.

(2)   Promote interagency coordination among State agencies responsible for services and support of individuals that have traumatic brain injury.

(3)   Study the needs of individuals with traumatic brain injury and their families.

(4)   Make recommendations to the Governor, the General Assembly, and the Secretary of Health and Human Services regarding the planning, development, funding, and implementation of a comprehensive statewide service delivery system.

(5)   Promote and implement injury prevention strategies across the State. (2003-114, s. 1; 2009-361, s. 3.)

§ 143B-216.66. North Carolina Brain Injury Advisory Council - membership; quorum; compensation.

(a)   The Council shall consist of 23 voting and 10 ex officio nonvoting members, appointed as follows:

(1)   Three members by the General Assembly, upon the recommendation of the President Pro Tempore of the Senate, as follows:

a.   A representative of the North Carolina Medical Society or other organization with interest in brain injury prevention or treatment.

b.   A nurse with expertise in trauma, neurosurgery, neuropsychology, physical medicine and rehabilitation, or emergency medicine.

c.   One at-large member who shall be a veteran or family member of a veteran who has suffered a brain injury.

(2) Three members by the General Assembly, upon the recommendation of the Speaker of the House of Representatives, as follows:

a. One at-large member who may have experience as a school nurse or rehabilitation specialist.

b. A representative of the North Carolina Hospital Association or other organization interested in brain injury prevention or treatment.

c. A physician with expertise in trauma, neurosurgery, neuropsychology, physical medicine and rehabilitation, or emergency medicine.

(3) Fourteen members by the Governor, as follows:

a. Three survivors of brain injury, one each representing the eastern, central, and western regions of the State.

b. Four family members of persons with brain injury with consideration for geographic representation.

c. A brain injury service provider in the private sector.

d. The director of a local management entity of mental health, developmental disabilities, and substance abuse services.

e. The Executive Director, or designee thereof, of North Carolina Advocates for Justice.

f. The Executive Director, or designee thereof, of the Brain Injury Association of North Carolina.

g. The Chair of the Board, or designee thereof, of the Brain Injury Association of North Carolina.

h. The Executive Director, or designee thereof, of the North Carolina Protection and Advocacy System.

i. One stroke survivor, as recommended by the American Heart Association.

(4)   Nine ex officio members by the Secretary of Health and Human Services, as follows:

a.   One member from the Division of Mental Health, Developmental Disabilities, and Substance Abuse Services.

b.   One member from the Division of Vocational Rehabilitation.

c.   One member from the Council on Developmental Disabilities.

d.   One member from the Division of Medical Assistance.

e.   Two members from the Division of Health Service Regulation.

f.   One member from the Division of Social Services.

g.   One member from the Office of Emergency Medical Services.

h.   One member from the Division of Public Health.

(5)   Two members by the Superintendent of Public Instruction, one of whom is ex officio, nonvoting, and employed with the Division of Exceptional Children.

(6)   One member by the Commissioner of Insurance, or the Commissioner's designee.

(7)   One member by the Secretary of Administration representing veterans affairs.

(b)   The terms of the initial members of the Council shall commence October 1, 2003. In his initial appointments, the Governor shall designate four members who shall serve terms of four years, four members who shall serve terms of three years, and three members who shall serve terms of two years. After the initial appointees' terms have expired, all members shall be appointed for a term of four years. No member appointed by the Governor shall serve more than two successive terms.

Any appointment to fill a vacancy on the Council created by the resignation, dismissal, death, or disability of a member shall be for the balance of the unexpired term. Terms for ex officio, nonvoting members do not expire.

(c) The initial chair of the Council shall be designated by the Secretary of the Department of Health and Human Services from the Council members. The chair shall hold this office for not more than four years. Subsequent chairs will be elected by the Council.

(d) The Council shall meet quarterly and at other times at the call of the chair. A majority of voting members of the Council shall constitute a quorum.

(e) Council members shall be reimbursed for expenses incurred in the performance of their duties in accordance with G.S. 138-5 and G.S. 138-6, as applicable.

(f) The Secretary of the Department of Health and Human Services shall provide clerical and other assistance as needed. (2003-114, s. 1; 2007-182, s. 1; 2009-361, s. 3.)

§ 143B-216.67: Reserved for future codification purposes.

§ 143B-216.68: Reserved for future codification purposes.

§ 143B-216.69: Reserved for future codification purposes.

Part 34. Office of Policy and Planning.

§ 143B-216.70. Office of Policy and Planning.

(a) To promote coordinated policy development and strategic planning for the State's health and human services systems, the Secretary of Health and Human Services shall establish an Office of Policy and Planning from existing resources across the Department. The Director of the Office of Policy and Planning shall report directly to the Secretary and shall have the following responsibilities:

(1) Coordinate the development of departmental policies, plans, and rules, in consultation with the Divisions of the Department.

(2) Development of a departmental process for the development and implementation of new policies, plans, and rules.

(3) Development of a departmental process for the review of existing policies, plans, and rules to ensure that departmental policies, plans, and rules are relevant.

(4) Coordination and review of all departmental policies before dissemination to ensure that all policies are well-coordinated within and across all programs.

(5) Implementation of ongoing strategic planning that integrates budget, personnel, and resources with the mission and operational goals of the Department.

(6) Review, disseminate, monitor, and evaluate best practice models.

(b) Under the direction of the Secretary of Health and Human Services, the Director of the Office of Policy and Planning shall have the authority to direct Divisions, offices, and programs within the Department to conduct periodic reviews of policies, plans, and rules and shall advise the Secretary when it is determined to be appropriate or necessary to modify, amend, and repeal departmental policies, plans, and rules. All policy and management positions within the Office of Policy and Planning are exempt positions as that term is defined in G.S. 126-5. (2005-276, s. 10.2.)

§ 143B-216.71: Reserved for future codification purposes.

§ 143B-216.72: Reserved for future codification purposes.

Part 34A. North Carolina Energy Assistance Act for Low-Income Persons.

§ 143B-216.72A: Recodified as G.S. 143B-472.121 through 143B-472.123 by Session Laws 2009-446, s. 2(a).

§ 143B-216.72B: Recodified as G.S. 143B-472.121 through 143B-472.123 by Session Laws 2009-446, s. 2(a).

§ 143B-216.72C: Recodified as G.S. 143B-472.121 through 143B-472.123 by Session Laws 2009-446, s. 2(a).

§ 143B-216.73: Reserved for future codification purposes.

§ 143B-216.74: Reserved for future codification purposes.

Part 35. Governor's Commission on Early Childhood Vision Care.

§ 143B-216.75: Repealed by Session Laws 2011-266, s. 1.40, effective July 1, 2011.

Article 4.

Department of Revenue.

Part 1. General Provisions.

§ 143B-217. Department of Revenue - creation.

There is hereby recreated and reestablished a department to be known as the "Department of Revenue" with the organization, duties, functions, and powers defined in the Executive Organization Act of 1973. (1973, c. 476, s. 184.)

§ 143B-218. Department of Revenue - duties.

It shall be the duty of the Department to collect and account for the State's tax funds, to insure uniformity of administration of the tax laws and regulations, to conduct research on revenue matters, and to exercise general and specific supervision over the valuation and taxation of property throughout the State. (1973, c. 476, s. 185; 1981, c. 859, s. 81; c. 1127, s. 53.)

§ 143B-218.1: Recodified as § 105-256(a)(6) by Session Laws 2001 414, s. 25.

§ 143B-219. Department of Revenue - functions.

(a) The functions of the Department of Revenue shall comprise, except as otherwise expressly provided by the Executive Organization Act of 1973 or by the Constitution of North Carolina, all executive functions of the State in relation to revenue collection, tax research, tax settlement, and property tax supervision including those prescribed powers, duties and functions enumerated in Article 16 of Chapter 143A of the General Statutes of this State.

(b) All functions, powers, duties, and obligations heretofore vested in any agency enumerated in Article 16 of Chapter 143A of the General Statutes are hereby transferred to and vested in the Department of Revenue, except as otherwise provided by the Executive Organization Act of 1973. They shall include, by way of extension and not of limitation, the functions of:

(1) The Commissioner and Department of Revenue,

(2) The Department of Tax Research, and

(3) The State Board of Assessment. (1973, c. 476, s. 186; 1981, c. 859, s. 82; c. 1127, s. 53.)

§ 143B-220. Department of Revenue - head.

The Secretary of Revenue shall be the head of the Department. (1973, c. 476, s. 187.)

§ 143B-221: Repealed by Session Laws 2001-414, s. 47.

Part 2. Property Tax Commission.

§§ 143B-222 through 143B-225: Repealed by Session Laws 1991, c. 110, s. 3.

§§ 143B-226 through 143B-245. Reserved for future codification purposes.

Article 5.

Department of Military and Veterans Affairs.

Part 1. General Provisions.

§§ 143B-246 through 143B-251. Repealed by Session Laws 1977, c. 70, s. 33.

Part 2. Veterans Affairs Commission.

§§ 143B-252 through 143B-253. Transferred to §§ 143B-399, 143B-400 by Session Laws 1977, c. 70, ss. 24, 25.

Part 3. Energy Division.

§§ 143B-254 through 143B-255. Repealed by Session Laws 1977, c. 23, s. 3.

§§ 143B-256 through 143B-259. Reserved for future codification purposes.

Article 6.

Department of Corrections.

Part 1. General Provisions.

§§ 143B-260 through 143B-264: Recodified and renumbered as Subpart A of Part 2 of Article 13, G.S. 143B-700 through 143B-711.

Part 2. Board of Correction.

§ 143B-265: Recodified and renumbered as Subpart B of Part 2 of Article 13, G.S. 143B-715.

Part 3. Parole Commission.

§§ 143B-266, 143B-267: Recodified and renumbered as Subpart C of Part 2 of Article 13, G.S. 143B-720, 143B-721.

§ 143B-268. Reserved for future codification purposes.

Part 4. Black Mountain Advancement Center for Women.

§ 143B-269: Repealed by Session Laws 2007-252, s. 1, effective July 1, 2007.

Part 5. Substance Abuse Advisory Council.

§ 143B-270: Repealed by Session Laws 2011-266, s. 1.17(a), effective July 1, 2011.

§ 143B-271: Repealed by Session Laws 2011-266, s. 1.17(a), effective July 1, 2011.

§ 143B-272: Reserved for future codification purposes.

Article 6A.

North Carolina State-County Criminal Justice Partnership Act.

§ 143B-273: Repealed by Session Laws 2011-192, s. 6(a), effective July 1, 2011.

§ 143B-273.1: Repealed by Session Laws 2011-192, s. 6(a), effective July 1, 2011.

§ 143B-273.2: Repealed by Session Laws 2011-192, s. 6(a), effective July 1, 2011.

§ 143B-273.3: Repealed by Session Laws 2011-192, s. 6(a), effective July 1, 2011.

§ 143B-273.4: Repealed by Session Laws 2011-192, s. 6(a), effective July 1, 2011.

§ 143B-273.5: Repealed by Session Laws 2011-192, s. 6(a), effective July 1, 2011.

§ 143B-273.6: Repealed by Session Laws 2011-192, s. 6(a), effective July 1, 2011.

§ 143B-273.7: Repealed by Session Laws 2011-192, s. 6(a), effective July 1, 2011.

§ 143B-273.8: Repealed by Session Laws 2011-192, s. 6(a), effective July 1, 2011.

§ 143B-273.9: Repealed by Session Laws 2011-192, s. 6(a), effective July 1, 2011.

§ 143B-273.10: Repealed by Session Laws 2011-192, s. 6(a), effective July 1, 2011.

§ 143B-273.11: Repealed by Session Laws 2011-192, s. 6(a), effective July 1, 2011.

§ 143B-273.12: Repealed by Session Laws 2011-192, s. 6(a), effective July 1, 2011.

§ 143B-273.13: Repealed by Session Laws 2011-192, s. 6(a), effective July 1, 2011.

§ 143B-273.14: Repealed by Session Laws 2011-192, s. 6(a), effective July 1, 2011.

§ 143B-273.15: Repealed by Session Laws 2011-192, s. 6(a), effective July 1, 2011.

§ 143B-273.15A: Repealed by Session Laws 2011-192, s. 6(a), effective July 1, 2011.

§ 143B-273.16: Repealed by Session Laws 2011-192, s. 6(a), effective July 1, 2011.

§ 143B-273.17: Repealed by Session Laws 2011-192, s. 6(a), effective July 1, 2011.

§ 143B-273.18: Repealed by Session Laws 2011-192, s. 6(a), effective July 1, 2011.

§ 143B-273.19: Repealed by Session Laws 2011-192, s. 6(a), effective July 1, 2011.

§ 143B-274. Reserved for future codification purposes.

Article 7.

Department of Environment and Natural Resources.

Part 1. General Provisions.

§§ 143B-275 through 143B-279: Repealed by Session Laws 1989, c. 727, s. 2.

§ 143B-279.1. Department of Environment and Natural Resources - creation.

(a) There is hereby created and constituted a department to be known as the Department of Environment and Natural Resources, with the organization, powers, and duties defined in this Article and other applicable provisions of law.

(b) The provisions of Article 1 of this Chapter not inconsistent with this Article shall apply to the Department of Environment and Natural Resources. (1989, c. 727, s. 3; 1997-443, s. 11A.119(a).)

§ 143B-279.2. Department of Environment and Natural Resources - duties.

It shall be the duty of the Department:

(1) To provide for the protection of the environment;

(1a) To administer the State Outer Continental Shelf (OCS) Task Force and coordinate State participation activities in the federal outer continental shelf resource recovery programs as provided under the OCS Lands Act Amendments of 1978 (43 USC §§ 1801 et seq.) and the OCS Lands Act Amendments of 1986 (43 USC §§ 1331 et seq.).

(1b) To provide for the protection of the environment and public health through the regulation of solid waste and hazardous waste management and the administration of environmental health programs.

(2) Repealed by Session Laws 1997-443, s. 11A.5, effective August 28, 1997.

(2a) To provide and keep a museum or collection of the natural history of the State and to maintain the North Carolina Biological Survey; and

(3) To provide for the management of the State's natural resources.

(4) Repealed by Session Laws 2011-145, s. 13.11, effective July 1, 2011. (1989, c. 727, s. 3; 1993, c. 321, s. 28(c); c. 561, s. 116(e); 1997-443, s. 11A.5; 2009-451, s. 13.1A; 2011-145, s. 13.11.)

§ 143B-279.3. Department of Environment and Natural Resources - structure.

(a) All functions, powers, duties, and obligations previously vested in the following subunits of the following departments are transferred to and vested in the Department of Environment and Natural Resources by a Type I transfer, as defined in G.S. 143A-6:

(1) Radiation Protection Section, Division of Health Service Regulation, Department of Health and Human Services.

(2), (3) Repealed by Session Laws 1997-443, s. 11A.6.

(4) Coastal Management Division, Department of Natural Resources and Community Development.

(5) Environmental Management Division, Department of Natural Resources and Community Development.

(6) Repealed by Session Laws 2011-145, s. 13.25(b), effective July 1, 2011.

(7) Land Resources Division, Department of Natural Resources and Community Development.

(8) Marine Fisheries Division, Department of Natural Resources and Community Development.

(9) Parks and Recreation Division, Department of Natural Resources and Community Development.

(10) Repealed by Session Laws 2011-145, s. 13.22A(c), effective July 1, 2011.

(11)   Water Resources Division, Department of Natural Resources and Community Development.

(12)   North Carolina Zoological Park, Department of Natural Resources and Community Development.

(13)   Albemarle-Pamlico Study.

(14)   Office of Marine Affairs, Department of Administration.

(15)   Environmental Health Section, Division of Health Services, Department of Health and Human Services.

(b)   All functions, powers, duties, and obligations previously vested in the following commissions, boards, councils, and committees of the following departments are transferred to and vested in the Department of Environment and Natural Resources by a Type II transfer, as defined in G.S. 143A-6:

(1)   Repealed by Session Laws 1993, c. 501, s. 27.

(2)   Radiation Protection Commission, Department of Health and Human Services.

(3)   Repealed by Session Laws 1997-443, s. 11A.6.

(4)   Water Treatment Facility Operators Board of Certification, Department of Health and Human Services.

(5)   through (8) Repealed by Session Laws 1997-443, s. 11A.6.

(9)   Coastal Resources Commission, Department of Natural Resources and Community Development.

(10)   Environmental Management Commission, Department of Natural Resources and Community Development.

(11)   Air Quality Council, Department of Natural Resources and Community Development.

(12)   Wastewater Treatment Plant Operators Certification Commission, Department of Natural Resources and Community Development.

(13) Repealed by Session Laws 2011-145, s. 13.25(e), effective July 1, 2011.

(14) North Carolina Mining and Energy Commission, Department of Natural Resources and Community Development.

(15) Advisory Committee on Land Records, Department of Natural Resources and Community Development.

(16) Marine Fisheries Commission, Department of Natural Resources and Community Development.

(17) Parks and Recreation Council, Department of Natural Resources and Community Development.

(18) Repealed by Session Laws 2013-360, s. 14.3(j), effective August 1, 2013.

(19) North Carolina Trails Committee, Department of Natural Resources and Community Development.

(20) Sedimentation Control Commission, Department of Natural Resources and Community Development.

(21) Repealed by Session Laws 2011-145, s. 13.22A(d), effective July 1, 2011.

(22) North Carolina Zoological Park Council, Department of Natural Resources and Community Development.

(23) Repealed by Session Laws 1997-286, s. 6.

(c) (1) Repealed by Session Laws 2002, ch. 70, s. 1, effective July 1, 2002.

(2) There is created a division within the environmental area of the Department of Environment and Natural Resources to be named the Division of Waste Management. All functions, powers, duties, and obligations of the Solid Waste Management Section of the Division of Health Services of the Department of Health and Human Services are transferred in their entirety to the

Division of Waste Management of the Department of Environment and Natural Resources.

(3)   Repealed by Session Laws 2011-145, s. 13.3(i), effective July 1, 2011.

(d)   The Department of Environment and Natural Resources is vested with all other functions, powers, duties, and obligations as are conferred by the Constitution and laws of this State. (1989, c. 727, s. 3; 1989 (Reg. Sess., 1990), c. 1004, s. 31; 1991, c. 342, ss. 16(a), (b); 1993, c. 321, ss. 28(a), (b); c. 501, s. 27; 1995 (Reg. Sess., 1996), c. 743, s. 20; 1997-286, s. 6; 1997-443, ss. 11A.6, 11A.123; 2002-70, s. 1; 2007-182, s. 1; 2011-145, ss. 13.3(i), 13.25(b), (e), 13.22A(c), (d); 2012-143, s. 1(d); 2013-360, s. 14.3(j).)

§ 143B-279.4. The Department of Environment and Natural Resources - Secretary; Deputy Secretaries.

(a)   The Secretary of Environment and Natural Resources shall be the head of the Department.

(b)   The Secretary may appoint two Deputy Secretaries. (1989, c. 727, s. 3; 1989 (Reg. Sess., 1990), c. 1004, s. 19(a); 1997-443, s. 11A.119(a).)

§ 143B-279.5. Biennial State of the Environment Report.

(a)   The Secretary of Environment and Natural Resources shall report on the state of the environment to the General Assembly, the Fiscal Research Division of the General Assembly, and the Environmental Review Commission no later than 15 February of each odd-numbered year. The report shall include:

(1)   An identification and analysis of current environmental protection issues and problems within or affecting the State and its people;

(2)   Trends in the quality and use of North Carolina's air and water resources;

(3)   An inventory of areas of the State where air or water pollution is in evidence or may occur during the upcoming biennium;

(4) Current efforts and resources allocated by the Department to correct identified pollution problems and an estimate, if necessary, of additional resources needed to study, identify, and implement solutions to solve potential problems;

(5) Departmental goals and strategies to protect the natural resources of the State;

(6) Any information requested by the General Assembly or the Environmental Review Commission;

(7) Suggested legislation, if necessary; and

(8) Any other information on the state of the environment the Secretary considers appropriate.

(b) Other State agencies involved in protecting the State's natural resources and environment shall cooperate with the Department of Environment and Natural Resources in preparing this report. (1989, c. 727, s. 3; 1989 (Reg. Sess., 1990), c. 1004, s. 19(b); 1991 (Reg. Sess., 1992), c. 990, s. 5; 1997-443, s. 11A.123; 2012-200, s. 27.)

§ 143B-279.6: Repealed by Session Laws 1997-443, s. 11A.2.

§ 143B-279.7. Fish kill response protocols; report.

(a) The Department of Environment and Natural Resources shall coordinate an intradepartmental effort to develop scientific protocols to respond to significant fish kill events utilizing staff from the Division of Water Resources, Division of Marine Fisheries, Department of Health and Human Services, Wildlife Resources Commission, the scientific community, and other agencies, as necessary. In developing these protocols, the Department of Environment and Natural Resources shall address the unpredictable nature of fish kills caused by both natural and man-made factors. The protocols shall contain written procedures to respond to significant fish kill events including:

(1) Developing a plan of action to evaluate the impact of fish kills on public health and the environment.

(2) Responding to fish kills within 24 hours.

(3) Investigating and collecting data relating to fish kill events.

(4) Summarizing and distributing fish kill information to participating agencies, scientists and other interested parties.

(b) The Secretary of Environment and Natural Resources shall take all necessary and appropriate steps to effectively carry out the purposes of this Part including:

(1) Providing adequate training for fish kill investigators.

(2) Taking immediate action to protect public health and the environment.

(3) Cooperating with agencies, scientists, and other interested parties, to help determine the cause of the fish kill.

(c) The Department of Environment and Natural Resources shall report annually to the Environmental Review Commission no later than December 1 of each year. This report shall include a summary of all fish kill activity within the last year, an overview of any trend analyses, a discussion of any new or modified methodologies or reporting protocols, and any other relevant information. (1995 (Reg. Sess., 1996), c. 633, s. 4; 1997-443, s. 11A.108A; 2001-452, s. 2.8; 2001-474, ss. 30, 31; 2013-413, s. 57(p).)

§ 143B-279.8. Coastal Habitat Protection Plans.

(a) The Department shall coordinate the preparation of draft Coastal Habitat Protection Plans for critical fisheries habitats. The goal of the Plans shall be the long-term enhancement of coastal fisheries associated with each coastal habitat identified in subdivision (1) of this subsection. The Department shall use the staff of those divisions within the Department that have jurisdiction over marine fisheries, water quality, and coastal area management in the preparation of the Coastal Habitat Protection Plans and shall request assistance from other federal and State agencies as necessary. The plans shall:

(1) Describe and classify biological systems in the habitats, including wetlands, fish spawning grounds, estuarine or aquatic endangered or

threatened species, primary or secondary nursery areas, shellfish beds, submerged aquatic vegetation (SAV) beds, and habitats in outstanding resource waters.

(2) Evaluate the function, value to coastal fisheries, status, and trends of the habitats.

(3) Identify existing and potential threats to the habitats and the impact on coastal fishing.

(4) Recommend actions to protect and restore the habitats.

(b) Once a draft Coastal Habitat Protection Plan has been prepared, the chairs of the Coastal Resources Commission, the Environmental Management Commission, and the Marine Fisheries Commission shall each appoint two members of the commission he or she chairs to a six-member review committee. The six-member review committee, in consultation with the Department, shall review the draft Plan and may revise the draft Plan on a consensus basis. The draft Plan, as revised by the six-member review committee, shall then be submitted to the Coastal Resources Commission, the Environmental Management Commission, and the Marine Fisheries Commission, each of which shall independently consider the Plan for adoption. If any of the three commissions is unable to agree to any aspect of a Plan, the chair of each commission shall refer that aspect of the Plan to a six-member conference committee to facilitate the resolution of any differences. The six-member conference committee shall be appointed in the same manner as a six-member review committee and may include members of the six-member review committee that reviewed the Plan. Each final Coastal Habitat Protection Plan shall consist of those provisions adopted by all three commissions. The three commissions shall review and revise each Coastal Habitat Protection Plan at least once every five years.

(c) In carrying out their powers and duties, the Coastal Resources Commission, the Environmental Management Commission, and the Marine Fisheries Commission shall ensure, to the maximum extent practicable, that their actions are consistent with the Coastal Habitat Protection Plans as adopted by the three commissions. The obligation to act in a manner consistent with a Coastal Habitat Protection Plan is prospective only and does not oblige any commission to modify any rule adopted, permit decision made, or other action taken prior to the adoption or revision of the Coastal Habitat Protection Plan by the three commissions. The Coastal Resources Commission, the Environmental

Management Commission, and the Marine Fisheries Commission shall adopt rules to implement Coastal Habitat Protection Plans in accordance with Chapter 150B of the General Statutes.

(d)   If any of the three commissions concludes that another commission has taken an action that is inconsistent with a Coastal Habitat Protection Plan, that commission may request a written explanation of the action from the other commission. A commission shall provide a written explanation: (i) upon the written request of one of the other two commissions, or (ii) upon its own motion if the commission determines that it must take an action that is inconsistent with a Coastal Habitat Protection Plan.

(e)   The Coastal Resources Commission, the Environmental Management Commission, and the Marine Fisheries Commission shall report to the Joint Legislative Commission on Governmental Operations and the Environmental Review Commission on progress in developing and implementing the Coastal Habitat Protection Plans, including the extent to which the actions of the three commissions are consistent with the Plans, on or before 1 September of each year.

(f)   The Secretary of Environment and Natural Resources shall report to the Environmental Review Commission and the Joint Legislative Commission on Governmental Operations within 30 days of the completion or substantial revision of each draft Coastal Habitat Protection Plan. The Environmental Review Commission and the Joint Legislative Commission on Governmental Operations shall concurrently review each draft Coastal Habitat Protection Plan within 30 days of the date the draft Plan is submitted by the Secretary. The Environmental Review Commission and the Joint Legislative Commission on Governmental Operations may submit comments and recommendations on the draft Plan to the Secretary within 30 days of the date the draft Plan is submitted by the Secretary. (1997-400, s. 3.1; 1997-443, s. 11A.119(b); 2011-291, ss. 2.52, 2.53; 2012-201, s. 6.)

§ 143B-279.9. Land-use restrictions may be imposed to reduce danger to public health at contaminated sites.

(a)   In order to reduce or eliminate the danger to public health or the environment posed by the presence of contamination at a site, an owner, operator, or other responsible party may impose restrictions on the current or future use of the real property comprising any part of the site where the contamination is located if the restrictions meet the requirements of this section.

The restrictions must be agreed to by the owner of the real property, included in a remedial action plan for the site that has been approved by the Secretary, and implemented as a part of the remedial action program for the site. The Secretary may approve restrictions included in a remedial action plan in accordance with standards that the Secretary determines to be applicable to the site. Except as provided in subsection (b) of this section, if the remedial action is risk-based or will not require that the site meet unrestricted use standards, the remedial action plan must include an agreement by the owner, operator, or other responsible party to record approved land-use restrictions that meet the requirements of this section as provided in G.S. 143B-279.10 or G.S. 143B-279.11, whichever applies. Restrictions may apply to activities on, over, or under the land, including, but not limited to, use of groundwater, building, filling, grading, excavating, and mining. Any approved restriction shall be enforced by any owner of the land, operator of the facility, or other party responsible for the contaminated site. Any land-use restriction may also be enforced by the Department through the remedies provided by any provision of law that is implemented or enforced by the Department or by means of a civil action. The Department may enforce any land-use restriction without first having exhausted any available administrative remedies. A land-use restriction may also be enforced by any unit of local government having jurisdiction over any part of the site. A land-use restriction shall not be declared unenforceable due to lack of privity of estate or contract, due to lack of benefit to particular land, or due to lack of any property interest in particular land. Any person who owns or leases a property subject to a land-use restriction under this Part shall abide by the land-use restriction.

(b) The definitions set out in G.S. 143-215.94A apply to this subsection. A remedial action plan for the cleanup of environmental damage resulting from a discharge or release of petroleum from an underground storage tank pursuant to Part 2A of Article 21A of Chapter 143 of the General Statutes must include an agreement by the owner, operator, or other party responsible for the discharge or release of petroleum to record a notice of any applicable land-use restrictions that meet the requirements of this subsection as provided in G.S. 143B-279.11. All of the provisions of this section shall apply except as specifically modified by this subsection and G.S. 143B-279.11. Any restriction on the current or future use of real property pursuant to this subsection shall be enforceable only with respect to: (i) real property on which the source of contamination is located and (ii) any real property on which contamination is located at the time the remedial action plan is approved and that was owned or controlled by any owner or operator of the underground storage tank or other responsible party at the time the discharge or release of petroleum is discovered or reported or at any time thereafter. No restriction on the current or future use of real property shall apply to any portion of any parcel or tract of land on which contamination is not located. This subsection shall not be construed to require any person to record any notice of restriction on the current or future use of real property other than the real property described in this subsection. For purposes of this subsection and G.S. 143B-279.11, the Secretary may restrict current or future use of real property only as set out in any one or more of the following subdivisions:

(1)   Where soil contamination will remain in excess of unrestricted use standards, the property may be used for a primary or secondary residence, school, daycare center, nursing home, playground, park, recreation area, or other similar use only with the approval of the Department.

(2)   Where soil contamination will remain in excess of unrestricted use standards and the property is used for a primary or secondary residence that was constructed before the release of petroleum that resulted in the contamination is discovered or reported, the Secretary may approve alternative restrictions that are sufficient to reduce the risk of exposure to contaminated soils to an acceptable level while allowing the real property to continue to be used for a residence.

(3)   Where groundwater contamination will remain in excess of unrestricted use standards, installation or operation of any well usable as a source of water shall be prohibited.

(4)   Any restriction on the current or future use of the real property that is agreed upon by both the owner of the real property and the Department.

(c)   This section does not alter any right, duty, obligation, or liability of any owner, operator, or other responsible party under any other provision of law.

(d)   As used in this section:

(1)   "Unrestricted use standards" means generally applicable standards, guidance, or established methods governing contaminants that are established by statute or adopted, published, or implemented by the Environmental Management Commission, the Commission for Public Health, or the Department. Cleanup or remediation of real property to unrestricted use standards means that the property is restored to a condition such that the property and any use that is made of the property does not pose a danger or risk to public health, the environment, or users of the property that is

significantly greater than that posed by use of the property prior to its having been contaminated.

(2) "Risk-based", when used in connection with cleanup, remediation, or similar terms, means cleanup or remediation of contamination of real property to a level that, although not in compliance with unrestricted use standards, does not pose a significant danger or risk to public health, the environment, or users of the real property so long as the property remains in the condition and is used in a manner that is consistent with the assumptions as to the condition and use of the property on which the determination that the level of risk is acceptable is based. (1999-198, s. 1; 2000-51, s. 1; 2001-384, ss. 1, 12; 2002-90, s. 1; 2007-182, s. 2.)

§ 143B-279.10. Recordation of contaminated sites.

(a) The owner of the real property on which a site is located that is subject to current or future use restrictions approved as provided in G.S. 143B-279.9(a) shall submit to the Department a survey plat as required by this section within 180 days after the owner is notified to do so. The survey plat shall identify areas designated by the Department, shall be prepared and certified by a professional land surveyor, and shall be entitled "NOTICE OF CONTAMINATED SITE". Where a contaminated site is located on more than one parcel or tract of land, a composite map or plat showing all parcels or tracts may be recorded. The Notice shall include a legal description of the site that would be sufficient as a description in an instrument of conveyance, shall meet the requirements of G.S. 47-30 for maps and plats, and shall identify:

(1) The location and dimensions of any disposal areas and areas of potential environmental concern with respect to permanently surveyed benchmarks.

(2) The type, location, and quantity of contamination known to the owner of the site to exist on the site.

(3) Any restriction approved by the Department on the current or future use of the site.

(b) The Department shall review the proposed Notice to determine whether the Notice meets the requirements of this section and rules adopted to implement this section, and shall provide the owner of the site with a notarized copy of the approved Notice. After the Department approves the Notice, the owner of the site shall file a notarized copy of the approved Notice in the register of deeds office in the county or counties in which the land is located within 15 days of the date on which the owner receives approval of the Notice from the Department.

(c)   Repealed by Session Laws 2012-18, s. 1.22, effective July 1, 2012.

(d)   In the event that the owner of the site fails to submit and file the Notice required by this section within the time specified, the Secretary may prepare and file the Notice. The costs thereof may be recovered by the Secretary from any responsible party. In the event that an owner of a site who is not a responsible party submits and files the Notice required by this section, the owner may recover the reasonable costs thereof from any responsible party.

(e)   When a contaminated site that is subject to current or future land-use restrictions is sold, leased, conveyed, or transferred, the deed or other instrument of transfer shall contain in the description section, in no smaller type than that used in the body of the deed or instrument, a statement that the property is a contaminated site and a reference by book and page to the recordation of the Notice.

(f)   A Notice of Contaminated Site filed pursuant to this section shall, at the request of the owner of the land, be cancelled by the Secretary after the contamination has been eliminated or remediated to unrestricted use standards. If requested in writing by the owner of the land and if the Secretary concurs with the request, the Secretary shall send to the register of deeds of each county where the Notice is recorded a statement that the contamination has been eliminated, or that the contamination has been remediated to unrestricted use standards, and request that the Notice be cancelled of record. The Secretary's statement shall contain the names of the owners of the land as shown in the Notice and reference the plat book and page where the Notice is recorded.

(g)   This section does not apply to the cleanup pursuant to a remedial action plan that addresses environmental damage resulting from a discharge or release of petroleum from an underground storage tank pursuant to Part 2A of Article 21A of Chapter 143 of the General Statutes.

(h)   The definitions set out in G.S. 143B-279.9 apply to this section. (1999-198, s. 1; 2000-51, s. 2; 2001-384, s. 2; 2002-90, s. 2; 2012-18, s. 1.22.)

§ 143B-279.11. Recordation of residual petroleum from an underground storage tank.

(a)   The definitions set out in G.S. 143-215.94A and G.S. 143B-279.9 apply to this section. This section applies only to a cleanup pursuant to a remedial action plan that addresses environmental damage resulting from a discharge or release of petroleum from an underground storage tank pursuant to Part 2A of Article 21A of Chapter 143 of the General Statutes.

(b)   The owner, operator, or other person responsible for a discharge or release of petroleum from an underground storage tank shall prepare and submit to the Department a proposed Notice that meets the requirements of this section. The proposed Notice shall be submitted to the Department (i) before the property is conveyed, or (ii) when the owner, operator, or other person responsible for the discharge or release requests that the Department issue a determination that no further action is required under the remedial action plan, whichever first occurs. The Notice shall be entitled "NOTICE OF RESIDUAL PETROLEUM". The Notice shall include a description that would be sufficient as a description in an instrument of conveyance of the (i) real property on which the source of contamination is located and (ii) any real property on which contamination is located at the time the remedial action plan is approved and that was owned or controlled by any owner or operator of the underground storage tank or other responsible party at the time the discharge or release of petroleum is discovered or reported or at any time thereafter. The Notice shall identify the location of any residual petroleum known to exist on the real property at the time the Notice is prepared. The Notice shall also identify the location of any residual petroleum known, at the time the Notice is prepared, to exist on other real property that is a result of the discharge or release. The Notice shall set out any restrictions on the current or future use of the real property that are imposed by the Secretary pursuant to G.S. 143B-279.9(b) to protect public health, the environment, or users of the property.

(c)   If the contamination is located on more than one parcel or tract of land, the Department may require that the owner, operator, or other person responsible for the discharge or release prepare a composite map or plat that shows all parcels or tracts. If the contamination is located on one parcel or tract of land, the owner, operator, or other person responsible for the discharge or release may prepare a map or plat that shows the parcel but is not required to do so. A map or plat shall be prepared and certified by a professional land surveyor, shall meet the requirements of G.S. 47-30, and shall be submitted to the Department for approval. When the Department has approved a map or plat, it shall be recorded in the office of the register of deeds and shall be incorporated into the Notice by reference.

(d) The Department shall review the proposed Notice to determine whether the Notice meets the requirements of this section and rules adopted to implement this section and shall provide the owner, operator, or other person responsible for the discharge or release of petroleum from an underground storage tank with a notarized copy of the approved Notice. After the Department approves the Notice, the owner, operator, or other person responsible for the discharge or release of petroleum from an underground storage tank shall file a notarized copy of the approved Notice in the register of deeds office in the county or counties in which the real property is located (i) before the property is conveyed or (ii) within 30 days after the owner, operator, or other person responsible for the discharge or release receives notice from the Department that no further action is required under the remedial action plan, whichever first occurs. If the owner, operator, or other person responsible for the discharge or release fails to file the Notice as required by this section, any determination by the Department that no further action is required is void. The owner, operator, or other person responsible for the discharge or release, may record the Notice required by this section without the agreement of the owner of the real property. The owner, operator, or other person responsible for the discharge or release shall submit a certified copy of the Notice as filed in the register of deeds office to the Department.

(e) Repealed by Session Laws 2012-18, s. 1.23, effective July 1, 2012.

(f) In the event that the owner, operator, or other person responsible for the discharge or release fails to submit and file the Notice required by this section within the time specified, the Secretary may prepare and file the Notice. The costs thereof may be recovered by the Secretary from any responsible party. In the event that an owner of the real property who is not a responsible party submits and files the Notice required by this section, the owner may recover the reasonable costs thereof from any responsible party.

(g) A Notice filed pursuant to this section shall, at the request of the owner of the real property, be cancelled by the Secretary after the residual petroleum has been eliminated or remediated to unrestricted use standards. If requested in writing by the owner of the land, the Secretary shall send to the register of deeds of each county where the Notice is recorded a statement that the residual petroleum has been eliminated, or that the residual petroleum has been remediated to unrestricted use standards, and request that the Notice be cancelled of record. The Secretary's statement shall contain the names of the owners of the land as shown in the Notice and reference the plat book and page where the Notice is recorded. (2001-384, s. 3; 2002-90, ss. 3-5; 2012-18, s. 1.23.)

§ 143B-279.12. One-stop permits for certain environmental permits.

(a) The Department of Environment and Natural Resources shall establish a one-stop environmental permit application assistance and tracking system program for all its regional offices. The Department shall provide to each person who submits an application for any environmental permit subject to this section to any regional office a time frame within which that applicant may expect a final decision regarding the issuance or denial of the permit. The Department shall identify the environmental permits that are subject to this section. The procedure regulating the time frame estimates and sanction for failing to honor the time frame shall be as set out in subsections (b) and (c) of this section.

(b) Upon receipt of a complete application for an environmental permit, the Department of Environment and Natural Resources shall provide to the applicant a good faith estimate of the date by which the Department expects to make the final decision of whether to issue or deny the permit.

(c) Unless otherwise provided by law, when an applicant has provided to the Department of Environment and Natural Resources the information and documentation required and requested by the Department and the Department fails to issue or deny the permit within 60 days of the date projected by the Department for the final decision of whether to issue or deny the permit, the permit shall be automatically granted to the applicant. This subsection does not apply when an applicant submits a substantial amendment to its application after the Department has provided the applicant the projected time frame as required by this section. This subsection does not apply when an applicant agrees to receive a final decision from the Department more than 60 days from the date projected by the Department under subsection (b) of this section.

(d) The Department of Environment and Natural Resources shall track the time required to process each complete environmental permit application that is subject to this section. The Department shall compare the time in which the permit was issued or denied with the projected time frame provided to the applicant by the Department as required by this section. The Department shall identify each permit that was issued or denied more than 90 days after receipt of a complete application by the Department and shall document the reasons for the delayed action.

(e)   Repealed by Session Laws 2008-198, s. 10.1, effective August 8, 2008.

(f)   The Department may adopt temporary rules to implement this section. (2004-124, s. 12.12(a); 2006-79, s. 14; 2008-198, s. 10.1.)

§ 143B-279.13. Express permit and certification reviews.

(a)   The Department of Environment and Natural Resources shall develop an express review program to provide express permit and certification reviews in all of its regional offices. Participation in the express review program is voluntary, and the program is to become supported by the fees determined pursuant to subsection (b) of this section. The Department of Environment and Natural Resources shall determine the project applications to review under the express review program from those who request to participate in the program. The express review program may be applied to any one or all of the permits, approvals, or certifications in the following programs: the erosion and sedimentation control program, the coastal management program, and the water quality programs, including water quality certifications and stormwater management. The express review program shall focus on the following permits or certifications:

(1)   Stormwater permits under Part 1 of Article 21 of Chapter 143 of the General Statutes.

(2)   Stream origination certifications under Article 21 of Chapter 143 of the General Statutes.

(3)   Water quality certification under Article 21 of Chapter 143 of the General Statutes.

(4)   Erosion and sedimentation control permits under Article 4 of Chapter 113A of the General Statutes.

(5)   Permits under the Coastal Area Management Act (CAMA), Part 4 of Article 7 of Chapter 113A of the General Statutes.

(b) The Department of Environment and Natural Resources may determine the fees for express application review under the express review program. Notwithstanding G.S. 143-215.3D, the maximum permit application fee to be charged under subsection (a) of this section for the express review of a project application requiring all of the permits under subdivisions (1) through (5) of subsection (a) of this section shall not exceed five thousand five hundred dollars ($5,500). Notwithstanding G.S. 143-215.3D, the maximum permit application fee to be charged for the express review of a project application requiring all of the permits under subdivisions (1) through (4) of subsection (a) of this section shall not exceed four thousand five hundred dollars ($4,500). Notwithstanding G.S. 143-215.3D, the maximum permit application fee charged for the express review of a project application for any other combination of permits under subdivisions (1) through (5) of subsection (a) of this section shall not exceed four thousand dollars ($4,000). Express review of a project application involving additional permits or certifications issued by the Department of Environment and Natural Resources other than those under subdivisions (1) through (5) of subsection (a) of this section may be allowed by the Department, and, notwithstanding G.S. 143-215.3D or any other statute or rule that sets a permit fee, the maximum permit application fee charged for the express review of a project application shall not exceed four thousand dollars ($4,000), plus one hundred fifty percent (150%) of the fee that would otherwise apply by statute or rule for that particular permit or certification. Additional fees, not to exceed fifty percent (50%) of the original permit application fee under this section, may be charged for subsequent reviews due to the insufficiency of the permit applications. The Department of Environment and Natural Resources may establish the procedure by which the amount of the fees under this subsection is determined, and the fees and procedures are not rules under G.S. 150B-2(8a) for the express review program under this section.

(c) Repealed by Session Laws 2008-198, s. 10.2, effective August 8, 2008. (2005-276, s. 12.2(a); 2008-198, s. 10.2.)

§ 143B-279.14. Express Review Fund.

The Express Review Fund is created as a special nonreverting fund. All fees collected under G.S. 143B-279.13 shall be credited to the Express Review Fund. The Express Review Fund shall be used for the costs of implementing the express review program under G.S. 143B-279.13 and the costs of administering the program, including the salaries and support of the program's staff. If the express review program is abolished, the funds in the Express Review Fund shall be credited to the General Fund. (2005-276, s. 12.2(a).)

§ 143B-279.15. Report on One-Stop Permitting Program and Express Permitting Program.

No later than 1 March of each year, the Department of Environment and Natural Resources shall report to the Fiscal Research Division of the General Assembly and the Environmental Review Commission on the One-Stop for Certain Environmental Permits Program established by G.S. 143B-279.12 and the Express Permit and Certification Reviews Program established by G.S. 143B-279.13. The report shall include:

(1)   The number of environmental permits subject to G.S. 143B-279.12 that took more than 90 days to issue or deny, the types of permits those were, the reasons for the extended processing time of those permits, and how the time within which the permit was actually issued or denied compared with the projected time frame provided to the applicant by the Department as provided by G.S. 143B-279.12. Based on the data gathered in this subdivision, the Department shall include recommendations regarding permit time frames for all major permits issued by the Department.

(2)   Findings on the success of the Express Permit and Certification Reviews program established by G.S. 143B-279.13 and any other findings or recommendations, including any legislative proposals that it deems pertinent. (2008-198, s. 10.3.)

§ 143B-279.16. Civil penalty assessments.

(a)   The purpose of this section is to provide to the person receiving a notice of violation of an environmental statute or an environmental rule a greater opportunity to understand what corrective action is needed, receive technical assistance from the Department of Environment and Natural Resources, and to take the needed corrective action. It is also the purpose of this section to provide to the person receiving the notice of violation a greater opportunity for informally resolving matters involving any such violation.

(b) In order to fulfill the purpose set forth in subsection (a) of this section, the Department of Environment and Natural Resources shall, effective July 1, 2011, extend the period of time by 10 days between the time the violator is sent a notice of violation of an environmental statute or an environmental rule and the subsequent date the violator is sent an assessment of the civil penalty for the violation. (2011-145, s. 13.6.)

§ 143B-279.17. Tracking and report on permit processing times.

The Department of Environment and Natural Resources shall track the time required to process all permit applications in the One-Stop for Certain Environmental Permits Programs established by G.S. 143B-279.12 and the Express Permit and Certification Reviews established by G.S. 143B-279.13 that are received by the Department. The processing time tracked shall include (i) the total processing time from when an initial permit application is received to issuance or denial of the permit and (ii) the processing time from when a complete permit application is received to issuance or denial of the permit. No later than March 1 of each year, the Department shall report to the Fiscal Research Division of the General Assembly and the Environmental Review Commission on the permit processing times required to be tracked pursuant to this section. (2012-187, s. 13(a).)

Part 2. Board of Natural Resources and Community Development.

§ 143B-280: Repealed by Session Laws 1989, c. 727, s. 2.

Part 3. Wildlife Resources Commission.

§ 143B-281: Repealed by Session Laws 1989, c. 727, s. 2.

§ 143B-281.1. Wildlife Resources Commission - transfer; independence preserved; appointment of Executive Director and employees.

The Wildlife Resources Commission, as established by Chapters 75A, 113, and 143 of the General Statutes and other applicable laws of this State, is hereby transferred to the Department of Environment and Natural Resources by a Type II transfer as defined in G.S. 143A-6. The Wildlife Resources Commission shall exercise all its prescribed statutory powers independently of the Secretary of Environment and Natural Resources and, other provisions of this Chapter notwithstanding, shall be subject to the direction and supervision of the Secretary only with respect to the management functions of coordinating and reporting. Any other provisions of this Chapter to the contrary notwithstanding, the Executive Director of the Wildlife Resources Commission shall be appointed by the Commission and the employees of the Commission shall be employed as now provided in G.S. 143-246. (1989, c. 727, s. 4; 1997-443, s. 11A.119(a).)

Part 4. Environmental Management Commission.

§ 143B-282. Environmental Management Commission - creation; powers and duties.

(a) There is hereby created the Environmental Management Commission of the Department of Environment and Natural Resources with the power and duty to promulgate rules to be followed in the protection, preservation, and enhancement of the water and air resources of the State.

(1) Within the limitations of G.S. 143-215.9 concerning industrial health and safety, the Environmental Management Commission shall have all of the following powers and duties:

a. To grant a permit or temporary permit, to modify or revoke a permit, and to refuse to grant permits pursuant to G.S. 143-215.1 and G.S. 143-215.108 with regard to controlling sources of air and water pollution.

b. To issue a special order pursuant to G.S. 143-215.2(b) and G.S. 143-215.110 to any person whom the Commission finds responsible for causing or contributing to any pollution of water within such watershed or pollution of the air within the area for which standards have been established.

c. To conduct and direct that investigations be conducted pursuant to G.S. 143-215.3 and G.S. 143-215.108(c)(5).

d. To conduct public hearings, institute actions in superior court, and agree upon or enter into settlements, all pursuant to G.S. 143-215.3.

e. To direct the investigation of any killing of fish and wildlife pursuant to G.S. 143-215.3.

f. To consult with any person proposing to construct, install, or acquire an air or water pollution source pursuant to G.S. 143-215.3 and G.S. 143-215.111.

g. To encourage local government units to handle air pollution problems and to provide technical and consultative assistance pursuant to G.S. 143-215.3 and G.S. 143-215.112.

h. To review and have general oversight and supervision over local air pollution control programs pursuant to G.S. 143-215.3 and G.S. 143-215.112.

i. To declare an emergency when it finds a generalized dangerous condition of water or air pollution pursuant to G.S. 143-215.3.

j. To render advice and assistance to local government regarding floodways pursuant to G.S. 143-215.56.

k. To declare and delineate and modify capacity use areas pursuant to G.S. 143-215.13.

l. To grant permits for water use within capacity use areas pursuant to G.S. 143-215.15.

m. To direct that investigations be conducted when necessary to carry out duties regarding capacity use areas pursuant to G.S. 143-215.19.

n. To approve, disapprove and approve subject to conditions all applications for dam construction pursuant to G.S. 143-215.28; to require construction progress reports pursuant to G.S. 143-215.29.

o. To halt dam construction pursuant to G.S. 143-215.29.

p. To grant final approval of dam construction work pursuant to G.S. 143-215.30.

q. To have jurisdiction and supervision over the maintenance and operation of dams pursuant to G.S. 143-215.31.

r. To direct the inspection of dams pursuant to G.S. 143-215.32.

s. To modify or revoke any final action previously taken by the Commission pursuant to G.S. 143-214.1 and G.S. 143-215.107.

t. To have jurisdiction and supervision over oil pollution and dry-cleaning solvent use, contamination, and remediation pursuant to Article 21A of Chapter 143 of the General Statutes.

u. To administer the State's authority under 33 U.S.C. § 1341 of the federal Clean Water Act.

v. To approve Coastal Habitat Protection Plans as provided in G.S. 143B-279.8.

(2) The Environmental Management Commission shall adopt rules:

a. For air quality standards, emission control standards and classifications for air contaminant sources pursuant to G.S. 143-215.107.

b. For water quality standards and classifications pursuant to G.S. 143-214.1 and G.S. 143-215.

c. To implement water and air quality reporting pursuant to Part 7 of Article 21 of Chapter 143 of the General Statutes.

d. To be applied in capacity use areas pursuant to G.S. 143-215.14.

e. To implement the issuance of permits for water use within capacity use areas pursuant to G.S. 143-215.15 and G.S. 143-215.16.

f. Repealed by Session Laws 1983, c. 222, s. 3.

g. For the protection of the land and the waters over which this State has jurisdiction from pollution by oil, oil products and oil by-products pursuant to Article 21A of Chapter 143.

h. Governing underground tanks used for the storage of oil or hazardous substances pursuant to Articles 21, 21A, or 21B of Chapter 143 of the General Statutes, including inspection and testing of these tanks and certification of persons who inspect and test tanks.

i. To implement the provisions of Part 2A of Article 21 of Chapter 143 of the General Statutes.

j. To implement the provisions of Part 6 of Article 21A of Chapter 143 of the General Statutes.

k. To implement basinwide water quality management plans developed pursuant to G.S. 143-215.8B.

l. For matters within its jurisdiction that allow for and regulate horizontal drilling and hydraulic fracturing for the purpose of oil and gas exploration and development.

(3) The Commission is authorized to make such rules, not inconsistent with the laws of this State, as may be required by the federal government for grants-in-aid for water and air resources purposes which may be made available to the State by the federal government. This section is to be liberally construed in order that the State and its citizens may benefit from such grants-in-aid.

(4) The Commission shall make rules consistent with the provisions of this Chapter. All rules adopted by the Commission shall be enforced by the Department of Environment and Natural Resources.

(5) The Environmental Management Commission shall have the power to adopt rules with respect to any State laws administered under its jurisdiction so as to accept evidence of compliance with corresponding federal law or regulation in lieu of a State permit, or otherwise modify a requirement for a State permit, upon findings by the Commission, and after public hearings, that there are:

a. Similar and corresponding or more restrictive federal laws or regulations which also require an applicant to obtain a federal permit based upon the same general standards or more restrictive standards as the State laws and rules require; and

b. That the enforcement of the State laws and rules would require the applicant to also obtain a State permit in addition to the required federal permit; and

c. That the enforcement of the State laws and rules would be a duplication of effort on the part of the applicant; and

d. Such duplication of State and federal permit requirements would result in an unreasonable burden not only on the applicant, but also on the citizens and resources of the State.

(6) The Commission may establish a procedure for evaluating renewable energy technologies that are, or are proposed to be, employed as part of a renewable energy facility, as defined in G.S. 62-133.8; establish standards to ensure that renewable energy technologies do not harm the environment, natural resources, cultural resources, or public health, safety, or welfare of the State; and, to the extent that there is not an environmental regulatory program, establish an environmental regulatory program to implement these protective standards.

(b) The Environmental Management Commission shall submit quarterly written reports as to its operation, activities, programs, and progress to the Environmental Review Commission. The Environmental Management Commission shall supplement the written reports required by this subsection with additional written and oral reports as may be requested by the Environmental Review Commission. The Environmental Management Commission shall submit the written reports required by this subsection whether or not the General Assembly is in session at the time the report is due.

(c) The Environmental Management Commission shall implement the provisions of subsections (d) and (e) of 33 U.S.C. § 1313 by identifying and prioritizing impaired waters and by developing appropriate total maximum daily loads of pollutants for those impaired waters. The Commission shall incorporate those total maximum daily loads approved by the United States Environmental Protection Agency into its continuing basinwide water quality planning process.

(d) The Environmental Management Commission may adopt rules setting out strategies necessary for assuring that water quality standards are met by any point or nonpoint source or by any category of point or nonpoint sources that is determined by the Commission to be contributing to the water quality impairment. These strategies may include, but are not limited to, additional monitoring, effluent limitations, supplemental standards or classifications, best management practices, protective buffers, schedules of compliance, and the establishment of and delegations to intergovernmental basinwide groups.

(e) In appointing the members of the Commission, the appointing authorities shall make every effort to ensure fair geographic representation of the Commission. (1973, c. 1262, s. 19; 1975, c. 512; 1977, c. 771, s. 4; 1983, c.

222, s. 3; 1985, c. 551, s. 1; 1989, c. 652, s. 2; c. 727, s. 218(128); 1989 (Reg. Sess., 1990), c. 1036, s. 1; 1991 (Reg. Sess., 1992), c. 990, s. 1; 1993, c. 348, s. 3; 1996, 2nd Ex. Sess., c. 18, s. 27.4(b); 1997-392, s. 2(a), (b); 1997-400, s. 3.2; 1997-443, s. 11A.119(a); 1997-458, ss. 8.4, 8.5; 1997-496, s. 16; 1998-212, s. 14.9H(f); 1999-328, s. 4.13; 2001-424, s. 19.13(a); 2002-165, s. 1.9; 2007-397, s. 2(c); 2012-143, s. 2(h).)

§ 143B-282.1. Environmental Management Commission - quasi-judicial powers; procedures.

(a) With respect to those matters within its jurisdiction, the Environmental Management Commission shall exercise quasi-judicial powers in accordance with the provisions of Chapter 150B of the General Statutes. This section and any rules adopted by the Environmental Management Commission shall govern such proceedings:

(1) Exceptions to recommended decisions in contested cases shall be filed with the Secretary within 30 days of the receipt by the Secretary of the official record from the Office of Administrative Hearings, unless additional time is allowed by the chairman of the Commission.

(2) Oral arguments by the parties may be allowed by the chairman of the Commission upon request of the parties.

(3) Deliberations of the Commission shall be conducted in its public meeting unless the Commission determines that consultation with its counsel should be held in a closed session pursuant to G.S. 143-318.11.

(b) The final agency decision in contested cases that arise from civil penalty assessments shall be made by the Commission. In the evaluation of each violation, the Commission shall recognize that harm to the natural resources of the State arising from the violation of standards or limitations established to protect those resources may be immediately observed through damaged resources or may be incremental or cumulative with no damage that can be immediately observed or documented. Penalties up to the maximum authorized may be based on any one or combination of the following factors:

(1) The degree and extent of harm to the natural resources of the State, to the public health, or to private property resulting from the violation;

(2) The duration and gravity of the violation;

(3) The effect on ground or surface water quantity or quality or on air quality;

(4) The cost of rectifying the damage;

(5) The amount of money saved by noncompliance;

(6) Whether the violation was committed willfully or intentionally;

(7) The prior record of the violator in complying or failing to comply with programs over which the Environmental Management Commission has regulatory authority; and

(8) The cost to the State of the enforcement procedures.

(c) The chairman shall appoint a Committee on Civil Penalty Remissions from the members of the Commission. No member of the Committee on Civil Penalty Remissions may hear or vote on any matter in which he has an economic interest. The Committee on Civil Penalty Remissions shall make the final agency decision on remission requests. In determining whether a remission request will be approved, the Committee shall consider the recommendation of the Secretary and the following factors:

(1) Whether one or more of the civil penalty assessment factors in subsection (b) of this section were wrongly applied to the detriment of the petitioner;

(2) Whether the violator promptly abated continuing environmental damage resulting from the violation;

(3) Whether the violation was inadvertent or a result of an accident;

(4) Whether the violator had been assessed civil penalties for any previous violations;

(5) Whether payment of the civil penalty will prevent payment for the remaining necessary remedial actions.

(d) The Committee on Civil Penalty Remissions may remit the entire amount of the penalty only when the violator has not been assessed civil penalties for previous violations, and when payment of the civil penalty will prevent payment for the remaining necessary remedial actions.

(e) If any civil penalty has not been paid within 30 days after the final agency decision or court order has been served on the violator, the Secretary of Environment and Natural Resources shall request the Attorney General to institute a civil action in the Superior Court of any county in which the violator resides or has his or its principal place of business to recover the amount of the assessment.

(f) As used in this section, "Secretary" means the Secretary of Environment and Natural Resources. (1989 (Reg. Sess., 1990), c. 1036, s. 2; 1993 (Reg. Sess., 1994), c. 570, s. 5; 1995 (Reg. Sess., 1996), c. 743, s. 21; 1997-443, s. 11A.119(a).)

§ 143B-283. Environmental Management Commission - members; selection; removal; compensation; quorum; services.

(a) Repealed by Session Laws 2013-360, s. 14.23(a), effective July 1, 2013.

(a1) The Environmental Management Commission shall consist of 15 members as follows:

(1) One appointed by the Governor who shall be a licensed physician.

(2) One appointed by the Governor who shall at the time of appointment have special training or scientific expertise in hydrology, water pollution control, or the effects of water pollution.

(3) One appointed by the Governor who shall at the time of appointment have special training or scientific expertise in hydrology, water pollution control, or the effects of water pollution.

(4) One appointed by the Governor who shall at the time of appointment have special training or scientific expertise in air pollution control or the effects of air pollution.

(5) One appointed by the Governor who shall at the time of appointment be actively connected with or have had experience in agriculture.

(6) One appointed by the Governor who shall at the time of appointment have special training and scientific expertise in freshwater, estuarine, marine biological, or ecological sciences or be actively connected with or have had experience in the fish and wildlife conservation activities of the State.

(7) One appointed by the Governor who shall at the time of appointment be actively employed by, or recently retired from, an industrial manufacturing facility and shall be knowledgeable in the field of industrial pollution control.

(8) One appointed by the Governor who shall at the time of appointment be a licensed engineer with specialized training and experience in water supply or water or air pollution control.

(9) One appointed by the Governor who shall serve at large.

(10) One appointed by the General Assembly upon recommendation of the Speaker of the House of Representatives in accordance with G.S. 120-121 who shall serve at large.

(11) One appointed by the General Assembly upon recommendation of the Speaker of the House of Representatives in accordance with G.S. 120-121 who shall serve at large.

(12) One appointed by the General Assembly upon recommendation of the Speaker of the House of Representatives in accordance with G.S. 120-121 who shall serve at large.

(13) One appointed by the General Assembly upon recommendation of the President Pro Tempore of the Senate in accordance with G.S. 120-121 who shall serve at large.

(14) One appointed by the General Assembly upon recommendation of the President Pro Tempore of the Senate in accordance with G.S. 120-121 who shall serve at large.

(15) One appointed by the General Assembly upon recommendation of the President Pro Tempore of the Senate in accordance with G.S. 120-121 who shall serve at large.

(b) Any appointment to fill a vacancy on the Commission created by the resignation, dismissal, death or disability of a member shall be for the balance of the unexpired term. The Governor may reappoint a member of the Commission to an additional term if, at the time of the reappointment, the member qualifies for membership on the Commission under subdivisions (1) through (9) of subsection (a1) of this section. Appointments by the General Assembly shall be made in accordance with G.S. 120-121, and vacancies in those appointments shall be filled in accordance with G.S. 120-122.

(b1) The Governor shall have the power to remove any member of the Commission from office for misfeasance, malfeasance, or nonfeasance in accordance with the provisions of G.S. 143B-13 of the Executive Organization Act of 1973.

(b2) The members of the Commission shall receive per diem and necessary travel and subsistence expenses in accordance with the provisions of G.S. 138-5.

(b3) A majority of the Commission shall constitute a quorum for the transaction of business.

(b4) All clerical and other services required by the Commission shall be supplied by the Secretary of Environment and Natural Resources.

(c) The Governor shall require adequate disclosure of potential conflicts of interest by members. The Governor, by executive order, shall promulgate criteria regarding conflicts of interest and disclosure thereof for determining the eligibility of persons under this subsection, giving due regard to the requirements of federal legislation, and for this purpose may promulgate rules, regulations or guidelines in conformance with those established by any federal agency interpreting and applying provisions of federal law.

(c1) All members of the Commission are covered persons for the purposes of Chapter 138A of the General Statutes, the State Government Ethics Act. As covered persons, members of the Commission shall comply with the applicable requirements of the State Government Ethics Act, including mandatory training, the public disclosure of economic interests, and ethical standards for covered persons. Members of the Commission shall comply with the provisions of the State Government Ethics Act to avoid conflicts of interest.

(d) Repealed by Session Laws 2013-360, s. 14.23(a), effective July 1, 2013.

(e) Members of the Commission shall serve terms of four years. (1973, c. 1262, s. 20; 1977, c. 771, s. 4; 1979, 2nd Sess., c. 1158, ss. 5, 6; 1981 (Reg. Sess., 1982), c. 1191, s. 19; 1989, c. 315; c. 727, s. 218(129); 1995, c. 490, s. 18; 1997-381, s. 1; 1997-443, s. 11A.119(a); 1998-217, s. 17; 2000-172, ss. 4.1, 4.2; 2001-486, s. 2.16; 2007-182, s. 2; 2013-360, s. 14.23(a).)

§ 143B-284. Environmental Management Commission - officers.

The Environmental Management Commission shall have a chairman and a vice-chairman. The chairman shall be designated by the Governor from among the members of the Commission to serve as chairman at the pleasure of the Governor. The vice-chairman shall be elected by and from the members of the Commission and shall serve for a term of two years or until the expiration of his regularly appointed term whichever comes first. (1973, c. 1262, s. 21.)

§ 143B-285. Environmental Management Commission - meetings.

The Environmental Management Commission shall meet at least once in each quarter and may hold special meetings at any time and place within the State at the call of the chairman or upon the written request of at least five members. (1973, c. 1262, s. 22.)

§§ 143B-285.1 through 143B-285.9. Reserved for future codification purposes.

Part 4A. Governor's Waste Management Board.

§§ 143B-285.10 through 143B-285.15: Repealed by Session Laws 1993, c. 501, s. 1.

§§ 143B-285.16 through 143B-285.19. Reserved for future codification purposes.

Part 4B. Office of Environmental Education and Public Affairs.

§ 143B-285.20. Short title.

This Part shall be known and cited as the Environmental Education Act of 1993. (1993, c. 501, s. 28.)

§ 143B-285.21. Declaration of purpose.

The purpose of this Part shall be to encourage, promote, and support the development of programs, facilities, and materials for the purpose of environmental education in North Carolina. (1993, c. 501, s. 28.)

§ 143B-285.22. Creation.

There is hereby created the Office of Environmental Education and Public Affairs (hereinafter referred to as "Office") within the Department of Environment and Natural Resources. (1993, c. 501, s. 28; 1997-443, s. 11A.119(a); 2010-31, s. 13.1A(c).)

§ 143B-285.23. Powers and duties of the Secretary of Environment and Natural Resources.

The Secretary of Environment and Natural Resources shall:

(1) Establish an Office of Environmental Education and Public Affairs to:

a. Serve as a clearinghouse of environmental information for the State.

b. Plan for the Department's future needs for environmental education materials and programs.

c. Maintain a computerized database of existing education materials and programs within the Department.

d. Maintain a speaker's bureau of environmental specialists to address environmental concerns and issues in communities across the State.

e. Evaluate opportunities for establishing regional environmental education centers.

f. Administer the Project Tomorrow Award Program to encourage school children to discover and explore ways to protect the environment.

g. Assist the Department of Public Instruction in integrating environmental education into course curricula.

h. Develop and implement a grants and award program for environmental education projects in schools and communities.

(2) Coordinate, through technical assistance and staff support and with participation of the Department of Public Instruction and other relevant agencies, institutions, and citizens, the planning and implementation of a statewide program of environmental education.

(3) Be responsible for such matters as the purchase of educational equipment, materials, and supplies; the construction or modification of facilities; and the employment of consultants and other personnel necessary to carry out the provisions of this Part.

(4) Encourage coordination between the various State and federal agencies, citizens groups, and the business and industrial community, in the dissemination of environmental information and education.

(5) Utilize existing programs, educational materials, or facilities, both public and private, wherever feasible. (1993, c. 501, s. 28; 1997-443, s. 11A.119(a); 2010-31, s. 13.1A(d).)

§ 143B-285.24. Grants and awards.

The objective of grants and awards made under the provisions of this Part shall be to promote the further development of local and regional environmental education and information dissemination to aid especially, but not be limited to, school-age children. The Office shall recommend each year to the Governor recipients for the Project Tomorrow Award, which the Governor shall award for outstanding environmental projects by elementary schools in North Carolina. (1993, c. 501, s. 28.)

§ 143B-285.25. Liaison between the Office of Environmental Education and Public Affairs and the Department of Public Instruction.

The Superintendent of the Department of Public Instruction shall identify an environmental education liaison within the Office of Instructional Services of the Department of Public Instruction to:

(1) Coordinate environmental education within the State curriculum and among the Department and other State agencies.

(2) Conduct teacher training in environmental education topics in conjunction with Department and other State agencies.

(3) Coordinate and integrate topics within the various curriculum areas of the standard course of study.

(4) Promote awareness of environmental issues to the public and to the school communities, including students, teachers, and administrators.

(5) Establish a repository of environmental education instructional materials and disseminate information on the availability of these materials to schools.

(6) Promote and facilitate the sharing of information through electronic networks to all schools. (1993, c. 501, s. 28; 2010-31, s. 13.1A(e).)

Part 5. Marine Fisheries Commission.

§§ 143B-286 through 143B-289: Repealed by Session Laws 1987, c. 641, s. 1.

Part 5A. Marine Fisheries Commission.

§§ 143B-289.1 through 143B-289.12: Repealed by Session Laws 1997-400, s. 6.3.

§§ 143B-289.13 through 143B-289.18: Reserved for future codification purposes.

Part 5B. Office of Marine Affairs.

§§ 143B-289.19 through 143B-289.23: Recodified as §§ 143B-289.40 through 143B-289.44 by Session Laws 1997-400, ss. 6, 6.3(b).

§§ 143B-289.24 through 143B-289.39: Reserved for future codification purposes.

Part 5C. Division of North Carolina Aquariums.

§ 143B-289.40. Division of North Carolina Aquariums - creation.

The Division of North Carolina Aquariums is created in the Department of Environment and Natural Resources. (1985, c. 202, s. 3; 1995, c. 509, s. 98; 1997-286, s. 2; 1997-400, s. 6.3(a), (b); 1997-443, s. 11A.119(b).)

§ 143B-289.41. Division of North Carolina Aquariums - organization; powers and duties.

(a)   The Division of North Carolina Aquariums shall be organized as prescribed by the Secretary of Environment and Natural Resources and shall exercise the following powers and duties:

(1)   Repealed by Session Laws 1991, c. 320, s. 3.

(1a) Establish and maintain the North Carolina Aquariums.

(1b) Administer the operations of the North Carolina Aquariums, such administrative duties to include, but not be limited to the following:

a.   Adopt goals and objectives for the Aquariums and review and revise these goals and objectives periodically.

b.   Review and approve requests for use of the Aquarium facilities and advise the Secretary of Environment and Natural Resources on the most appropriate use consistent with the goals and objectives of the Aquariums.

c. Continually review and evaluate the types of projects and programs being carried out in the Aquarium facilities and determine if the operation of the facilities is in compliance with the established goals and objectives.

d. Recommend to the Secretary of Environment and Natural Resources any policies and procedures needed to assure effective staff performance and proper liaison among Aquarium facilities in carrying out the overall purposes of the Aquarium programs.

e. Review Aquarium budget submissions to the Secretary of Environment and Natural Resources.

f. Recruit and recommend to the Secretary of Environment and Natural Resources candidates for the positions of directors of the Aquariums.

g. Create local advisory committees in accordance with the provisions of G.S. 143B-289.43.

(1c) Notwithstanding Article 3A of Chapter 143 of the General Statutes, and G.S. 143-49(4), dispose of any exhibit, exhibit component, or object from the collections of the North Carolina Aquariums by sale, lease, or trade. A sale, lease, or trade under this subdivision shall be conducted in accordance with generally accepted practices for zoos and aquariums that are accredited by the American Association of Zoos and Aquariums. After deducting the expenses attributable to the sale or lease, the net proceeds of any sale or lease shall be credited to the North Carolina Aquariums Fund.

(2), (3) Repealed by Session Laws 1993, c. 321, s. 28(e).

(4) through (6) Repealed by Session Laws 1991, c. 320, s. 3.

(7) Assume any other powers and duties assigned to it by the Secretary.

(b) The Secretary may adopt any rules and procedures necessary to implement this section. (1985, c. 202, s. 3; 1991, c. 320, s. 3; 1993, c. 321, ss. 28(d), 28(e); 1997-286, s. 3; 1997-400, s. 6.3(b), (c); 1997-443, ss. 11A.119(a), 11A.123; 1999-49, s. 1.)

§ 143B-289.42. North Carolina Aquariums; purpose.

The purpose of establishing and maintaining the North Carolina Aquariums is to promote an awareness, understanding, and appreciation of the diverse natural and cultural resources associated with North Carolina's oceans, estuaries, rivers, streams, and other aquatic environments. (1991, c. 320, s. 4; 1993, c. 321, s. 28(d); 1997-400, s. 6.3(b).)

§ 143B-289.43. Local advisory committees; duties; membership.

Local advisory committees created pursuant to G.S. 143B-289.41(a)(1b) shall assist each North Carolina Aquarium in its efforts to establish projects and programs and to assure adequate citizen-consumer input into those efforts. Members of these committees shall be appointed by the Secretary of Environment and Natural Resources for three-year terms from nominations made by the Director of the Office of Marine Affairs. Each committee shall select one of its members to serve as chairperson. Members of the committees shall serve without compensation for services or expenses. (1991, c. 320, s. 4; 1993, c. 321, ss. 28(d), 28(f); 1997-286, s. 4; 1997-400, s. 6.3(b), (d); 1997-443, ss. 11A.119(a), 11A.123.)

§ 143B-289.44. North Carolina Aquariums; fees; fund.

(a) Fees. - The Secretary of Environment and Natural Resources may adopt a schedule of fees for the aquariums and piers operated by the North Carolina Aquariums, including:

(1) Gate admission fees.

(2) Facility rental fees.

(3) Educational programs.

(b) Fund. - The North Carolina Aquariums Fund is hereby created as a special and nonreverting fund. The North Carolina Aquariums Fund shall be used for repair, renovation, expansion, maintenance, educational exhibit construction, and operational expenses at existing aquariums, to pay the debt service and lease payments related to the financing of expansions of aquariums, and to match private funds that are raised for these purposes.

(c) Disposition of Fees. - All entrance fee receipts shall be credited to the North Carolina Aquariums Fund.

(d) The Division of North Carolina Aquariums shall submit to the Joint Legislative Commission on Governmental Operations, the House and Senate Appropriations Subcommittees on Natural and Economic Resources, and the Fiscal Research Division by September 30 of each year a report on the North Carolina Aquariums Fund that shall include the source and amounts of all funds credited to the Fund and the purpose and amount of all expenditures from the Fund during the prior fiscal year. (1997-286, s. 5; 1997-400, s. 6.3(b); 1997-443, s. 11A.119(b); 1999-49, s. 2; 2002-159, s. 46; 2005-276, s. 12.10; 2012-142, s. 12.5(a); 2013-413, s. 42(a).)

§ 143B-289.45. Satellite areas prohibited absent General Assembly authorization.

Notwithstanding any other provision of law, State funds shall not be used for any of the following purposes unless specifically authorized by the General Assembly:

(1) Construction of any satellite area.

(2) Commencement of any capital project in connection with the construction or acquisition of any satellite area.

(3) Operation of any satellite area.

For purposes of this section, the term "satellite area" means any property or facility that is to be operated by the Division of North Carolina Aquariums that is located somewhere other than on the site of the aquariums at Pine Knoll Shores, Roanoke Island, and Fort Fisher. (2012-142, s. 12.5(c).)

§ 143B-289.46. Reserved for future codification purposes.

§ 143B-289.47. Reserved for future codification purposes.

§ 143B-289.48. Reserved for future codification purposes.

§ 143B-289.49. Reserved for future codification purposes.

Part 5D. Marine Fisheries Commission.

§ 143B-289.50. Definitions.

(a)   As used in this part:

(1)   "Commission" means the Marine Fisheries Commission.

(2)   "Department" means the Department of Environment and Natural Resources.

(3)   "Fisheries Director" means the Director of the Division of Marine Fisheries of the Department of Environment and Natural Resources.

(4)   "Secretary" means the Secretary of Environment and Natural Resources.

(b)   The definitions set out in G.S. 113-129 and G.S. 113-130 shall apply throughout this Part. (1997-400, s. 2.1; 1997-443, s. 11A.123.)

§ 143B-289.51. Marine Fisheries Commission - creation; purposes.

(a)   There is hereby created the Marine Fisheries Commission in the Department of Environment and Natural Resources.

(b)   The functions, purposes, and duties of the Marine Fisheries Commission are to:

(1)   Manage, restore, develop, cultivate, conserve, protect, and regulate the marine and estuarine resources within its jurisdiction, as described in G.S. 113-132.

(2)   Implement the laws relating to coastal fisheries, coastal fishing, shellfish, crustaceans, and other marine and estuarine resources enacted by the General Assembly by the adoption of rules and policies, to provide a sound, constructive, comprehensive, continuing, and economical coastal fisheries program directed by citizens who are knowledgeable in the protection, restoration, proper use, and management of marine and estuarine resources.

(3) Implement management measures regarding ocean and marine fisheries in the Atlantic Ocean consistent with the authority conferred on the State by the United States.

(4) Advise the State regarding ocean and marine fisheries within the jurisdiction of the Atlantic States Marine Fisheries Compact, the South Atlantic Fishery Management Council, the Mid-Atlantic Fishery Management Council, and other similar organizations established to manage or regulate fishing in the Atlantic Ocean. (1997-400, s. 2.1; 1997-443, s. 11A.119(b).)

§ 143B-289.52. Marine Fisheries Commission - powers and duties.

(a) The Marine Fisheries Commission shall adopt rules to be followed in the management, protection, preservation, and enhancement of the marine and estuarine resources within its jurisdiction, as described in G.S. 113-132, including commercial and sports fisheries resources. The Marine Fisheries Commission shall have the power and duty:

(1) To authorize, license, regulate, prohibit, prescribe, or restrict all forms of marine and estuarine resources in coastal fishing waters with respect to:

a. Time, place, character, or dimensions of any methods or equipment that may be employed in taking fish.

b. Seasons for taking fish.

c. Size limits on and maximum quantities of fish that may be taken, possessed, bailed to another, transported, bought, sold, or given away.

(2) To provide fair regulation of commercial and recreational fishing groups in the interest of the public.

(3) To adopt rules and take all steps necessary to develop and improve mariculture, including the cultivation, harvesting, and marketing of shellfish and other marine resources in the State, involving the use of public grounds and private beds as provided in G.S. 113-201.

(4) To close areas of public bottoms under coastal fishing waters for such time as may be necessary in any program of propagation of shellfish as provided in G.S. 113-204.

(5) In the interest of conservation of the marine and estuarine resources of the State, to institute an action in the superior court to contest the claim of title or claimed right of fishery in any navigable waters of the State registered with the Department as provided in G.S. 113-206(d).

(6) To make reciprocal agreements with other jurisdictions respecting any of the matters governed in this Subchapter as provided by G.S. 113-223.

(7) To adopt relevant provisions of federal laws and regulations as State rules pursuant to G.S. 113-228.

(8) To delegate to the Fisheries Director the authority by proclamation to suspend or implement, in whole or in part, a particular rule of the Commission that may be affected by variable conditions as provided in G.S. 113-221.1.

(9) To comment on and otherwise participate in the determination of permit applications received by State agencies that may have an effect on the marine and estuarine resources of the State.

(10) To adopt Fishery Management Plans as provided in G.S. 113-182.1, to establish a Priority List to determine the order in which Fishery Management Plans are developed, to establish a Schedule for the development and adoption of each Fishery Management Plan, and to establish guidance criteria as to the contents of Fishery Management Plans.

(11) To approve Coastal Habitat Protection Plans as provided in G.S. 143B-279.8.

(12) Except as may otherwise be provided, to make the final agency decision in all contested cases involving matters within the jurisdiction of the Commission.

(13) To adopt rules to define fishing gear as either recreational gear or commercial gear.

(b) The Marine Fisheries Commission shall have the power and duty to establish standards and adopt rules:

(1) To implement the provisions of Subchapter IV of Chapter 113 as provided in G.S. 113-134.

(2) To manage the disposition of confiscated property as set forth in G.S. 113-137.

(3) To govern all license requirements prescribed in Article 14A of Chapter 113 of the General Statutes.

(4) To regulate the importation and exportation of fish, and equipment that may be used in taking or processing fish, as necessary to enhance the conservation of marine and estuarine resources of the State as provided in G.S. 113-170.

(5) To regulate the possession, transportation, and disposition of seafood, as provided in G.S. 113-170.4.

(6) To regulate the disposition of the young of edible fish, as provided by G.S. 113-185.

(7) To manage the leasing of public grounds for mariculture, including oysters and clam production, as provided in G.S. 113-202.

(8) To govern the utilization of private fisheries, as provided in G.S. 113-205.

(9) To impose further restrictions upon the throwing of fish offal in any coastal fishing waters, as provided in G.S. 113-265.

(10) To regulate the location and utilization of artificial reefs in coastal waters.

(11) To regulate the placement of nets and other sports or commercial fishing apparatus in coastal fishing waters with regard to navigational or recreational safety as well as from a conservation standpoint.

(c) The Commission is authorized to authorize, license, prohibit, prescribe, or restrict:

(1) The opening and closing of coastal fishing waters, except as to inland game fish, whether entirely or only as to the taking of particular classes of fish, use of particular equipment, or as to other activities.

(2) The possession, cultivation, transportation, importation, exportation, sale, purchase, acquisition, and disposition of all marine and estuarine resources and all related equipment, implements, vessels, and conveyances as necessary to carry out its duties.

(d) The Commission may adopt rules required by the federal government for grants-in-aid for coastal resource purposes that may be made available to the State by the federal government. This section is to be liberally construed in order that the State and its citizens may benefit from federal grants-in-aid.

(d1) The Commission may regulate participation in a fishery that is subject to a federal fishery management plan if that plan imposes a quota on the State for the harvest or landing of fish in the fishery. The Commission may use any additional criteria aside from holding a Standard Commercial Fishing License to develop limited-entry fisheries. The Commission may establish a fee for each license established pursuant to this subsection in an amount that does not exceed five hundred dollars ($500.00).

(d2) To ensure an orderly transition from one permit year to the next, the Division may issue a permit prior to July 1 of the permit year for which the permit is valid. Revenue that the Division receives for the issuance of a permit prior to the beginning of a permit year shall not revert at the end of the fiscal year in which the revenue is received and shall be credited and available to the Division for the permit year in which the permit is valid.

(e) The Commission may adopt rules to implement or comply with a fishery management plan adopted by the Atlantic States Marine Fisheries Commission or adopted by the United States Secretary of Commerce pursuant to the Magnuson-Stevens Fishery Conservation and Management Act, 16 U.S.C. § 1801, et seq. Notwithstanding G.S. 150B-21.1(a), the Commission may adopt temporary rules under this subsection at any time within six months of the adoption or amendment of a fishery management plan or the notification of a change in management measures needed to remain in compliance with a fishery management plan.

(e1) A supermajority of the Commission shall be six members. A supermajority shall be necessary to override recommendations from the Division of Marine Fisheries regarding measures needed to end overfishing or to rebuild overfished stocks.

(f)   The Commission shall adopt rules as provided in this Chapter. All rules adopted by the Commission shall be enforced by the Department of Environment and Natural Resources.

(g)   As a quasi-judicial agency, the Commission, in accordance with Article IV, Section 3 of the Constitution of North Carolina, has those judicial powers reasonably necessary to accomplish the purposes for which it was created.

(h)   Social security numbers and identifying information obtained by the Commission or the Division of Marine Fisheries shall be treated as provided in G.S. 132-1.10. For purposes of this subsection, "identifying information" also includes a person's mailing address, residence address, date of birth, and telephone number.

(i)   The Commission may adopt rules to exempt individuals who participate in organized fishing events held in coastal or joint fishing waters from recreational fishing license requirements for the specified time and place of the event when the purpose of the event is consistent with the conservation objectives of the Commission. (1997-400, ss. 2.1, 2.2; 1997-443, s. 11A.123; 1998-217, s. 18(a); 1998-225, ss. 1.3, 1.4, 1.5; 2001-474, s. 32; 2003-154, s. 3; 2004-187, ss. 7, 8; 2006-255, ss. 11.2, 12; 2012-190, s. 5; 2012-200, s. 17; 2013-360, ss. 14.8(v), (w).)

§ 143B-289.53. Marine Fisheries Commission - quasi-judicial powers; procedures.

(a)   With respect to those matters within its jurisdiction, the Marine Fisheries Commission shall exercise quasi-judicial powers in accordance with the provisions of Chapter 150B of the General Statutes. This section and any rules adopted by the Marine Fisheries Commission shall govern the following proceedings:

(1)   Exceptions to recommended decisions in contested cases shall be filed with the Secretary within 30 days of the receipt by the Secretary of the official record from the Office of Administrative Hearings, unless additional time is allowed by the Chair of the Commission.

(2) Oral arguments by the parties may be allowed by the Chair of the Commission upon request of the parties.

(3) Deliberations of the Commission shall be conducted in its public meeting unless the Commission determines that consultation with its counsel should be held in a closed session pursuant to G.S. 143-318.11.

(b) The final agency decision in contested cases that arise from civil penalty assessments shall be made by the Commission. In the evaluation of each violation, the Commission shall recognize that harm to the marine and estuarine resources within its jurisdiction, as described in G.S. 113-132, arising from the violation of a statute or rule enacted or adopted to protect those resources may be immediately observed through damaged resources or may be incremental or cumulative with no damage that can be immediately observed or documented. Penalties up to the maximum authorized may be based on any one or combination of the following factors:

(1) The degree and extent of harm to the marine and estuarine resources within the jurisdiction of the Commission, as described in G.S. 113-132; to the public health; or to private property resulting from the violation.

(2) The frequency and gravity of the violation.

(3) The cost of rectifying the damage.

(4) Whether the violation was committed willfully or intentionally.

(5) The prior record of the violator in complying or failing to comply with programs over which the Marine Fisheries Commission has regulatory authority.

(6) The cost to the State of the enforcement procedures.

(c) The Chair shall appoint a Committee on Civil Penalty Remissions from the members of the Commission. No member of the Committee on Civil Penalty Remissions may hear or vote on any matter in which the member has an economic interest. The Committee on Civil Penalty Remissions shall make the final agency decision on remission requests. In determining whether a remission request will be approved, the Committee shall consider the recommendation of the Secretary and the following factors:

(1) Whether one or more of the civil penalty assessment factors in subsection (b) of this section were wrongly applied to the detriment of the petitioner.

(2) Whether the violator promptly abated continuing environmental damage resulting from the violation.

(3) Whether the violation was inadvertent.

(4) Whether the violator had been assessed civil penalties for any previous violations.

(5) Whether payment of the civil penalty will prevent payment for the remaining necessary remedial actions.

(d) The Committee on Civil Penalty Remissions may remit the entire amount of the penalty only when the violator has not been assessed civil penalties for previous violations and when payment of the civil penalty will prevent payment for the remaining necessary remedial actions.

(e) If any civil penalty has not been paid within 30 days after the final agency decision or court order has been served on the violator, the Secretary of Environment and Natural Resources shall request the Attorney General to institute a civil action in the superior court of any county in which the violator resides or has his or its principal place of business to recover the amount of the assessment.

(f) The Secretary may delegate his powers and duties under this section to the Fisheries Director. (1997-400, s. 2.1; 1997-443, s. 11A.119(a).)

§ 143B-289.54. Marine Fisheries Commission - members; appointment; term; oath; ethical standards; removal; compensation; staff.

(a) Members, Selection. - The Marine Fisheries Commission shall consist of nine members appointed by the Governor as follows:

(1) One person actively engaged in, or recently retired from, commercial fishing as demonstrated by currently or recently deriving at least fifty percent (50%) of annual earned income from taking and selling fishery resources in

coastal fishing waters of the State. The spouse of a commercial fisherman who meets the criteria of this subdivision may be appointed under this subdivision.

(2) One person actively engaged in, or recently retired from, commercial fishing as demonstrated by currently or recently deriving at least fifty percent (50%) of annual earned income from taking and selling fishery resources in coastal fishing waters of the State. The spouse of a commercial fisherman who meets the criteria of this subdivision may be appointed under this subdivision.

(3) One person actively connected with, and experienced as, a licensed fish dealer or in seafood processing or distribution as demonstrated by deriving at least fifty percent (50%) of annual earned income from activities involving the buying, selling, processing, or distribution of seafood landed in this State. The spouse of a person qualified under this subdivision may be appointed provided that the spouse is actively involved in the qualifying business.

(4) One person actively engaged in recreational sports fishing in coastal waters in this State. An appointee under this subdivision may not derive more than ten percent (10%) of annual earned income from sports fishing activities.

(5) One person actively engaged in recreational sports fishing in coastal waters in this State. An appointee under this subdivision may not derive more than ten percent (10%) of annual earned income from sports fishing activities.

(6) One person actively engaged in the sports fishing industry as demonstrated by deriving at least fifty percent (50%) of annual earned income from selling goods or services in this State. The spouse of a person qualified under this subdivision may be appointed provided that the spouse is actively involved in the qualifying business.

(7) One person having general knowledge of and experience related to subjects and persons regulated by the Commission.

(8) One person having general knowledge of and experience related to subjects and persons regulated by the Commission.

(9) One person who is a fisheries scientist having special training and expertise in marine and estuarine fisheries biology, ecology, population dynamics, water quality, habitat protection, or similar knowledge. A person appointed under this subdivision may not receive more than ten percent (10%)

of annual earned income from either the commercial or sports fishing industries, including the processing and distribution of seafood.

(b) Residential Qualifications. - For purposes of providing regional representation on the Commission, the following three coastal regions of the State are designated: (i) Northeast Coastal Region comprised of Bertie, Camden, Chowan, Currituck, Dare, Gates, Halifax, Hertford, Martin, Northampton, Pasquotank, Perquimans, Tyrrell, and Washington Counties, (ii) Central Coastal Region comprised of Beaufort, Carteret, Craven, Hyde, Jones, and Pamlico Counties; and (iii) Southeast Coastal Region comprised of Bladen, Brunswick, Columbus, New Hanover, Onslow, and Pender Counties. Persons appointed under subdivisions (1), (2), (3), (4), and (8) of subsection (a) of this section shall be residents of one of the coastal regions of the State. The membership of the Commission shall include at least one person who is a resident of each of the three coastal regions of the State.

(c) Additional Considerations. - In making appointments to the Commission, the Governor shall provide for appropriate representation of women and minorities on the Commission.

(d) Terms. - The term of office of members of the Commission is three years. A member may be reappointed to any number of successive three-year terms. Upon the expiration of a three-year term, a member shall continue to serve until a successor is appointed and duly qualified as provided by G.S. 128-7. The term of members appointed under subdivisions (1), (4), and (7) of subsection (a) of this section shall expire on 30 June of years evenly divisible by three. The term of members appointed under subdivisions (2), (5), and (8) of subsection (a) of this section shall expire on 30 June of years that precede by one year those years that are evenly divisible by three. The term of members appointed under subdivisions (3), (6), and (9) of subsection (a) of this section shall expire on 30 June of years that follow by one year those years that are evenly divisible by three.

(e) Vacancies. - An appointment to fill a vacancy shall be for the unexpired balance of the term.

(f) Oath of Office. - Each member of the Commission, before assuming the duties of office, shall take an oath of office as provided in Chapter 11 of the General Statutes.

(g) Ethical Standards. -

(1) Disclosure statements. - Any person under consideration for appointment to the Commission shall provide both a financial disclosure statement and a potential bias disclosure statement to the Governor. A financial disclosure statement shall include statements of the nominee's financial interests in and related to State fishery resources use, licenses issued by the Division of Marine Fisheries held by the nominee or any business in which the nominee has a financial interest, and uses made by the nominee or by any business in which the nominee has a financial interest of the regulated resources. A potential bias disclosure statement shall include a statement of the nominee's membership or other affiliation with, including offices held, in societies, organizations, or advocacy groups pertaining to the management and use of the State's coastal fishery resources. Disclosure statements shall be treated as public records under Chapter 132 of the General Statutes and shall be updated on an annual basis.

(2) Voting/conflict of interest. - A member of the Commission shall not vote on any issue before the Commission that would have a "significant and predictable effect" on the member's financial interest. For purposes of this subdivision, "significant and predictable effect" means there is or may be a close causal link between the decision of the Commission and an expected disproportionate financial benefit to the member that is shared only by a minority of persons within the same industry sector or gear group. A member of the Commission shall also abstain from voting on any petition submitted by an advocacy group of which the member is an officer or sits as a member of the advocacy group's board of directors. A member of the Commission shall not use the member's official position as a member of the Commission to secure any special privilege or exemption of substantial value for any person. No member of the Commission shall, by the member's conduct, create an appearance that any person could improperly influence the member in the performance of the member's official duties.

(3) Regular attendance. - It shall be the duty of each member of the Commission to regularly attend meetings of the Commission.

(h) Removal. - The Governor may remove, as provided in G.S. 143B-13, any member of the Commission for misfeasance, malfeasance, or nonfeasance.

(i) Office May Be Held Concurrently With Others. - The office of member of the Marine Fisheries Commission may be held concurrently with any other elected or appointed office, as authorized by Article VI, Section 9, of the Constitution of North Carolina.

(j)   Compensation. - Members of the Commission who are State officers or employees shall receive no per diem compensation for serving on the Commission, but shall be reimbursed for their expenses in accordance with G.S. 138-6. Members of the Commission who are full-time salaried public officers or employees other than State officers or employees shall receive no per diem compensation for serving on the Commission, but shall be reimbursed for their expenses in accordance with G.S. 138-6 in the same manner as State officers or employees. All other Commission members shall receive per diem compensation and reimbursement in accordance with the compensation rate established in G.S. 93B-5.

(k)   Staff. - All clerical and other services required by the Commission shall be supplied by the Fisheries Director and the Department.

(l)   Legal Services. - The Attorney General shall: (i) act as attorney for the Commission; (ii) at the request of the Commission, initiate actions in the name of the Commission; and (iii) represent the Commission in any appeal or other review of any order of the Commission. (1997-400, s. 2.1; 1998-225, ss. 1.6, 1.7; 2001-213, s. 5; 2013-360, s. 14.7(b).)

§ 143B-289.55. Marine Fisheries Commission - officers; organization; seal.

(a)   The Governor shall appoint a member of the Commission to serve as Chair. The Chair shall serve at the pleasure of the Governor. The Commission shall elect one of its members to serve as Vice-Chair. The Vice-Chair shall serve a one-year term beginning 1 July and ending 30 June of the following year. The Vice-Chair may serve any number of consecutive terms.

(b)   The Chair shall guide and coordinate the activities of the Commission in fulfilling its duties as set out in this Article. The Chair shall report to and advise the Governor and the Secretary on the activities of the Commission, on marine and estuarine conservation matters, and on all marine fisheries matters.

(c)   The Commission shall determine its organization and procedure in accordance with the provisions of this Article. The provisions of the most recent edition of Robert's Rules of Order shall govern any procedural matter for which no other provision has been made.

(d)   The Commission may adopt a common seal and may alter it as necessary. (1997-400, s. 2.1.)

§ 143B-289.56. Marine Fisheries Commission - meetings; quorum.

(a)   The Commission shall meet at least once each calendar quarter and may hold additional meetings at any time and place within the State at the call of the Chair or upon the written request of at least four members. At least three of the four quarterly meetings of the Commission shall be held in one of the coastal regions designated in G.S. 143B-289.54.

(b)   (1)   Six members of the Commission shall constitute a quorum for the transaction of business.

(2)   A quorum of the Commission may transact business only if one member, other than the Chair, appointed pursuant to subdivision (1), (2), or (3) of G.S. 143B-289.54(a) and one member, other than the Chair, appointed pursuant to subdivision (4), (5), or (6) of G.S. 143B-289.54(a) are present.

(c)   If the Commission is unable to transact business because the requirements of subdivision (2) of subsection (b) of this section are not met, the Chair shall call another meeting of the Commission within 30 days and shall place on the agenda for that meeting every matter with respect to which the Commission was unable to transact business. Five members of the Commission shall constitute a quorum for the transaction of business at a meeting called under this subsection. The requirements of subdivision (2) of subsection (b) of this section shall not apply to a meeting called under this subsection. (1997-400, s. 2.1; 1998-225, s. 1.8.)

§ 143B-289.57. Marine Fisheries Commission Advisory Committees established; members; selection; duties.

(a)   The Commission shall be assisted in the performance of its duties by four standing advisory committees and four regional advisory committees. Each standing and regional advisory committee shall consist of no more than 11 members. The Chair of the Commission shall designate one member of each advisory committee to serve as Chair of the committee. Members shall serve staggered three-year terms as determined by the Commission. The Commission shall establish other policies and procedures for standing and regional advisory committees that are consistent with those governing the Commission as set out in this Part.

(b) The Chair of the Commission shall appoint the following standing advisory committees:

(1) The Finfish Committee, which shall consider matters concerning finfish.

(2), (3) Repealed by Session Laws 2012-190, s. 4(a), and Session Laws 2012-200, s. 16(a), effective July 1, 2012.

(3a) The Shellfish/Crustacean Advisory Committee, which shall consider matters concerning oysters, clams, scallops, other molluscan shellfish, shrimp, and crabs.

(4) The Habitat and Water Quality Committee, which shall consider matters concerning habitat and water quality that may affect coastal fisheries resources.

(c) Each standing advisory committee shall be composed of commercial and recreational fishermen, scientists, and other persons who have expertise in the matters to be considered by the advisory committee to which they are appointed. In making appointments to advisory committees, the Chair of the Commission shall ensure that both commercial and recreational fishing interests are fairly represented and shall consider for appointment persons who are recommended by groups representing commercial fishing interests, recreational fishing interests, environmental protection and conservation interests, and other groups interested in coastal fisheries management.

(d) Each standing advisory committee shall review all matters referred to the committee by the Commission and shall make findings and recommendations on these matters. A standing advisory committee may, on its own motion, make findings and recommendations as to any matter related to its subject area. The Commission, in the performance of its duties, shall consider all findings and recommendations submitted by standing advisory committees.

(e) The Chair of the Commission shall appoint a Northern Regional Advisory Committee, encompassing areas from the Virginia line south through Hyde and Pamlico Counties and any counties to the west, and a Southern Regional Advisory Committee, encompassing areas from Carteret County south to the South Carolina line and any counties to the west. In making appointments to regional advisory committees, the Chair of the Commission shall ensure that both commercial and recreational fishing interests are fairly represented. (1997-400, s. 2.1; 2012-190, s. 4(a); 2012-200, s. 16(a).)

§ 143B-289.58: Repealed by Session Laws 2013-360, s. 14.10, effective July 1, 2013.

§ 143B-289.59. Conservation Fund; Commission may accept gifts.

(a) The Marine Fisheries Commission may accept gifts, donations, or contributions from any sources. These funds shall be held in a separate account and used solely for the purposes of marine and estuarine conservation and management. These funds shall be administered by the Marine Fisheries Commission and shall be used for marine and estuarine resources management, including education about the importance of conservation, in a manner consistent with marine and estuarine conservation management principles.

(b) The Marine Fisheries Commission is hereby authorized to issue and sell appropriate emblems by which to identify recipients thereof as contributors to a special marine and estuarine resources Conservation Fund that shall be made available to the Marine Fisheries Commission for conservation, protection, enhancement, preservation, and perpetuation of marine and estuarine species that may be endangered or threatened with extinction and for education about these issues. The special Conservation Fund is subject to oversight of the State Auditor pursuant to Article 5A of Chapter 147 of the General Statutes. Emblems of different sizes, shapes, types, or designs may be used to recognize contributions in different amounts, but no emblem shall be issued for a contribution amounting in value to less than five dollars ($5.00). (1997-400, s. 2.1.)

§ 143B-289.60. Article subject to Chapter 113.

Nothing in this Article shall be construed to affect the jurisdictional division between the Marine Fisheries Commission and the Wildlife Resources Commission contained in Subchapter IV of Chapter 113 of the General Statutes or in any way to alter or abridge the powers and duties of the two agencies conferred in that Subchapter. (1997-400, s. 2.1.)

§ 143B-289.61. Jurisdictional questions.

In the event of any question arising between the Wildlife Resources Commission and the Marine Fisheries Commission or between the Department of Environment and Natural Resources and the Marine Fisheries Commission as to any duty, responsibility, or authority imposed upon any of these bodies by law or with respect to conflict involving rules or administrative practices, the question or conflict shall be resolved by the Governor, whose decision shall be binding. (1997-400, s. 2.1; 1997-443, s. 11A.123.)

§§ 143B-289.62 through 143B-289.65. Reserved for future codification purposes.

Part 6. North Carolina Mining Commission.

§ 143B-290: Repealed by Session Laws 2012-143, s. 1(a), effective August 1, 2012.

§ 143B-291: Repealed by Session Laws 2012-143, s. 1(a), effective August 1, 2012.

§ 143B-292: Repealed by Session Laws 2012-143, s. 1(a), effective August 1, 2012.

§ 143B-293: Repealed by Session Laws 2012-143, s. 1(a), effective August 1, 2012.

Part 6A. North Carolina Mining and Energy Commission.

§ 143B-293.1. North Carolina Mining and Energy Commission - creation; powers and duties.

(a) There is hereby created the North Carolina Mining and Energy Commission of the Department of Environment and Natural Resources with the power and duty to adopt rules necessary to administer the Oil and Gas

Conservation Act pursuant to G.S. 113-391 and for the development of the oil, gas, and mining resources of the State. The Commission shall make such rules consistent with the provisions of this Chapter. All rules adopted by the Commission shall be enforced by the Department of Environment and Natural Resources.

(b) The Commission shall have the authority to make determinations and issue orders pursuant to the Oil and Gas Conservation Act to (i) regulate the spacing of wells and to establish drilling units as provided in G.S. 113-393; (ii) require the operation of wells with efficient gas-oil ratios and to fix such ratios; (iii) limit and prorate the production of oil or gas, or both, from any pool or field for the prevention of waste as provided in G.S. 113-394; and (iv) require integration of interests as provided in G.S. 113-393.

(c) The Commission shall submit quarterly written reports as to its operation, activities, programs, and progress to the Joint Legislative Commission on Energy Policy and the Environmental Review Commission. The Commission shall supplement the written reports required by this subsection with additional written and oral reports as may be requested by the Joint Legislative Commission on Energy Policy and the Environmental Review Commission. The Commission shall submit the written reports required by this subsection whether or not the General Assembly is in session at the time the report is due. (1973, c. 1262, s. 29; 1977, c. 771, s. 4; 1983, c. 279, s. 2; 1989, c. 727, s. 193; 1989 (Reg. Sess., 1990), c. 944, s. 1; 1991 (Reg. Sess., 1992), c. 1039, s. 16; 1997-443, s. 11A.119(a); 2002-165, s. 1.10; 2012-143, s. 1(b).)

§ 143B-293.2. North Carolina Mining and Energy Commission - members; selection; removal; compensation; quorum; services.

(a) Members Selection. - The North Carolina Mining and Energy Commission shall consist of 15 members appointed as follows:

(1) The Chair of the North Carolina State University Minerals Research Laboratory Advisory Committee, or the Chair's designee, ex officio.

(2) The State Geologist, or other designee of the Secretary of Environment and Natural Resources.

(3) Repealed by Session Laws 2013-365, s. 3(a), effective July 29, 2013.

(3a)   One appointed by the Governor, at large.

(4)   One appointed by the General Assembly upon recommendation of the Speaker of the House of Representatives who is a member of a nongovernmental conservation interest.

(5)   One appointed by the General Assembly upon recommendation of the Speaker of the House of Representatives who, at the time of initial appointment, is an elected official of a municipal government located in a region of North Carolina that has oil and gas potential. A person serving in this seat may complete a term on the Commission even if the person is no longer serving as an elected official of a municipal government but may not be reappointed to a subsequent term.

(6)   One appointed by the General Assembly upon recommendation of the Speaker of the House of Representatives who is a representative of the mining industry.

(7)   One appointed by the General Assembly upon recommendation of the Speaker of the House of Representatives who shall be a geologist with experience in oil and gas exploration and development.

(8)   One appointed by the General Assembly upon recommendation of the President Pro Tempore of the Senate who is a member of a nongovernmental conservation interest.

(9)   One appointed by the General Assembly upon recommendation of the President Pro Tempore of the Senate who, at the time of initial appointment, is a member of a county board of commissioners of a county located in a region of North Carolina that has oil and gas potential. A person serving in this seat may complete a term on the Commission even if the person is no longer serving as county commissioner but may not be reappointed to a subsequent term.

(10)   One appointed by the General Assembly upon recommendation of the President Pro Tempore of the Senate who is a representative of the mining industry.

(11)   One appointed by the General Assembly upon recommendation of the President Pro Tempore of the Senate who shall be an engineer with experience in oil and gas exploration and development.

(12) One appointed by the Governor who shall be a representative of a publicly traded natural gas company.

(13) One appointed by the Governor who shall be a licensed attorney with experience in legal matters associated with oil and gas exploration and development.

(14) One appointed by the Governor who is a member of the Environmental Management Commission.

(15) One appointed by the Governor who is a member of the Commission for Public Health.

(b) Terms. - The term of office of members of the Commission is three years. A member may be reappointed to no more than two consecutive three-year terms. The term of a member who no longer meets the qualifications of their respective appointment, as set forth in subsection (a) of this section, shall terminate but the member may continue to serve until a new member who meets the qualifications is appointed. The terms of members appointed under subdivisions (4), (6), (9), and (12) of subsection (a) of this section shall expire on June 30 of years evenly divisible by three. The terms of members appointed under subdivisions (7), (10), (13), and (14) of subsection (a) of this section shall expire on June 30 of years that precede by one year those years that are evenly divisible by three. The terms of members appointed under subdivisions (5), (8), (11), and (15) of subsection (a) of this section shall expire on June 30 of years that follow by one year those years that are evenly divisible by three.

(c) Vacancies; Removal from Office. -

(1) Any appointment by the Governor to fill a vacancy on the Commission created by the resignation, dismissal, death, or disability of a member shall be for the balance of the unexpired term. The Governor shall have the power to remove any member of the Commission from office for misfeasance, malfeasance, or nonfeasance in accordance with the provisions of G.S. 143B-13 of the Executive Organization Act of 1973.

(2) Members appointed by the President Pro Tempore of the Senate and the Speaker of the House of Representatives shall be made in accordance with G.S. 120-121, and vacancies in those appointments shall be filled in accordance with G.S. 120-122. In accordance with Section 10 of Article VI of the North

Carolina Constitution, a member may continue to serve until a successor is duly appointed.

(d) Compensation. - The members of the Commission shall receive per diem and necessary traveling and subsistence expenses in accordance with the provisions of G.S. 138-5.

(e) Quorum. - A majority of the Commission shall constitute a quorum for the transaction of business.

(f) Staff. - All staff support required by the Commission shall be supplied by the Division of Energy, Mineral, and Land Resources and the North Carolina Geological Survey.

(g) Committees. - In addition to the Committee on Civil Penalty Remissions required to be established under G.S. 143B-293.6, the chair may establish other committees from members of the Commission to address specific issues as appropriate. No member of a committee may hear or vote on any matter in which the member has an economic interest. A majority of a committee shall constitute a quorum for the transaction of business. At a minimum, the chair shall establish a Committee on Mining, which shall consist of members appointed under subdivisions (1), (4), (6), (8), (10), (14), and (15) of subsection (a) of this section. The Committee on Mining shall have exclusive responsibility and authority over matters pertaining to mining and implementation of the Mining Act of 1971, including all of the following powers and duties:

(1) To act as the advisory body to the Governor pursuant to Article V(a) of the Interstate Mining Compact, as set out in G.S. 74-37.

(2) To adopt rules necessary to administer the Mining Act of 1971 pursuant to G.S. 74-63.

(3) To adopt rules necessary to administer the Control of Exploration for Uranium in North Carolina Act of 1983 pursuant to G.S. 74-86.

(4) To adopt rules, not inconsistent with the laws of this State, as may be required by the federal government for grants-in-aid for mining resource purposes which may be made available to the State by the federal government. This section is to be liberally construed in order that the State and its citizens may benefit from such grants-in-aid.

(h) Office May Be Held Concurrently With Others. - Membership on the Mining and Energy Commission is hereby declared to be an office that may be held concurrently with other elective or appointive offices in addition to the maximum number of offices permitted to be held by one person under G.S. 128-1.1. (1973, c. 1262, s. 30; 1997-496, s. 8; 2006-79, ss. 3, 4; 2012-143, s. 1(b); 2012-187, s. 1.1; 2013-365, s. 3(a).)

§ 143B-293.3: Reserved for future codification purposes.

§ 143B-293.4. North Carolina Mining and Energy Commission - officers.

The Mining and Energy Commission shall have a chair and a vice-chair. The Commission shall elect one of its members to serve as chair and one of its members to serve as vice-chair. The chair and vice-chair shall serve one-year terms beginning August 1 and ending July 31 of the following year. The chair and vice-chair may serve any number of terms, but not more than two terms consecutively. (1973, c. 1262, s. 31; 2006-79, s. 5; 2012-143, s. 1(b).)

§ 143B-293.5. North Carolina Mining and Energy Commission - meetings.

The North Carolina Mining and Energy Commission shall meet at least quarterly and may hold special meetings at any time and place within the State at the call of the chair or upon the written request of at least nine members. (1973, c. 1262, s. 32; 2006-79, s. 6; 2012-143, s. 1(b).)

§ 143B-293.6. North Carolina Mining and Energy Commission - quasi-judicial powers; procedures.

(a) With respect to those matters within its jurisdiction, the Mining and Energy Commission shall exercise quasi-judicial powers in accordance with the provisions of Chapter 150B of the General Statutes.

(b) The chair shall appoint a Committee on Civil Penalty Remissions from the members of the Commission. No member of the Committee on Civil Penalty Remissions may hear or vote on any matter in which the member has an economic interest. In determining whether a remission request will be approved, the Committee shall consider the recommendation of the Secretary or the Secretary's designee and all of the following factors:

(1)   Whether one or more of the civil penalty assessment factors in subsection (b) of this section were wrongly applied to the detriment of the petitioner.

(2)   Whether the violator promptly abated continuing environmental damage resulting from the violation.

(3)   Whether the violation was inadvertent or a result of an accident.

(4)   Whether the violator had been assessed civil penalties for any previous violations.

(5)   Whether payment of the civil penalty will prevent payment for the remaining necessary remedial actions.

(c)   The Committee on Civil Penalty Remissions may remit the entire amount of the penalty only when the violator has not been assessed civil penalties for previous violations and when payment of the civil penalty will prevent payment for the remaining necessary remedial actions. (2012-143, s. 1(b).)

Part 7. Soil and Water Conservation Commission.

§§ 143B-294 through 143B-297.1: Recodified as Article 71 of Chapter 106, G.S. 106-840 through G.S. 106-844, by Session Laws 2011-145, s. 13.22A(e), effective July 1, 2011.

Part 8. Sedimentation Control Commission.

§ 143B-298. Sedimentation Control Commission - creation; powers and duties.

There is hereby created the Sedimentation Control Commission of the Department of Environment and Natural Resources with the power and duty to develop and administer a sedimentation control program as herein provided.

The Sedimentation Control Commission has the following powers and duties:

(1)   In cooperation with the Secretary of the Department of Transportation and Highway Safety and other appropriate State and federal agencies, develop,

promulgate, publicize, and administer a comprehensive State erosion and sedimentation control program.

(2)   Develop and adopt on or before July 1, 1974, rules and regulations for the control of erosion and sedimentation pursuant to G.S. 113A-54.

(3)   Conduct public hearings pursuant to G.S. 113A-54.

(4)   Assist local governments in developing erosion and sedimentation control programs pursuant to G.S. 113A-60.

(5)   Assist and encourage other State agencies in developing erosion and sedimentation control programs pursuant to G.S. 113A-56.

(6)   Develop recommended methods of control of sedimentation and prepare and make available for distribution publications and other materials dealing with sedimentation control techniques pursuant to G.S. 113A-54. (1973, c. 1262, s. 39; 1977, c. 771, s. 4; 1989, c. 727, s. 218(137); 1997-443, s. 11A.119(a).)

§ 143B-299. Sedimentation Control Commission - members; selection; compensation; meetings.

(a)   Creation; Membership. - There is hereby created in the Department of Environment and Natural Resources the North Carolina Sedimentation Control Commission, which is charged with the duty of developing and administering the sedimentation control program provided for in this Article. The Commission shall consist of the following members:

(1)   A person to be nominated jointly by the boards of the North Carolina League of Municipalities and the North Carolina Association of County Commissioners.

(2)   A person to be nominated by the Board of the North Carolina Home Builders Association.

(3)   A person to be nominated by the Carolinas Branch, Associated General Contractors of America.

(4) A representative of a North Carolina public utility company.

(5) The Director of the North Carolina Water Resources Research Institute.

(6) A member of the North Carolina Mining and Energy Commission who shall be a representative of nongovernmental conservation interests, as required by G.S. 74-38(b).

(7) A member of the State Soil and Water Conservation Commission.

(8) A member of the Environmental Management Commission.

(9) A soil scientist from the faculty of North Carolina State University.

(10) Two persons who shall be representatives of nongovernmental conservation interests.

(11) A professional engineer registered under the provisions of Chapter 89C of the General Statutes nominated by the Professional Engineers of North Carolina, Inc.

(b) Appointment. - The Commission members shall be appointed by the Governor. All Commission members, except the person appointed under subdivision (5) of subsection (a) of this section, shall serve staggered terms of three years and until their successors are appointed and duly qualified. The person appointed under subdivision (5) of subsection (a) of this section shall serve as a member of the Commission, subject to removal by the Governor as hereinafter specified in this section, so long as the person continues as Director of the Water Resources Research Institute. The terms of members appointed under subdivisions (2), (4), (7), and (8) of subsection (a) of this section shall expire on 30 June of years evenly divisible by three. The terms of members appointed under subdivisions (1), (3), and (10) of subsection (a) of this section shall expire on 30 June of years that follow by one year those years that are evenly divisible by three. The terms of members appointed under subdivisions (6), (9), and (11) of subsection (a) of this section shall expire on 30 June of years that precede by one year those years that are evenly divisible by three. Except for the person appointed under subdivision (5) of subsection (a) of this section, no member of the Commission shall serve more than two complete consecutive three-year terms. Any member appointed by the Governor to fill a vacancy occurring in any of the appointments shall be appointed for the remainder of the term of the member causing the vacancy. The Governor may at any time remove any member of the Commission for inefficiency, neglect of duty, malfeasance, misfeasance, nonfeasance, or because they no longer possess the required qualifications for membership. The office of the North Carolina Sedimentation Control Commission is declared to be an office that may be held concurrently with any other elective or appointive office, under the authority of Article VI, Sec. 9, of the North Carolina Constitution.

(b1)   Chair. - The Governor shall designate a member of the Commission to serve as chair.

(c)   Compensation. - The members of the Commission shall receive the usual and customary per diem allowed for the other members of boards and commissions of the State and as fixed in the Biennial Appropriation Act, and, in addition, the members of the Commission shall receive subsistence and travel expenses according to the prevailing State practice and as allowed and fixed by statute for such purposes, which said travel expenses shall also be allowed while going to or from any place of meeting or when on official business for the Commission. The per diem payments made to each member of the Commission shall include necessary time spent in traveling to and from their places of residence within the State to any place of meeting or while traveling on official business for the Commission.

(d)   Meetings of Commission. - The Commission shall meet at the call of the chair and shall hold special meetings at the call of a majority of the members. (1973, c. 1262, s. 40; 1977, c. 771, s. 4; 1981, c. 248, ss. 1, 2; 1989, c. 727, s. 218(138); 1989 (Reg. Sess., 1990), c. 1004, s. 19(b); 1991, c. 551, s. 1; 1997-443, s. 11A.119(a); 2006-79, s. 9; 2010-180, s. 10; 2012-143, s. 1(d).)

Part 9. Water Pollution Control System Operators Certification Commission.

§ 143B-300. Water Pollution Control System Operators Certification Commission - creation; powers and duties.

(a)   There is hereby created the Water Pollution Control System Operators Certification Commission to be located in the Department of Environment and Natural Resources. The Commission shall adopt rules with respect to the certification of water pollution control system operators as provided by Article 3 of Chapter 90A of the General Statutes.

(b)   The Commission shall adopt such rules, not inconsistent with the laws of this State, as may be required by the federal government for grants-in-aid for programs concerned with the certification of water pollution control system operators which may be made available to the State by the federal government. This section is to be liberally construed in order that the State and its citizens may benefit from such grants-in-aid.

(c)   The Commission may by rule delegate any of its powers, other than the power to adopt rules, to the Secretary of Environment and Natural Resources or the Secretary's designee. (1973, c. 1262, s. 42; 1977, c. 771, s. 4; 1989, c. 727, s. 195; 1991, c. 623, s. 15; 1997-443, s. 11A.119(a); 2006-79, s. 10.)

§ 143B-301. Water Pollution Control System Operators Certification Commission - members; selection; removal; compensation; quorum; services.

(a)   The Water Pollution Control System Operators Certification Commission shall consist of 11 members. Two members shall be from the animal agriculture industry and shall be appointed by the Commissioner of Agriculture. Nine members shall be appointed by the Secretary of Environment and Natural Resources with the approval of the Environmental Management Commission with the following qualifications:

(1)   Two members shall be currently employed as water pollution control facility operators, water pollution control system superintendents or directors, water and sewer superintendents or directors, or equivalent positions with a North Carolina municipality;

(2)   One member shall be manager of a North Carolina municipality having a population of more than 10,000 as of the most recent federal census;

(3)   One member shall be manager of a North Carolina municipality having a population of less than 10,000 as of the most recent federal census;

(4)   One member shall be employed by a private industry and shall be responsible for supervising the treatment or pretreatment of industrial wastewater;

(5)   One member who is a faculty member of a four-year college or university and whose major field is related to wastewater treatment;

(6) One member who is employed by the Department of Environment and Natural Resources and works in the field of water pollution control, who shall serve as Chairman of the Commission;

(7) One member who is employed by a commercial water pollution control system operating firm; and

(8) One member shall be currently employed as a water pollution control system collection operator, superintendent, director, or equivalent position with a North Carolina municipality.

(b) Appointments to the Commission shall be for a term of three years. Terms shall be staggered so that three terms shall expire on 30 June of each year, except that members of the Commission shall serve until their successors are appointed and duly qualified as provided by G.S. 128-7.

(c) The Commission shall elect a Vice-Chairman from among its members. The Vice-Chairman shall serve from the time of his election until 30 June of the following year, or until his successor is elected.

(d) Any appointment to fill a vacancy on the Commission created by the resignation, dismissal, death or disability of a member shall be for the balance of the unexpired term.

(e) The Governor shall have the power to remove any member of the Commission from office for misfeasance, malfeasance, and nonfeasance according to the provisions of G.S. 143B-13.

(f) The members of the Commission shall receive per diem and necessary travel and subsistence expenses in accordance with the provisions of G.S. 138-5 and G.S. 143B-15.

(g) A majority of the Commission shall constitute a quorum for the transaction of business.

(h) All clerical and other services required by the Commission shall be supplied by the Secretary of Environment and Natural Resources. (1973, c. 1262, s. 43; 1977, c. 771, s. 4; 1989, c. 372, s. 10; c. 727, s. 196, 197; 1989 (Reg. Sess., 1990), c. 850, s. 1; c. 1004, s. 19(b); 1991, c. 623, ss. 1, 16; 1995 (Reg. Sess., 1996), c. 626, s. 5; 1997-443, s. 11A.119(a).)

§ 143B-301.1. Definitions.

The definitions set out in G.S. 90A-46 shall apply throughout this Part. (1991, c. 623, s. 17; 1991 (Reg. Sess., 1992), c. 890, s. 21.)

§§ 143B-301.2 through 143B-301.9. Reserved for future codification purposes.

Part 9A. Well Contractors Certification Commission.

§ 143B-301.10. Definitions.

The definitions in G.S. 87-85 and G.S. 87-98.2 apply in this Part. (1997-358, s. 1.)

§ 143B-301.11. Creation, powers, and duties of the Commission.

(a) Creation and Duties. - The Well Contractors Certification Commission is created within the Department. The Commission shall:

(1) Adopt rules with respect to the certification of well contractors as provided by Article 7A of Chapter 87 of the General Statutes.

(2) Exercise quasi-judicial powers in accordance with the provisions of Chapter 150B of the General Statutes. The Commission shall make the final agency decision on any matter involving the certification of well contractors pursuant to Article 7A of Chapter 87 of the General Statutes and on civil penalties assessed for violations of that Article or rules adopted pursuant to that Article.

(3) Adopt rules as may be required to secure a federal grant-in-aid for a program concerned with the certification of well contractors. This subdivision is to be liberally construed in order that the State and its citizens may benefit from federal grants-in-aid.

(b) Delegation. - The Commission may, by rule, delegate to the Secretary any of its powers, other than the power to adopt rules. (1997-358, s. 1.)

§ 143B-301.12. Membership of Commission.

(a) Appointments. - The Commission shall consist of seven members appointed as follows:

(1) One member appointed by the General Assembly upon recommendation of the Speaker of the House of Representatives who, at the time of appointment, is (i) engaged in well contractor activities, (ii) certified as a well contractor under Article 7A of Chapter 87 of the General Statutes, (iii) engaged primarily in the construction, installation, repair, alteration, or abandonment of domestic water supply wells, and (iv) a resident of a county that is located east of or is traversed by Interstate 95.

(2) One member appointed by the General Assembly upon recommendation of the Speaker of the House of Representatives who, at the time of appointment, is (i) engaged in well contractor activities, (ii) certified as a well contractor under Article 7A of Chapter 87 of the General Statutes, (iii) engaged primarily in the construction, installation, repair, alteration, or abandonment of domestic water supply wells, and (iv) a resident of a county that is located wholly west of Interstate 95.

(3) One member appointed by the General Assembly upon recommendation of the President Pro Tempore of the Senate who, at the time of appointment, is (i) engaged in well contractor activities, (ii) certified as a well contractor under Article 7A of Chapter 87 of the General Statutes, and (iii) engaged primarily in the construction, installation, repair, alteration, or abandonment of industrial, municipal, or other large capacity water supply wells.

(4) One member appointed by the General Assembly upon recommendation of the President Pro Tempore of the Senate who, at the time of appointment, is (i) engaged in well contractor activities, (ii) certified as a well contractor under Article 7A of Chapter 87 of the General Statutes, and (iii) engaged primarily in the construction, installation, repair, alteration, or abandonment of nonwater supply wells, such as monitoring or recovery wells.

(5) One member appointed by the General Assembly upon recommendation of the Speaker of the House of Representatives who, at the time of appointment, is (i) employed by a local county health department and (ii) actively engaged in well inspection and permitting.

(6) One member appointed by the General Assembly upon recommendation of the President Pro Tempore of the Senate who, at the time of

appointment, is (i) employed by a local county health department and (ii) actively engaged in well inspection and permitting.

(7)   One member appointed by the Governor who is (i) appointed from the public at large, (ii) not engaged in well contractor activities, and (iii) not an employee of a firm or corporation engaged in well contractor activities or a State or county governmental agency.

(b)   Additional Qualifications. - Appointment of members to fill positions (1), (2), (3), and (4) shall be made from among all those persons who are recommended for appointment to the Commission by any person who is engaged in well contractor activities and who is certified as a well contractor under Article 7A of Chapter 87 of the General Statutes. No person shall be appointed to the Commission who is a resident of, or has a principal place of business in, the same county as another member of the Commission.

(c)   Terms. - Appointments to the Commission shall be for terms of three years. The terms of members appointed to fill positions (1), (2), and (7) shall expire on 30 June of years evenly divisible by three. The terms of members appointed to fill positions (3) and (4) shall expire on 30 June of years that follow y one year those years that are evenly divisible by three. The terms of members appointed to fill positions (5) and (6) shall expire on 30 June of years that precede by one year those years that are evenly divisible by three. Members shall serve until their successors are appointed and qualified. No member shall serve more than two consecutive terms.

(d)   Officers. - The Commission shall elect a Chair and a Vice-Chair from among its members. These officers shall serve from the time of their election until 30 June of the following year, or until a successor is elected.

(e)   Vacancies. - An appointment to fill a vacancy on the Commission created by the resignation, dismissal, disability, or death of a member shall be for the balance of the unexpired term. Vacancies in appointments made by the General Assembly shall be filled as provided in G.S. 120-122.

(f)   Removal. - The Governor may remove any member of the Commission from office for misfeasance, malfeasance, or nonfeasance, as provided in G.S. 143B-13.

(g) Compensation. - The members of the Commission shall receive per diem and necessary travel and subsistence expenses in accordance with the provisions of G.S. 138-5.

(h) Quorum. - A majority of the membership of the Commission constitutes a quorum for the transaction of business.

(i) Services. - All clerical and other services required by the Commission shall be supplied by the Secretary. (1997-358, s. 1; 2002-165, s. 1.11.)

Part 10. Earth Resources Council.

§§ 143B-302 through 143B-304: Repealed by Session Laws 1983, c. 667, s. 1.

Part 11. Community Development Council.

§§ 143B-305 through 143B-307: Recodified as §§ 143B-437.1 through 143B-437.3 by Session Laws 1989, c. 727, s. 199.

Part 12. Forestry Council.

§§ 143B-308 through 143B-310: Recodified as G.S. 143A-66.1 through 143A-66.3, in Article 7 of Chapter 143A, by Session Laws 2011-145, s. 13.25(f), effective July 1, 2011.

Part 13. Parks and Recreation Council.

§§ 143B-311 through 143B-313: Repealed by Session Laws 1995, c. 456, s. 4.

Part 13A. North Carolina Parks and Recreation Authority.

§ 143B-313.1. North Carolina Parks and Recreation Authority; creation; powers and duties.

The North Carolina Parks and Recreation Authority is created, to be administered by the Department of Environment and Natural Resources. The North Carolina Parks and Recreation Authority shall have at least the following powers and duties:

(1)   To receive public and private donations, appropriations, grants, and revenues for deposit into the Parks and Recreation Trust Fund.

(2)   To allocate funds for land acquisition from the Parks and Recreation Trust Fund.

(3)   To allocate funds for repairs, renovations, improvements, construction, and other capital projects from the Parks and Recreation Trust Fund.

(4)   To solicit financial and material support from public and private sources.

(5)   To develop effective public and private support for the programs and operations of the parks and recreation areas.

(6)   To consider and to advise the Secretary of Environment and Natural Resources on any matter the Secretary may refer to the North Carolina Parks and Recreation Authority. (1995, c. 456, s. 1; 1997-443, s. 11A.119(a).)

§ 143B-313.2. North Carolina Parks and Recreation Authority; members; selection; compensation; meetings.

(a)   Membership. - The North Carolina Parks and Recreation Authority shall consist of nine members. The members shall include persons who are knowledgeable about park and recreation issues in North Carolina or with expertise in finance. In making appointments, each appointing authority shall specify under which subdivision of this subsection the person is appointed. Members shall be appointed as follows:

(1)   One member appointed by the Governor.

(2)   One member appointed by the Governor.

(3)   One member appointed by the Governor.

(3a) Repealed by Session Laws 2013-360, s. 14.5(a), effective July 1, 2013.

(3b) Repealed by Session Laws 2013-360, s. 14.5(a), effective July 1, 2013.

(4) One member appointed by the General Assembly upon the recommendation of the Speaker of the House of Representatives, as provided in G.S. 120-121.

(5) One member appointed by the General Assembly upon the recommendation of the Speaker of the House of Representatives, as provided in G.S. 120-121.

(6) One member appointed by the General Assembly upon the recommendation of the Speaker of the House of Representatives, as provided in G.S. 120-121.

(7) Repealed by Session Laws 2013-360, s. 14.5(a), effective July 1, 2013.

(7a) Repealed by Session Laws 2013-360, s. 14.5(a), effective July 1, 2013.

(8) One member appointed by the General Assembly upon the recommendation of the President Pro Tempore of the Senate, as provided in G.S. 120-121.

(9) One member appointed by the General Assembly upon the recommendation of the President Pro Tempore of the Senate, as provided in G.S. 120-121.

(10) One member appointed by the General Assembly upon the recommendation of the President Pro Tempore of the Senate, as provided in G.S. 120-121.

(11) Repealed by Session Laws 2013-360, s. 14.5(a), effective July 1, 2013.

(12) Repealed by Session Laws 2013-360, s. 14.5(a), effective July 1, 2013.

(b) Terms. - Members shall serve staggered terms of office of three years. Members shall serve no more than two consecutive three-year terms. After serving two consecutive three-year terms, a member is not eligible for appointment to the Authority for at least one year after the expiration date of that member's most recent term. Upon the expiration of a three-year term, a member may continue to serve until a successor is appointed and duly qualified as provided by G.S. 128-7. The terms of members appointed under subdivision (1), (5), or (9) of subsection (a) of this section shall expire on July 1 of years that are evenly divisible by three. The terms of members appointed under subdivision (2), (4), or (8) of subsection (a) of this section shall expire on July 1 of years that follow by one year those years that are evenly divisible by three. The terms of members appointed under subdivision (3), (6), or (10) of subsection (a) of this section shall expire on July 1 of years that precede by one year those years that are evenly divisible by three.

(c)   Chair. - The Governor shall appoint one member of the North Carolina Parks and Recreation Authority to serve as Chair.

(d)   Vacancies. - A vacancy on the North Carolina Parks and Recreation Authority shall be filled by the appointing authority responsible for making the appointment to that position as provided in subsection (a) of this section. An appointment to fill a vacancy shall be for the unexpired balance of the term.

(e)   Removal. - The Governor may remove, as provided in Article 10 of Chapter 143C of the General Statutes any member of the North Carolina Parks and Recreation Authority appointed by the Governor for misfeasance, malfeasance, or nonfeasance. The General Assembly may remove any member of the North Carolina Parks and Recreation Authority appointed by the General Assembly for misfeasance, malfeasance, or nonfeasance.

(f)   Compensation. - The members of the North Carolina Parks and Recreation Authority shall receive per diem and necessary travel and subsistence expenses according to the provisions of G.S. 138-5.

(g)   Meetings. - The North Carolina Parks and Recreation Authority shall meet at least quarterly at a time and place designated by the Chair.

(h)   Quorum. - A majority of the North Carolina Parks and Recreation Authority shall constitute a quorum for the transaction of business.

(i)   Staff. - All clerical and other services required by the North Carolina Parks and Recreation Authority shall be provided by the Secretary of Environment and Natural Resources. (1995, c. 456, s. 1; 1996, 2nd Ex. Sess., c. 15, s. 16.1; 1997-443, s. 11A.119(a); 1997-496, s. 10; 2001-424, s. 19.3(a); 2006-203, s. 105; 2007-437, s. 2; 2013-360, s. 14.5(a).)

Part 14. North Carolina Water Safety Council.

§§ 143B-314 through 143B-316: Repealed by Session Laws 1983 (Regular Session 1984), c. 995, s. 12.

Part 15. Small Business Environmental Advisory Panel.

§ 143B-317: Repealed by Session Laws 2011-266, ss. 1.35(a) and 3.3(a), effective July 1, 2011.

§ 143B-318: Repealed by Session Laws 2011-266, ss. 1.35(a) and 3.3(a), effective July 1, 2011.

§ 143B-319: Repealed by Session Laws 2011-266, ss. 1.35(a) and 3.3(a), effective July 1, 2011.

Part 16. Water Quality Council.

§§ 143B-320 through 143B-321: Repealed by Session Laws 1983 (Regular Session 1984), c. 995, s. 14.

Part 17. North Carolina National Park, Parkway and Forests Development Council.

§§ 143B-322 through 143B-324: Recodified as §§ 143B-446 through 143B-447.1 by Session Laws 1977, c. 198, s. 26.

Part 17A. Western North Carolina Public Lands Council.

§ 143B-324.1. Western North Carolina Public Lands Council creation; powers; duties.

The Western North Carolina Public Lands Council is created within the Department of Environment and Natural Resources. The North Carolina

National Park, Parkway and Forests Development [Western North Carolina Public Lands Council] Council shall:

(1)   Endeavor to promote the development of that part of the Smoky Mountains National Park lying in North Carolina, the completion and development of the Blue Ridge Parkway in North Carolina, the development of the Nantahala and Pisgah national forests, and the development of other recreational areas in that part of North Carolina immediately affected by the Great Smoky Mountains National Park, the Blue Ridge Parkway or the Pisgah or Nantahala national forests.

(2)   Study the development of these areas and to recommend a policy that will promote the development of the entire area generally designated as the mountain section of North Carolina, with particular emphasis upon the development of the scenic and recreational resources of the region, and the encouragement of the location of tourist facilities along lines designed to develop to the fullest these resources in the mountain section.

(3)   Confer with the various departments, agencies, commissioners and officials of the federal government and governments of adjoining states in connection with the development of the federal areas and projects named in this section.

(4)   Advise and confer with the various officials, agencies or departments of the State of North Carolina that may be directly or indirectly concerned in the development of the resources of these areas.

(5)   Advise and confer with the various interested individuals, organizations or agencies that are interested in developing this area.

(6)   Use its facilities and efforts in formulating, developing and carrying out overall programs for the development of the area as a whole.

(7)   Study the need for additional entrances to the Great Smoky Mountains National Park, together with the need for additional highway approaches and connections.

(8)   File its findings in this connection as recommendations with the National Park Service of the federal government, and the North Carolina Department of Transportation.

(9)   Advise the Secretary of Environment and Natural Resources upon any matter the Secretary of Environment and Natural Resources may refer to it. (1973, c. 1262, s. 66; 1977, c. 198, ss. 5, 26; 1989, c. 751, s. 9(c); 1991 (Reg. Sess., 1992), c. 959, s. 85; 1997-443, ss. 11A.123, 15.36(b), (c); 2010-180, s. 7(b).)

§ 143B-324.2. Western North Carolina Public Lands Council members; selection; officers; removal; compensation; quorum; services.

(a)   Members; Selection; and Terms of Service. - The Western North Carolina Public Lands Council within the Department of Environment and Natural Resources shall consist of seven members appointed by the Governor. The composition of the Council shall be as follows:

(1)   One member shall be a resident of Buncombe County.

(2)   One member shall be a resident of Haywood County.

(3)   One member shall be a resident of Jackson County.

(4)   One member shall be a resident of Swain County.

(5)   One member shall be a resident of Cherokee County.

(6)   Two members shall be residents of counties adjacent to the Blue Ridge Parkway, the Great Smoky Mountains National Park or the Pisgah or Nantahala national forests.

The appointment of members shall be for terms of four years, or until their successors are appointed and qualify. Any appointment to fill a vacancy on the Council created by the resignation, dismissal, death or disability of a member shall be for the balance of the unexpired term.

(b)   Officers. - The Council shall elect a chair, a vice-chair, and a secretary. The chair and vice-chair shall all be members of the Council, but the secretary need not be a member of the Council. These officers shall perform the duties usually pertaining to such offices and when elected shall serve for a period of one year, but may be reelected. In case of vacancies by resignation or death, the office shall be filled by the Council for the unexpired term of said officer.

(c) Removal. - The Governor shall have the power to remove any member of the Council from office in accordance with the provisions of G.S. 143B-16 of the Executive Organization Act of 1973.

(d) Compensation. - Members of the Council shall receive per diem and necessary travel and subsistence expenses in accordance with the provisions of G.S. 138-5 and G.S. 143B-15 of the Executive Organization Act of 1973.

(e) Quorum. - Five members of the Council shall constitute a quorum for the transaction of business. (1973, c. 1262, s. 67; 1977, c. 198, ss. 5, 26; 1997-443, ss. 11A.123, 15.36(b), (d); 2010-180, s. 7(c).)

§ 143B-324.3. Western North Carolina Public Lands Council meetings.

The Western North Carolina Public Lands Council shall meet monthly and may hold special meetings at any time and place within the State at the call of the chair or upon written request of at least a majority of the members. (1973, c. 1262, s. 68; 1977, c. 198, s. 26; 1997-443, s. 15.36(b); 2010-180, s. 7(d).)

Part 18. Commercial and Sports Fisheries Advisory Committee.

§§ 143B-325 through 143B-327: Repealed by Session Laws 1983 (Regular Session 1984), c. 995, s. 11.

Part 19. John H. Kerr Reservoir Committee.

§§ 143B-328 through 143B-330: Repealed by Session Laws 1985 (Regular Session 1986), c. 1028, s. 30.

Part 20. Science and Technology Committee.

§§ 143B-331 through 143B-332: Recodified as §§ 143B-440, 143B-441 by Session Laws 1977, c. 198, s. 26.

Part 21. North Carolina Trails Committee.

§ 143B-333. North Carolina Trails Committee - creation; powers and duties.

There is hereby created the North Carolina Trails Committee of the Department of Environment and Natural Resources. The Committee shall have the following functions and duties:

(1) To meet not less than two times annually to advise the Department on all matters directly or indirectly pertaining to trails, their use, extent, location, and the other objectives and purposes of G.S. 113A-88.

(2) To coordinate trail development among local governments, and to assist local governments in the formation of their trail plans and advise the Department of its findings.

(3) To advise the Secretary of trail needs and potentials pursuant to G.S. 113A-88. (1973, c. 1262, s. 80; 1977, c. 771, s. 4; 1989, c. 727, s. 218(145); 1997-443, s. 11A.119(a).)

§ 143B-334. North Carolina Trails Committee - members; selection; removal; compensation.

The North Carolina Trails Committee shall consist of seven members appointed by the Secretary of Environment and Natural Resources. Two members shall be from the mountain section, two from the Piedmont section, two from the coastal plain, and one at large. They shall as much as possible represent various trail users.

The initial members of the North Carolina Trails Committee shall be the members of the current North Carolina Trails Committee who shall serve for a period equal to the remainder of their current term on the North Carolina Trails Committee. At the end of the respective terms of office of the initial members of the Committee, the appointment of their successors shall be for staggered terms of four years and until their successors are appointed and qualify. Any appointment to fill a vacancy on the Committee created by the resignation, dismissal, death or disability of a member shall be for the balance of the unexpired term.

The Governor shall have the power to remove any member of the Committee from office in accordance with the provisions of G.S. 143B-16 of the Executive Organization Act of 1973.

The Secretary of Environment and Natural Resources shall designate a member of the Committee to serve as chairman at the pleasure of the Governor.

Members of the Committee shall receive per diem and necessary travel and subsistence expenses in accordance with the provisions of G.S. 138-5 and G.S. 143B-15 of the Executive Organization Act of 1973. (1973, c. 1262, s. 81; 1977, c. 771, s. 4; 1989, c. 727, s. 218(146); 1997-443, s. 11A.119(a).)

Part 22. North Carolina Zoological Park Council.

§ 143B-335. North Carolina Zoological Park Council - creation; powers and duties.

There is hereby created the North Carolina Zoological Park Council of the Department of Environment and Natural Resources. The North Carolina Zoological Park Council shall have the following functions and duties:

(1) To advise the Secretary on the basic concepts of and for the Zoological Park, approve conceptual plans for the Zoological Park and its buildings;

(2) To advise on the construction, furnishings, equipment and operations of the North Carolina Zoological Park;

(2a) To establish and set admission fees with the approval of the Secretary of Environment and Natural Resources as provided in G.S. 143-177.3(b);

(3) To recommend programs to promote public appreciation of the North Carolina Zoological Park;

(4) To disseminate information on animals and the park as deemed necessary;

(5) To develop effective public support of the North Carolina Zoological Park through whatever means are desirable and necessary;

(6) To solicit financial and material support from various private sources within and without the State of North Carolina; and

(7) To advise the Secretary of Environment and Natural Resources upon any matter the Secretary may refer to it. (1973, c. 1262, s. 83; 1977, c. 771, s. 4; 1981, c. 278, s. 2; 1989, c. 727, s. 218(147); 1997-443, s. 11A.119(a).)

§ 143B-336. North Carolina Zoological Park Council - members; selection; removal; chairman; compensation; quorum; services.

The North Carolina Zoological Park Council of the Department of Environment and Natural Resources shall consist of 15 members appointed by the Governor, one of whom shall be the Chairman of the Board of Directors of the North Carolina Zoological Society.

The initial members of the Council shall be the members of the Board of Directors of the North Carolina Zoo Authority who shall serve for a period equal to the remainder of their current terms on the Board of Directors of the North Carolina Zoological Authority, all of whose terms expire July 15, 1975. At the end of the respective terms of office of the initial members of the Council, the Governor, to achieve staggered terms, shall appoint five members for terms of two years, five members for terms of four years and five members for terms of six years. Thereafter, the appointment of their successors shall be for terms of six years and until their successors are appointed and qualify. Any appointment to fill a vacancy on the Council created by the resignation, dismissal, death or disability of a member shall be for the balance of the unexpired term.

The Governor shall have the power to remove any member of the Council from office in accordance with the provisions of G.S. 143B-16 of the Executive Organization Act of 1973.

The Governor shall designate a member of the Council to serve as chairman at his pleasure.

Members of the Council shall receive per diem and necessary travel and subsistence expenses in accordance with the provisions of G.S. 138-5.

A majority of the Council shall constitute a quorum for the transaction of business.

All clerical and other services required by the Council shall be supplied by the Secretary of Environment and Natural Resources. (1973, c. 1262, s. 84; 1977, c. 771, s. 4; 1979, c. 30, s. 1; 1989, c. 727, s. 218(148); 1997-443, s. 11A.119(a).)

§ 143B-336.1. Special Zoo Fund.

A special continuing and nonreverting fund, to be called the Special Zoo Fund, is created. The North Carolina Zoological Park shall retain unbudgeted receipts at the end of each fiscal year, beginning June 30, 1989, and deposit these receipts into this Fund. This Fund shall be used for maintenance, repairs, and renovations of exhibits in existing habitat clusters and visitor services facilities, construction of visitor services facilities and support facilities such as greenhouses and temporary animal holding areas, for the replacement of tram equipment as required to maintain adequate service to the public, and for marketing the Zoological Park. The Special Zoo Fund may also be used to match private funds that are raised for these purposes. Funds may be expended for these purposes by the Department of Environment and Natural Resources on the advice of the North Carolina Zoological Park Council and with the approval of the Office of State Budget and Management. The Department of Environment and Natural Resources shall provide a report on or before October 1 of each year to the Office of State Budget and Management, the Fiscal Research Division of the General Assembly, and to the Joint Legislative Commission on Governmental Operations on the use of fees collected pursuant to this section. (1989, c. 752, s. 154; 1995, c. 324, s. 26.11; 1997-443, s. 11A.119(a); 2000-140, s. 93.1(a); 2001-424, s. 12.2(b); 2005-386, s. 5; 2010-142, s. 4.)

Part 23. Governor's Law and Order Commission.

§§ 143B-337 through 143B-339: Recodified as §§ 143B-478 to 143B-480.

Part 24. North Carolina Employment and Training Council.

§§ 143B-340 through 143B-341. Repealed by Session Laws 1985, c. 543, s. 6, effective July 1, 1985.

Part 25. Triad Park Commission.

§§ 143B-342 through 143B-344.2. Repealed by Session Laws 1983 (Regular Session 1984), c. 995, s. 13, effective June 27, 1984.

Part 26. Economic Opportunity Agencies.

§§ 143B-344.3 through 143B-344.10. Repealed by Session Laws 1981, c. 1127, s. 70.

Part 27. Employment and Training Act of 1985.

§§ 143B-344.11 through 143B-344.15: Recodified as §§ 143B-438.1 to 143B-438.5 by Session Laws 1989, c. 727, s. 202.

Part 28. North Carolina Aquariums Commission.

§§ 143B-344.16 through 143B-344.17: Repealed by Session Laws 1997, c. 286, s. 1.

Part 29. Advisory Commission for North Carolina State Museum of Natural Sciences.

§ 143B-344.18. Commission created; membership.

There is created an Advisory Commission for the North Carolina State Museum of Natural Sciences which shall determine its own organization. It shall consist of at least nine members, which shall include the Director of the North Carolina State Museum of Natural Sciences, the Commissioner of Agriculture, the State Geologist and Secretary of Environment and Natural Resources, the Director of the Institute of Fisheries Research of the University of North Carolina, the Director of the Wildlife Resources Commission, the Superintendent of Public Instruction, or qualified representative of any or all of the above-named members, and at least three persons representing the East, the Piedmont, and the Western areas of the State. Members appointed by the Governor shall serve for four-year staggered terms. Terms shall begin on 1 September. Members appointed by the Governor shall not serve more than three consecutive four-year terms. Any member may be removed by the Governor for cause. (1961, c. 1180, s. 1; 1973, c. 1262, s. 86; 1977, c. 771, s. 4; 1989, c. 727, s. 218(119); 1989 (Reg. Sess., 1990), c. 1004, s. 19(b); 1993, c. 561, ss. 116(b), (f); 1997-443, s. 11A.119(a); 2007-495, s. 4(a).)

§ 143B-344.19. Duties of Commission; meetings, formulation of policies and recommendations to Governor and General Assembly.

It shall be the duty of the Advisory Commission for the North Carolina State Museum of Natural Sciences to meet at least twice each year, to formulate policies for the advancement of the Museum, to make recommendations to the Governor and to the General Assembly concerning the Museum, and to assist in promoting and developing wider and more effective use of the North Carolina State Museum of Natural Sciences as an educational, scientific and historical exhibit. (1961, c. 1180, s. 2; 1993, c. 561, ss. 116(b), (f).)

§ 143B-344.20. No compensation of members; reimbursement for expenses.

Members of the Advisory Commission shall serve without compensation and shall be reimbursed for actual expenses incurred while in attendance at meetings of the Commission at the same rate as that established for reimbursement of State employees. Payment for such reimbursement for actual expense shall be made from the Contingency and Emergency Fund. (1961, c. 1180, s. 3; 1993, c. 561, s. 116(b).)

§ 143B-344.21. Reports to General Assembly.

The Commission shall prepare and submit a report outlining the needs of the North Carolina State Museum of Natural Sciences and recommendations for improvement of the effectiveness of the North Carolina State Museum of Natural Sciences for the purpose hereinabove set forth to the 1995 General Assembly, and to each succeeding General Assembly, to the Fiscal Research Division of the General Assembly, and to the Joint Legislative Commission on Governmental Operations on or before October 1 of each year. (1961, c. 1180, s. 4; 1993, c. 561, ss. 116(b), (f); 2010-142, s. 5.)

§ 143B-344.22. Museum of Natural Sciences; disposition of objects.

Notwithstanding Article 3A of Chapter 143 of the General Statutes, G.S. 143-49(4), or any other law pertaining to surplus State property, the Department of Environment and Natural Resources may sell or exchange any object from the collection of the Museum of Natural Sciences when it would be in the best interest of the Museum to do so. Sales or exchanges shall be conducted in accordance with generally accepted practices for accredited museums. If an object is sold, the net proceeds of the sale shall be deposited in the State treasury to the credit of a special fund to be used for the improvement of the Museum's collections or exhibits. (1998-212, s. 21(a)).

§ 143B-344.23. North Carolina Museum of Forestry; satellite museum.

The Department of Environment and Natural Resources shall establish and administer the North Carolina Museum of Forestry in Columbus County as a satellite museum of the North Carolina State Museum of Natural Sciences. (1998-212, s. 14.1(a).)

§§ 143B-344.24 through 143B-344.29. Reserved for future codification purposes.

Part 30. State Infrastructure Council.

§§ 143B-344.30 through 143B-344.33: Repealed by Session Laws 2005-454, s. 9, effective January 1, 2006.

Part 31. North Carolina Sustainable Communities Task Force.

§§ 143B-344.34 through 143B-344.38: Expired pursuant to Session Laws 2010-31, s. 13.5(e), as amended by Session Laws 2013-360, s. 14.2, effective July 31, 2013.

§ 143B-344.39: Reserved for future codification purposes.

§ 143B-344.40: Reserved for future codification purposes.

§ 143B-344.41: Reserved for future codification purposes.

Part 32. Energy Loan Fund.

§ 143B-344.42. Short title.

This Part shall be known as the Energy Loan Fund. (2000-140, s. 76(i); 2001-338, s. 1; 2009-475, s. 13; 2010-96, s. 21; 2013-360, s. 15.22(b).)

§ 143B-344.43. Legislative findings and purpose.

The General Assembly finds and declares that it is in the best interest of the citizens of North Carolina to promote and encourage energy efficiency within the State in order to conserve energy, promote economic competitiveness, and expand employment in the State. (2000-140, s. 76(i); 2001-338, s. 1; 2010-96, s. 21; 2013-360, s. 15.22(b).)

§ 143B-344.44. Lead agency; powers and duties.

(a) For the purposes of this Part, the Department of Environment and Natural Resources, State Energy Office, is designated as the lead State agency in matters pertaining to energy efficiency.

(b) The Department shall have the following powers and duties with respect to this Part:

(1) To provide industrial and commercial concerns doing business in North Carolina, local governmental units, nonprofit organizations, and residents in North Carolina with information and assistance in undertaking energy conserving capital improvement projects to enhance efficiency.

(2) To establish one or more revolving funds within the Department for the purpose of providing secured loans in amounts not greater than one million dollars ($1,000,000) per entity to install or to an entity that installs energy-efficient and renewable energy improvements (i) within business or nonprofit organizations located within or translocating to North Carolina, (ii) within local governmental units, (iii) within buildings classified as multifamily residential, (iv)

within buildings designated as multiuse that include residential units, and (v) within single family residences, however, in this instance the amount of the loan shall not exceed fifty thousand dollars ($50,000). In providing these loans, priority shall be given to entities already located in the State.

(3)   To develop and adopt rules to allow State-regulated financial institutions to provide secured loans to corporate entities, nonprofit organizations, and local governmental units and residents in accordance with terms and criteria established by the State Energy Office.

(4)   To work with appropriate State and federal agencies to develop and implement rules and regulations to facilitate this program.

(5)   To contract with persons or entities, including other State agencies and United States Treasury certified Community Development Financial Institutions (CDFI), to administer the Energy Loan Fund. Contracts for the procurement of services to manage, administer, and operate the Energy Loan Fund shall be awarded on a competitive basis through the solicitation of proposals and through the procedures established by statute and the Division of Purchase and Contract.

(c)   The annual interest rate charged for the use of the funds from the revolving fund established pursuant to subdivision (b)(2) of this section shall be a percentage not to exceed three percent (3%) per annum, to be established by the State Energy Office, excluding other fees required for loan application review and origination. The term of any loan originated under this section may not be greater than 20 years.

(d)   Notwithstanding subsection (c) of this section, the State Energy Office shall adopt rules to allow loans to be made from the revolving loan fund and by State-regulated financial institutions at interest rates as low as zero percent (0%) per annum for certain renewable energy, recycling, and energy efficient and conservation projects to encourage their development and use.

(e)   In accordance with the terms of the Stripper Well Settlement, administrative expenses for activities under this section that are subject to the Stripper Well Settlement shall be limited to five percent (5%) of funds allocated for this purpose. In accordance with the provisions of the American Recovery and Reinvestment Act of 2009 (ARRA) (Public Law 111-5), administrative expenses for activities under this section that are subject to the ARRA shall be limited to ten percent (10%) of funds allocated for this purpose.

(f) For purposes of this section:

(1) "Local governmental unit" means any board or governing body of a political subdivision of the State, including any board of a community college, any school board, or an agency, commission, or authority of a political subdivision of the State.

(2) "Nonprofit organization" means an organization that is exempt from federal income taxation under section 501(c)(3) of the Internal Revenue Code. (2000-140, s. 76(i); 2001-338, s. 1; 2009-446, s. 1(b); 2009-475, s. 13; 2010-96, s. 21; 2013-360, s. 15.22(b), (c).)

§ 143B-344.45: Reserved for future codification purposes.

Part 33. Weatherization Assistance Program and Heating/Air Repair and Replacement Program.

§ 143B-344.46. Weatherization Assistance Program and Heating/Air Repair and Replacement Program.

The State Energy Office within the Department may administer the Weatherization Assistance Program for Low-Income Families and the Heating/Air Repair and Replacement Program functions. Nothing in this Part shall be construed as obligating the General Assembly to appropriate funds for the Program or as entitling any person to services under the Program. (2003-284, s. 10.3; 2013-360, s. 15.22(h), (i).)

§ 143B-344.47: Reserved for future codification purposes.

Part 34. North Carolina Energy Assistance Act for Low-Income Persons.

§ 143B-344.48. Legislative findings and purpose.

(a) The General Assembly finds that:

(1) Maintaining the general health, welfare, and prosperity of the people of this State requires that all citizens receive essential levels of heat and electric service regardless of their economic circumstances.

(2) Serving the State's most vulnerable citizens, its low-income elderly, persons with disabilities, families with children, high residential energy users, and households with a high-energy burden, is a priority.

(3) Conserving energy benefits all citizens and the environment.

(4) Ensuring proper payment to public utilities and other entities providing energy services actually rendered is a responsibility of this State.

(5) Declining federal low-income energy assistance funding necessitates a State response to ensure the continuity and further development of energy assistance and related policies and programs in this State.

(6) Current energy assistance policies and programs have benefited North Carolina citizens and should be continued with the modifications provided in this Part.

(b) The General Assembly declares that it is the policy of this State that weatherization, replacement of heating and cooling systems, and other energy-related assistance programs be utilized to increase the energy efficiency of dwellings owned or occupied by low-income persons, reduce their total residential expenditures, and improve their health and safety. The State shall utilize all appropriate and available means to fund the Weatherization Assistance Program for Low-Income Families and the Heating/Air Repair and Replacement Program under G.S. 143B-344.46, and any other energy-related assistance program for low-income persons while, to the extent possible, identifying and utilizing sources of funding to achieve the objectives of this Part. (2006-206, s. 2; 2009-446, s. 2(a); 2013-360, s. 15.22(j).)

§ 143B-344.49. Definitions.

The following definitions apply to this Part:

(1) Applicant. - A member of the family residing in the dwelling unit, the owner, or designated agent of the owner of a dwelling unit applying for program services.

(2) Department. - The Environment and Natural Resources.

(3) Secretary. - The Secretary of the Department of Environment and Natural Resources.

(4) Subgrantee. - An entity managing a weatherization project that receives a federal grant of funds awarded pursuant to 10 C.F.R. § 440 (1 January 2006 edition) from this State or other entity named in the Notification of Grant Award and otherwise referred to as the grantee.

(5) Weatherization. - The modification of homes and home heating and cooling systems to improve heating and cooling efficiency by caulking and weather stripping, as well as insulating ceilings, attics, walls, and floors. (2006-206, s. 2; 2009-446, s. 2(a), (b); 2013-360, s. 15.22(j), (k).)

§ 143B-344.50. The State Energy Office designated agency; powers and duties.

(a) The State Energy Office in the Department of Environment and Natural Resources shall administer the Weatherization Assistance Program for Low-Income Families established by 42 U.S.C. § 6861, et seq., and 42 U.S.C. § 7101, et seq.; the Heating/Air Repair and Replacement Program established by the Secretary under G.S. 143B-344.46; and any other energy-related assistance program for the benefit of low-income persons in existing housing. The State Energy Office shall exercise the following powers and duties:

(1) Establish standards and criteria to carry out the provisions and purposes of this Part.

(2) Develop policy, criteria, and standards for receiving and processing applications for weatherization assistance.

(3) Make decisions and pursue appeals from decisions to accept or deny applications for weatherization, replacement of heating and cooling systems, and other energy-related assistance programs or otherwise participate in the State plan as a subgrantee or contractor.

(4) Adopt rules, consistent with the laws of this State, that may be required by the federal government for grants-in-aid for the Weatherization Assistance Program for Low-Income Families, the Heating/Air Repair and Replacement Program, or other energy-related assistance programs for the benefit of low-

income residents in existing housing. This section shall be liberally construed in order that this State and its citizens may benefit from such grants-in-aid.

(5) Establish procedures for the submission of periodic reports by any community action agency or other agency or entity authorized to manage a weatherization project, replacement of heating and cooling systems, or other energy-related assistance project.

(6) Implement criteria for periodic review of weatherization, replacement of heating and cooling systems, or other energy-related programs in existing housing for low-income households.

(7) Solicit, accept, hold, and administer on behalf of this State any grants or devises of money, securities, or property for the benefit of low-income residents in existing housing for use by the Department or other agencies in the administration of this Part.

(8) Create a Policy Advisory Council within the State Energy Office that shall advise the State Energy Office with respect to the development and implementation of a Weatherization Program for Low-Income Families, the Heating/Air Repair and Replacement Program, and any other energy-related assistance program for the benefit of low-income persons in existing housing.

(b) The Secretary shall have final decision-making authority with regard to all functions described in this Part. (2006-206, s. 2; 2009-446, s. 2(a); 2011-284, s. 101; 2013-360, ss. 15.22(j), (k).)

Part 35. Energy Policy Council.

§ 143B-344.55. Energy Policy Council - transfer.

The Energy Policy Council, as established by Chapter 113B of the General Statutes and other applicable laws of this State, is hereby transferred to the Department of Environment and Natural Resources by a Type II transfer as defined in G.S. 143A-6. (2013-365, s. 8(m).)

Article 8.

Department of Transportation.

Part 1. General Provisions.

§ 143B-345. Department of Transportation - creation.

There is hereby created and established a department to be known as the "Department of Transportation" with the organization, powers, and duties defined in Article 1 of Chapter 143B, except as modified in this Article. (1975, c. 716, s. 1.)

§ 143B-346. Department of Transportation - purpose and functions.

The general purpose of the Department of Transportation is to provide for the necessary planning, construction, maintenance, and operation of an integrated statewide transportation system for the economical and safe transportation of people and goods as provided for by law. The Department shall also provide and maintain an accurate register of transportation vehicles as provided by statutes, and the Department shall enforce the laws of this State relating to transportation safety assigned to the Department. The Department of Transportation shall be responsible for all of the transportation functions of the executive branch of the State as provided by law except those functions delegated to the Utilities Commission and the Commissioners of Navigation and Pilotage as provided for by Chapter 76. The major transportation functions include aeronautics, highways, mass transportation, motor vehicles, and transportation safety as provided for by State law. The Department of Transportation shall succeed to all functions vested in the Board of Transportation and the Department of Motor Vehicles on July 1, 1977. (1975, c. 716, s. 1; 1977, c. 464, s. 2; 2011-145, s. 14.6(e).)

§ 143B-347. Repealed by Session Laws 1977, c. 464, s. 3.

§ 143B-348. Department of Transportation - head; rules, regulations, etc., of Board of Transportation.

The Secretary of Transportation shall be the head of the Department of Transportation. He shall carry out the day-to-day operations of the Department and shall be responsible for carrying out the policies, programs, priorities, and projects approved by the Board of Transportation. He shall be responsible for all other transportation matters assigned to the Department of Transportation, except those reserved to the Board of Transportation by statute. Except as otherwise provided for by statute, the Secretary shall have all the powers and duties as provided for in Article 1 of Chapter 143B including the responsibility for all management functions for the Department of Transportation. The Secretary shall be vested with authority to adopt design criteria, construction specifications, and standards as required for the Department of Transportation to construct and maintain highways, bridges, and ferries. The Secretary or the Secretary's designee shall be vested with authority to promulgate rules and regulations concerning all transportation functions assigned to the Department.

All rules, regulations, ordinances, specifications, standards, and criteria adopted by the Board of Transportation and in effect on July 1, 1977, shall continue in effect until changed by the Board of Transportation or the Secretary of Transportation. The Secretary shall have complete authority to modify any of these matters existing on July 1, 1977, except as specifically restricted by the Board. Whenever any such criteria, rule, regulation, ordinance, specification, or standards are continued in effect under this section and the words "Board of Transportation" are used, the words shall mean the "Department of Transportation" unless the context makes such meaning inapplicable. All actions pending in court by or against the Board of Transportation may continue to be prosecuted in that name without the necessity of formally amending the name to the Department of Transportation. (1975, c. 716, s. 1; 1977, c. 464, s. 4; 2010-165, s. 11.)

§ 143B-349: Repealed by Session Laws 1977, c. 464, s. 5.

Part 2. Board of Transportation.

§ 143B-350. Board of Transportation - organization; powers and duties, etc.

(a) Board of Transportation. - There is hereby created a Board of Transportation. The Board shall carry out its duties consistent with the needs of the State as a whole. The diversity and size of the State require that regional differences be considered by Board members as they develop transportation policy and projects for the benefit of the citizens of the State.

(b) Membership of the Board. -

(1) Number, appointment. - The Board of Transportation shall have 19 voting members. Fourteen of the members shall be division members appointed by the Governor. Five shall be at-large members appointed by the Governor. At least three members of the Board shall be registered voters of a political party other than the political party of the Governor. The Secretary of Transportation shall serve as an ex officio nonvoting member of the Board. No more than two members of the Board may reside in the same highway division.

(2) Division members. - One member shall be appointed from and be a resident of each of the 14 highway divisions. The Governor, in selecting division members, shall consider for appointment persons suggested by the Transportation Advisory Committees located within each division. Division members shall direct their primary effort to developing transportation policy and addressing transportation problems in the region they represent. Division members shall regularly consult with and consider the views of local government units and Transportation Advisory Committees in the region they represent.

(3) At-large members. - Five members shall be appointed by the Governor from the State at large. At-large members appointed pursuant to this subdivision shall develop transportation policy and address transportation problems with a statewide perspective. At-large members appointed under this subdivision shall possess the following qualifications:

a. One at-large member shall be a person with expertise in environmental issues affecting the State;

b. One at-large member shall be a person familiar with the State ports and aviation issues;

c. One at-large member shall be a person residing in a rural area of the State with broad knowledge of and experience in transportation issues affecting rural areas;

d. One at-large member shall be a person residing in an urban area with broad knowledge of and expertise in mass transit;

e. One at-large member shall be a person with broad knowledge of and expertise in government-related finance and accounting.

(c) Staggered Terms. - The terms of all Board members serving on the Board prior to January 15, 2001, shall expire on January 14, 2001. A new board of 19 members shall be appointed with terms beginning on January 15, 2001. The Board shall serve the following terms: division members representing divisions 1, 3, 5, 7, 9, 11, and 13 and the three at-large members filling the positions designated in sub-subdivisions (b)(3)a., b., and e. of this section shall serve four-year terms beginning on January 15, 2001, and four-year terms thereafter; and division members representing divisions 2, 4, 6, 8, 10, 12, and 14 and the two at-large members filling the positions designated in sub-subdivisions (b)(3)c. and d. of this section shall serve two-year terms beginning January 15, 2001, and four-year terms thereafter.

(d) Holdover Terms; Vacancies; Removal. - Members shall continue to serve until their successors are appointed. The Governor may appoint a member to serve out the unexpired term of any Board member. The Governor may remove any member of the Board for any cause the Governor finds sufficient. The Governor shall remove any member of the Board upon conviction of a felony, conviction of any offense involving a violation of the Board member's official duties, or for a violation of the provisions of subsections (i), (j), and (k) of this section or any other code of ethics applicable to members of the Board as determined by the Governor or the Governor's designee.

(e) Organization and Meetings of the Board. - Within 60 days after January 15, 2001, and thereafter within 60 days following the beginning of the regular term of the Governor, the Governor or his designee shall call the Board into session. The Board shall select a chair and vice-chair from among its membership for two-year terms. The Board may select a chair or vice-chair for one additional two-year term. The Board of Transportation shall meet once in each 60 days at such regular meeting times as the Board may by rule provide and at any place in the State as the Board may provide. The Board may hold special meetings at any time at the call of the chairman or any three members. The Board shall have the power to adopt and enforce rules and regulations for the government of its business and proceedings. The Board shall keep minutes of its meetings, which shall at all times be open to public inspection. The majority of the Board shall constitute a quorum for the transaction of business. Board members shall receive per diem and necessary travel and subsistence expenses in accordance with G.S. 138-5 and G.S. 138-6, as appropriate.

(f) Duties of the Board. - The Board of Transportation has the following duties and powers:

(1)   To formulate policies and priorities for all modes of transportation under the Department of Transportation.

(2)   To advise the Secretary on matters to achieve the maximum public benefit in the performance of the functions assigned to the Department.

(3)   To ascertain the transportation needs and the alternative means to provide for these needs through an integrated system of transportation taking into consideration the social, economic and environmental impacts of the various alternatives.

(4)   To approve a schedule of all major transportation improvement projects and their anticipated cost. This schedule is designated the Transportation Improvement Program; it must be published and copies must be available for distribution. The document that contains the Transportation Improvement Program, or a separate document that is published at the same time as the Transportation Improvement Program, must include the anticipated funding sources for the improvement projects included in the Program, a list of any changes made from the previous year's Program, and the reasons for the changes.

(5)   To consider and advise the Secretary of Transportation upon any other transportation matter that the Secretary may refer to it.

(6)   To assist the Secretary of Transportation in the performance of his duties in the development of programs and approve priorities for programs within the Department.

(7)   To allocate all highway construction and maintenance funds appropriated by the General Assembly as well as federal-aid funds which may be available.

(8)   To approve all highway construction programs.

(9)   To approve all highway construction projects and construction plans for the construction of projects.

(10) To review all statewide maintenance functions.

(11) To award all highway construction contracts

(12) To authorize the acquisition of rights-of-way for highway improvement projects, including the authorization for acquisition of property by eminent domain.

(12a) To approve partnership agreements with the North Carolina Turnpike Authority, private entities, and authorized political subdivisions to finance, by tolls, contracts, and other financing methods authorized by law, the cost of acquiring, constructing, equipping, maintaining, and operating transportation infrastructure in this State, with priority given to highways, roads, streets, and bridges.

(13) Repealed by Session Laws 2010-165, s. 13, effective August 2, 2010.

(f1) Local Government Participation. - The ability of a local government to pay in part or whole for any transportation improvement project shall not be a factor considered by the Board of Transportation in its development and approval of a schedule of major State highway system improvement projects to be undertaken by the Department under G.S. 143B-350(f)(4).

(f2) Approval of aircraft and ferry purposes. - Before approving the purchase of an aircraft from the Equipment Fund or a ferry in a Transportation Improvement Program, the Board of Transportation shall prepare an estimate of the operational costs and capital costs associated with the addition of the aircraft or ferry and shall report those additional costs to the General Assembly pursuant to G.S. 136-12(b), and to the Joint Legislative Commission on Governmental Operations.

(g) Delegation of Board Duties. - The Board of Transportation shall delegate to the Secretary of Transportation the authority under subdivisions (1) and (2) of this subsection, and may delegate the authority under subdivision (3) of this subsection:

(1) To approve all highway construction projects and construction plans for the construction of projects;

(2) To award all highway construction contracts;

(3) To promulgate rules, regulations, and ordinances concerning all transportation functions assigned to the Department.

The Secretary may, in turn, subdelegate these duties and powers.

(h) Consultation of Board Members. - Each member of the Board of Transportation who is appointed to represent a transportation engineering division or who resides in a division shall be consulted before the Board makes a decision affecting that division.

(i) Disclosure of Contributions. - Any person serving on the Board of Transportation or as Secretary of Transportation on December 1, 1998, shall disclose on that date any contributions the person or the person's immediate family made to the political campaign of the appointing Governor in the two years preceding December 1, 1998. A person appointed to the Board of Transportation and a person appointed as Secretary of Transportation after December 1, 1998, shall disclose at the time the appointment of the person is officially made public any contributions the person or the person's immediate family made to the political campaign of the appointing Governor in the two years preceding the date of appointment. The term "immediate family", as used in this subsection, means a person's spouse, children, parents, brothers, and sisters. Disclosure forms shall be filed with the State Ethics Commission as a supplemental filing to the Statement of Economic Interest filed under Article 3 of Chapter 138A of the General Statutes. Disclosure forms shall not be a public record under the provisions of Chapter 132 of the General Statutes until such time as the appointment of the person filing the statement is officially made public.

(j) Disclosure of Campaign Fund-Raising. - A person appointed to the Board of Transportation on or after January 1, 2001, and a person appointed as Secretary of Transportation on or after January 1, 2001, shall disclose at the time the appointment of the person is officially made public any contributions the person personally acquired in the two years prior to appointment for: any political campaign for a statewide or legislative elected office in North Carolina; any political party executive committee or political committee acting on behalf of a candidate for statewide or legislative office. Disclosure forms shall be filed with the State Ethics Commission as a supplemental filing to the Statement of Economic Interest filed under Article 3 of Chapter 138A of the General Statutes. Disclosure forms shall not be a public record under the provisions of Chapter 132 of the General Statutes until such time as the appointment of the person filing the statement is officially made public.

(k) Ethics Policy. - The Board shall adopt by December 1, 1998, a code of ethics applicable to members of the Board, including the Secretary. Any code of ethics adopted by the Board shall be supplemental to the provisions of Chapter

138A of the General Statutes. A code of ethics adopted pursuant to this subsection shall include a prohibition against a member taking action as a Board member when a conflict of interest, or the appearance of a conflict of interest, exists. The ethics policy adopted pursuant to this subsection shall specify that a conflict of interest exists when the use of the Board member's position, or any official action taken by the Board member, would result in financial benefit, direct or indirect, to the Board member, a member of the Board member's immediate family, or an individual with whom, or business with which, the Board member is associated. The ethics policy adopted pursuant to this subsection shall specify that an appearance of a conflict of interest exists when a reasonable person would conclude from the circumstances that the Board member's ability to protect the public interest, or perform public duties, would be compromised by personal interest, even in the absence of an actual conflict of interest. The performance of usual and customary duties associated with the public position or the advancement of public policy goals or constituent services, without compensation, shall not constitute the use of the Board member's position for financial benefit. The conflict of interest provision of the ethics policy adopted pursuant to this subsection shall not apply to financial or other benefits derived by a Board member that the Board member would enjoy to an extent no greater than that which other citizens of the State would or could enjoy.

(l)   Additional Requirements for Disclosure Statements. - All disclosure statements required under subsections (i), (j), and (k) of this section must be sworn written statements.

(m)   Ethics and Board Duties Education. - The Board shall institute by January 1, 1999, and conduct annually an education program on ethics and on the duties and responsibilities of Board members. The training session shall be comprehensive in nature, conducted in conjunction with the State Ethics Commission, and shall include input from the School of Government at the University of North Carolina at Chapel Hill, the Attorney General's Office, the University of North Carolina Highway Safety Research Center, and senior career employees of the various divisions of the Department. This program shall include an initial orientation for new members of the Board and continuing education programs for Board members at least once each year.

(n)   Review of Appointments by the Joint Legislative Transportation Oversight Committee. - The Governor shall submit the names of all proposed Board of Transportation appointees, along with the disclosure statements required under subsections (i), (j), and (k) of this section, to the Joint Legislative Transportation Oversight Committee prior to Board members' taking office. The

Committee shall have 30 days to review and submit comments to the Governor on the proposed appointees before they take office. The Governor shall consider the views expressed by the Committee concerning the appointees to the Board. If the Committee does not review or submit comments to the Governor on the proposed Board appointees within the 30 days, the Governor may proceed to appoint the proposed members to the Board.

(o)   Additional Ethics Requirements. - Board members shall sign a sworn statement that they will abide by the disclosure, ethics, and education requirements of this section and of Chapter 138A of the General Statutes. Following the convening of each Board of Transportation meeting, and prior to the conduct of business, each Board member shall sign a sworn statement that the member has no financial, professional, or other interest in any project being considered on the meeting agenda. To the extent the Board member has such an interest, the chair and member shall take all appropriate steps to ensure that the interest is properly evaluated and addressed in accordance with law and that the member is not permitted to act on any matter in which the member has a disqualifying conflict of interest. (1975, c. 716, s. 1; 1977, c. 464, s. 6; 1981 (Reg. Sess., 1982), c. 1191, ss. 9, 10; 1985, c. 479, s. 185; 1987, c. 738, s. 170(b), (c); c. 747, s. 4.1; 1989, c. 500, s. 53; c. 692, s. 1.10; 1993, c. 483, s. 4; 1995, c. 490, s. 60; 1997-443, s. 32.1; 1997-495, s. 88(a); 1998-169, ss. 1, 2; 2006-201, s. 15; 2006-230, s. 1(c); 2006-264, s. 29(n); 2007-439, s. 2; 2008-180, s. 1; 2010-165, ss. 12, 13; 2012-84, ss. 1, 3.)

§§ 143B-351 through 143B-352: Repealed by Session Laws 1977, c. 464, s. 7.

Part 3. North Carolina State Ports Authority Transfer.

§ 143B-353: Repealed by Session Laws 1977, c. 65, s. 3.

Part 4. Navigation and Pilotage Commission.

§ 143B-354: Recodified as § 143B-451 by Session Laws 1977, c. 198, s. 26.

Part 5. Division of Aeronautics.

§ 143B-355. Division of Aeronautics.

There is hereby created the Division of Aeronautics of the Department of Transportation. The Division of Aeronautics shall carry out the duties assigned to the Department of Transportation by Article 1B of Chapter 113 of the General Statutes. (1975, c. 716, s. 1.)

§ 143B-356: Repealed by Session Laws 2011-145, s. 28.17(a), effective July 1, 2011 and Session Laws 2011-266, s. 1.21(a), effective July 1, 2011.

§ 143B-357: Repealed by Session Laws 2011-145, s. 28.17(a), effective July 1, 2011 and Session Laws 2011-266, s. 1.21(a), effective July 1, 2011.

Part 6. North Carolina Railroad and Atlantic and North Carolina Railroad.

§ 143B-358: Repealed by Session Laws 1991 (Regular Session 1992), c. 1030, s. 45, effective July 24, 1992.

Part 7. North Carolina Traffic Safety Authority.

§ 143B-359: Repealed by Session Laws 1981, c. 90, s. 2.

Part 8. Highway Safety Program.

§ 143B-360. Powers and duties of Department and Secretary.

The Department of Transportation is hereby empowered to contract on behalf of the State with the government of the United States to the extent allowed by the laws of North Carolina for the purpose of securing the benefits available to this State under the Federal Highway Safety Act of 1966. To that end, the Secretary of Transportation shall coordinate, with the Governor's approval, the activities of any and all departments and agencies of the State and its subdivisions relating thereto.

All of the duties and responsibilities of the Governor's Highway Safety Program, established pursuant to this section, are transferred to the Office of the Secretary of Transportation. (1975, c. 716, s. 1; 2001-424, s. 27.11(a).)

Part 9. North Carolina Rail Council.

§ 143B-361: Repealed by Session Laws 2011-145, s. 28.17(c), effective July 1, 2011 and Session Laws 2011-266, s. 1.14, effective July 1, 2011.

§ 143B-362: Repealed by Session Laws 2011-145, s. 28.17(c), effective July 1, 2011 and Session Laws 2011-266, s. 1.14, effective July 1, 2011.

§ 143B-363: Repealed by Session Laws 2011-145, s. 28.17(c), effective July 1, 2011 and Session Laws 2011-266, s. 1.14, effective July 1, 2011.

§ 143B-364. Reserved for future codification purposes.

§ 143B-365. Reserved for future codification purposes.

Article 9.

Department of Administration.

Part 1. General Provisions.

§ 143B-366. Department of Administration - creation.

There is hereby recreated and reestablished a department to be known as the "Department of Administration," with the organization, powers, and duties defined in the Executive Organization Act of 1973. (1975, c. 879, s. 2.)

§ 143B-367. Duties of the Department.

It shall be the duty of the Department of Administration to serve as a staff agency to the Governor and to provide for such ancillary services as the other departments of State government might need to insure efficient and effective operations. (1975, c. 879, s. 3.)

§ 143B-368. Functions of the Department.

(a)   The functions of the Department of Administration shall comprise, except as otherwise expressly provided by the Executive Organization Act of 1973 or by the Constitution of North Carolina, all functions of the executive branch of the State in relation to interdepartmental administration previously delineated and further including those prescribed powers, duties, functions, and responsibilities enumerated in Article 10 of Chapter 143A of the General Statutes of North Carolina.

(b)   Repealed by Session Laws 1991, c. 542, s. 11. (1975, c. 879, s. 4; 1991, c. 134, s. 2, c. 542, s. 11.)

§ 143B-369. Head of the Department.

The Secretary of Administration shall be the head of the Department. (1975, c. 879, s. 5.)

§ 143B-370: Repealed by Session Laws 1991, c. 542, s. 12.

§ 143B-370.1. Defibrillators in State buildings.

(a)   Subject to the receipt of public-private funds for this purpose, the Department of Administration shall, in consultation with OEMS, AHA, and a qualified vendor/provider of AEDs and training services, develop and adopt policies and procedures relative to the placement and use of automated external defibrillators in State-owned and State-leased buildings. The Department of Administration shall also require that all State buildings, facilities, and institutions shall develop a Medical Emergency Response Plan that facilitates the following:

(1)   Effective and efficient communication throughout the State-owned and State-leased buildings.

(2) Coordinated and practiced response plans.

(3) Training and equipment for first aid and CPR.

(4) Implementation of a lay rescuer AED program.

(b) In addition, for each State building, facility, or institution there shall be developed and periodically updated a maintenance plan that takes the following into account:

(1) Implementation of an appropriate training course in the use of AEDs, including the role of CPR.

(2) Proper maintenance and testing of the devices.

(3) Ensuring coordination with appropriate licensed professionals in the oversight of training of the devices.

(4) Ensuring coordination with local emergency medical systems regarding the placement of AEDs in State buildings, facilities, or institutions where such devices are to be used. (2012-198, s. 3(a), (b).)

Part 2. State Goals and Policy Board.

§§ 143B-371 through 143B-372: Repealed by Session Laws 1995, c. 117, s. 2.

Part 2A. North Carolina Progress Board.

§ 143B-372.1: Repealed by Session Laws 2007-323, s. 9.11, effective July 1, 2007.

§ 143B-372.2: Repealed by Session Laws 2007-323, s. 9.11, effective July 1, 2007.

§ 143B-372.3: Repealed by Session Laws 2007-323, s. 9.11, effective July 1, 2007.

Part 3. North Carolina Capital Planning Commission.

§ 143B-373. North Carolina Capital Planning Commission - creation; powers and duties.

(a) There is hereby recreated the North Carolina Capital Planning Commission of the Department of Administration.

(1) The Commission shall have the following powers and duties:

a. To obtain and maintain up-to-date building requirements for State governmental agencies in Wake County;

b. To formulate a long-range capital improvement program as required for State central governmental agencies in Wake County and maintain this program up-to-date;

c. To recommend the acquisition of land as required;

d. To recommend to the Governor the locations for State government buildings, monuments, memorials and improvements in Wake County, except for buildings occupied by the General Assembly; and

e. To recommend to the Governor the name for any new State government building or any building hereafter acquired by the State of North Carolina in Wake County, with the exception of buildings comprising a part of the North Carolina State University, the Dorothea Dix Hospital, the General Assembly or the Governor Morehead School;

(2) The Commission is authorized and empowered to adopt such rules and regulations, not inconsistent with the laws of this State, as may be required by the federal government for grants-in-aid for capital improvement purposes which may be made available to the State by the federal government. This section is to be liberally construed in order that the State and its citizens may benefit from such grants-in-aid.

(3) The Commission shall adopt rules and regulations consistent with the provisions of this Chapter. All rules and regulations not inconsistent with the provisions of this Chapter heretofore adopted by the existing North Carolina Capital Planning Commission shall remain in full force and effect unless and until repealed or superseded by action of the recreated Commission. All rules and regulations adopted by the Commission shall be enforced by the Department of Administration.

(b) Any:

(1) City exercising any jurisdiction in Wake County under Article 19 of Chapter 160A of the General Statutes (or under any local act of similar nature); and

(2) County exercising any jurisdiction in Wake County under Article 18 of Chapter 153A of the General Statutes (or under any local act of similar nature)

shall provide to the North Carolina Capital Planning Commission no later than August 1, 1989, a copy of any ordinance adopted under that Article and in effect on July 1, 1989, and shall provide a copy of any additional ordinance adopted or amended under such Article or similar local act after July 1, 1989, within 30 days of adoption; provided that no ordinance adopted under G.S. 160A-441 shall be so provided unless it applies to a structure owned by the State.

(c) Any:

(1) City exercising any jurisdiction in Wake County under Article 19 of Chapter 160A of the General Statutes (or under any local act of similar nature); and

(2) County exercising any jurisdiction in Wake County under Article 18 of Chapter 153A of the General Statutes (or under any local act of similar nature)

shall provide to the North Carolina Capital Planning Commission within seven days of first consideration by the governing body any proposal under either of those Articles or local acts which, if adopted would affect property within Wake County owned by the State.

(d) The North Carolina Capital Planning Commission may, by resolution, further define what types of proposals are required to be submitted under subsection (c) of this section, and may define the meaning of "first consideration" differently as to different types of actions, and may require similar notice of proposals before planning boards, boards of adjustment, and planning commissions. The North Carolina Capital Planning Commission may, in lieu of the specific requirements of subsection (c) and this subsection, adopt a different schedule for submission of proposals and ordinances, and the schedule may be different for different jurisdictions, so as to carry out the intent of this section. (1975, c. 879, s. 10; 1981 (Reg. Sess., 1982), c. 1191, s. 66; 1989, c. 32.)

§ 143B-374. North Carolina Capital Planning Commission - members; selection; quorum; compensation.

(a) The North Carolina Capital Planning Commission of the Department of Administration shall consist of the following ex officio members: the Governor of North Carolina who shall serve as chairman; all members of the Council of State including the Lieutenant Governor (or a person designated by the Lieutenant Governor), who shall serve as vice-chairman; the Speaker (or a person designated by the Speaker), and four members of the North Carolina House of Representatives, and four members of the North Carolina Senate; and a representative of the City of Raleigh to be designated by the City Council of Raleigh to serve a two-year term to expire at the same date city council members' terms expire. The President Pro Tempore of the Senate shall appoint the four members of the Senate on or before July 1, 1975, for two-year terms to expire at the same date General Assembly members' terms expire. The Speaker of the House of Representatives shall appoint the four members of the House on or before July 1, 1975, for two-year terms to expire at the same date General Assembly members' terms expire.

Public officers who are made members of the Commission shall be deemed to serve ex officio.

(b) The members of the Commission shall receive per diem and necessary travel and subsistence expenses in accordance with the provisions of G.S. 138-5.

A majority of the Commission shall constitute a quorum for the transaction of business.

All clerical and other services required by the Commission shall be supplied by the Secretary of Administration.

All minutes, records, plans, and all other documents of public record of the State Capital Planning Commission, the Heritage Square Commission, and the former North Carolina Capital Planning Commission shall be turned over to the Department of Administration.

The Commission shall meet quarterly, and at other times at the call of the chairman. (1975, c. 879, s. 11; 1981, c. 47, s. 3; 1991, c. 739, s. 28.)

Part 4. Child Day-Care Licensing Commission.

§§ 143B-375 through 143B-376: Recodified as §§ 143B-168.1, 143B-168.2 by Session Laws 1985, c. 757, s. 155(f).

Part 5. North Carolina Drug Commission.

§§ 143B-377 through 143B-378: Repealed by Session Laws 1977, c. 667, s. 1.

Part 6. North Carolina Council on Interstate Cooperation.

§ 143B-379 through 143B-384: Repealed by Session Laws 1991 (Regular Session, 1992), c. 912, s. 1, effective July 9, 1992.

Part 7. Youth Councils.

§ 143B-385. State Youth Advisory Council - creation; powers and duties.

There is hereby created the State Youth Advisory Council of the Department of Administration. The State Youth Advisory Council shall have the following functions and duties:

(1)   To advise the youth councils of North Carolina;

(2)   To encourage State and local councils to take active part in governmental and civic affairs, promote and participate in leadership and citizenship programs, and cooperate with other youth-oriented groups;

(3)   To receive on behalf of the Department of Administration and to recommend expenditure of gifts and grants from public and private donors;

(4)   To establish procedures for the election of its youth representatives by the State Youth Council; and

(5)   To advise the Secretary of Administration upon any matter the Secretary may refer to it. (1975, c. 879, s. 26.)

§ 143B-386. State Youth Advisory Council - members; selection; quorum; compensation.

The State Youth Advisory Council of the Department of Administration shall consist of 20 members. The composition and appointment of the Council shall be as follows:

Ten youths to be elected by the procedure adopted by the Youth Advisory Council, which shall include a requirement that four of the members represent youth organizations; and 10 adults to be appointed by the Governor at least four of whom shall be individuals working on youth programs through youth organizations. Provided that no person shall serve on the Board for more than two complete consecutive terms.

The initial members of the Council shall be the appointed members of the Youth Advisory Board who shall serve for a period equal to the remainder of their current terms on the Youth Advisory Board. The current terms of the youth members expire July 1, 1976, the current terms of four of the adult members expire April 7, 1976, and the remaining four adult members' terms expire May 1, 1978. At the end of the respective terms of office of the initial members of the Council, the appointment of their successors shall be as follows:

(1) Eight youth members to serve for terms beginning on July 1, 1976, and expiring on June 30, 1977, and two additional youth members to serve for terms beginning on July 1, 1977, and expiring on June 30, 1978. At the end of the terms of office of these youth members of the Council, the appointment of their successors shall be for terms of two years and until their successors are appointed and qualify.

(2) Four adult members to serve for terms beginning on April 8, 1976, and expiring on June 30, 1979; four adult members to serve for terms beginning on May 1, 1978, and expiring on June 30, 1980; one additional adult member to serve for a term beginning July 1, 1977, and expiring June 30, 1978; and one additional adult member to serve for a term beginning July 1, 1977, and expiring June 30, 1979. At the end of the respective terms of office of these adult members of the Council, the appointment of their successors shall be for terms of two years and until their successors are appointed and qualify. At least one adult member shall be an advisor of a local youth council at appointment and for the duration of the term. The total membership shall reasonably reflect the socioeconomic, ethnic, sexual and sectional composition of the State.

Any appointment to fill a vacancy on the Council created by the resignation, dismissal, death, or disability of a member shall be for the balance of the unexpired term.

The Governor shall have the power to remove any member of the Council from office in accordance with the provisions of G.S. 143B-16 of the Executive Organization Act of 1973.

The Governor shall designate an adult member of the Council to serve as chairman at the pleasure of the Governor. The Council shall elect a youth member to serve as vice-chairman for a one-year term.

A majority of the Council shall constitute a quorum for the transaction of business.

Members of the Council who are not officers or employees of the State shall receive per diem and necessary travel and subsistence expenses in accordance with provisions of G.S. 138-5.

All clerical and other services required by the Council shall be supplied by the Secretary of Administration. (1975, c. 879, s. 27; 1977, c. 510; 1979, c. 410; 1991, c. 128.)

§ 143B-387. State Youth Council.

There shall be a State Youth Council. It shall be established within one year of July 1, 1975, in accordance with the methods and procedures established by the Youth Advisory Council. The State Youth Council is authorized and empowered to do the following:

(1)   To consider problems affecting youth and recommend solutions or approaches to these problems to State and local governments and their officials;

(2)   To promote statewide activities for the benefit of youth; and,

(3)   To elect the youth representatives to the Youth Advisory Council. (1975, c. 879, s. 28.)

§ 143B-387.1. North Carolina Youth Advocacy and Involvement Fund.

The North Carolina Youth Advocacy and Involvement Fund is created as a special and nonreverting fund. Conference registration fees, gifts, donations, or contributions to or for the North Carolina Youth Legislative Assembly (YLA) and the North Carolina Students Against Destructive Decisions (SADD) programs shall be credited to the Fund.

The Fund shall be used solely to support planning and execution of the YLA and SADD programs. The Department shall maintain separate cost centers for each program. (2000-67, s. 23.1; 2004-124, s. 19.10.)

§ 143B-388. Local youth councils.

The primary purpose of local youth councils is to promote participation by youth in programs affecting civic and governmental affairs. (1975, c. 879, s. 29.)

Part 8. North Carolina Marine Science Council.

§§ 143B-389 through 143B-390: Repealed by Session Laws 1991, c. 320, s. 1.

Part 8A. Office of Marine Affairs.

§ 143B-390.1: Recodified as § 143B-289.19 by Session Laws 1995, c. 509, s. 98.

§§ 143B-390.2 through 143B-390.4: Recodified as §§ 143B-289.20 through 143B-289.22 by Session Laws 1993, c. 321, s. 28.

§§ 143B-390.5 through 143B-390.9. Reserved for future codification purposes.

Part 8B. North Carolina Council on Ocean Affairs.

§§ 143B-390.10 through 143B-390.11: Repealed by Session Laws 1993, c. 321, s. 28.

§ 143B-390.12. Reserved for future codification purposes.

§ 143B-390.13. Reserved for future codification purposes.

§ 143B-390.14. Reserved for future codification purposes.

Part 8C. North Carolina Aquariums Commission.

§§ 143B-390.15 through 143B-390.16: Recodified as §§ 143B-344.16, 143B-344.17 by Session Laws 1993, c. 321, s. 28(h).

Part 9. North Carolina Human Relations Commission.

§ 143B-391. North Carolina Human Relations Commission - Creation; powers and duties.

There is hereby created the North Carolina Human Relations Commission of the Department of Administration. The North Carolina Human Relations Commission shall have the following functions and duties:

(1)   To study problems concerning human relations;

(2)   To promote equality of opportunity for all citizens;

(3)   To promote understanding, respect, and goodwill among all citizens;

(4)   To provide channels of communication among the races;

(5)   To encourage the employment of qualified people without regard to race;

(6)   To encourage youths to become better trained and qualified for employment;

(7)   To receive on behalf of the Department of Administration and to recommend expenditure of gifts and grants from public and private donors;

(8) To enlist the cooperation and assistance of all State and local government officials in the attainment of the objectives of the Commission;

(9) To assist local good neighborhood councils and biracial human relations committees in promoting activities related to the functions of the Commission enumerated above;

(10) To advise the Secretary of Administration upon any matter the Secretary may refer to it;

(11) To administer the provisions of the State Fair Housing Act as outlined in Chapter 41A of the General Statutes;

(12) To administer the provisions of Chapter 99D of the General Statutes. (1975, c. 879, s. 34; 1983, c. 522, s. 2; 1989 (Reg. Sess., 1990), c. 979, s. 1(6); 1991, c. 433, s. 3; 2011-145, s. 20.1A(b); 2011-391, s. 45(a).)

§ 143B-392. North Carolina Human Relations Commission - Members; selection; quorum; compensation.

(a) The Human Relations Commission of the Department of Administration shall consist of 22 members. The Governor shall appoint one member from each of the 13 congressional districts, plus five members at large, including the chairperson. The Speaker of the North Carolina House of Representatives shall appoint two members to the Commission. The President Pro Tempore of the Senate shall appoint two members to the Commission. The terms of four of the members appointed by the Governor shall expire June 30, 1988. The terms of four of the members appointed by the Governor shall expire June 30, 1987. The terms of four of the members appointed by the Governor shall expire June 30, 1986. The terms of four of the members appointed by the Governor shall expire June 30, 1985. The terms of the members appointed by the Speaker of the North Carolina House of Representatives shall expire June 30, 1986. The terms of the members appointed by the Lieutenant Governor shall expire June 30, 1986. The initial term of office of the person appointed to represent the 12th Congressional District shall commence on January 3, 1993, and expire on June 30, 1996. At the end of the respective terms of office of the initial members of the Commission, the appointment of their successors shall be for terms of four years. No member of the commission shall serve more than two consecutive terms. A member having served two consecutive terms shall be eligible for reappointment one year after the expiration of his second term. Any appointment to fill a vacancy on the Commission created by the resignation, dismissal, death, or disability of a member shall be filled in the manner of the original appointment for the unexpired term.

(b)   Members of the Commission shall receive per diem and necessary travel and subsistence expenses in accordance with the provisions of G.S. 138-5.

(c)   A majority of the Commission shall constitute a quorum for the transaction of business.

(d)   All clerical and support services required by the Commission shall be supplied by the Secretary of the Department of Administration. (1975, c. 879, s. 35; 1983, c. 461; 1989 (Reg. Sess., 1990), c. 979, s. 1(7); 1991 (Reg. Sess., 1992), c. 1038, s. 20; 1995, c. 490, s. 26; 2001-486, s. 2.19; 2011-145, s. 20.1A(b); 2011-391, s. 45(a).)

Part 10. North Carolina Council for Women.

§ 143B-393. North Carolina Council for Women - creation; powers and duties.

There is hereby created the North Carolina Council for Women of the Department of Administration. The North Carolina Council for Women shall have the following functions and duties:

(1)   To advise the Governor, the principal State departments, and the State legislature concerning the education and employment of women in the State of North Carolina.

(2)   To advise the Secretary of Administration upon any matter the Secretary may refer to the Council.

(3)   Repealed by Session Laws 2013-360, s. 30.2(b), effective July 1, 2013. (1975, c. 879, s. 37; 1979, c. 1016, s. 1; 1991, c. 134, s. 4; 2013-360, s. 30.2(b).)

§ 143B-394. North Carolina Council for Women - members; selection; quorum; compensation.

The North Carolina Council for Women of the Department of Administration shall consist of 20 members appointed by the Governor. The initial members of the Council shall be the appointed members of the North Carolina Council for Women, three of whose appointments expire June 30, 1977, and four of whose appointments expire June 30, 1978. Thirteen additional members shall be appointed in 1977, six of whom shall serve terms expiring June 30, 1978, and seven of whom shall serve terms expiring June 30, 1979. At the ends of the respective terms of office of the initial members of the Council and of the 13 members added in 1977, the appointment of their successors shall be for terms of two years and until their successors are appointed and qualify. Any appointment to fill a vacancy on the Council created by the resignation, dismissal, death, or disability of a member shall be for the balance of the unexpired term. Members of the Council shall be representative of age, sex, ethnic and geographic backgrounds.

The Governor shall have the power to remove any member of the Council from office in accordance with the provisions of G.S. 143B-16 of the Executive Organization Act of 1973.

The Governor shall designate a member of the Council to serve as chairman at the pleasure of the Governor.

Members of the Council shall receive per diem and necessary travel and subsistence expenses in accordance with the provisions of G.S. 138-5.

A majority of the Council shall constitute a quorum for the transaction of business.

All clerical and other services required by the Council shall be supplied by the Secretary of Administration. (1975, c. 879, s. 38; 1977, c. 818; 1991, c. 134, s. 4.)

Part 10A. Office of Coordinator of Services for Victims of Sexual Assault.

§ 143B-394.1. Office of Coordinator of Services for Victims of Sexual Assault - purpose.

The ultimate goal of this Article is to establish a network of coordinated public and private services for victims of sexual assault, incorporating existing programs as well as aiding in the development of new programs. (1977, c. 997, s. 1.)

§ 143B-394.2. Office of Coordinator of Services for Victims of Sexual Assault - office created.

(a) The office of Coordinator of Services for Victims of Sexual Assault is hereby created in the Department of Administration. The office shall be under the direction and supervision of a full-time salaried State employee who shall be designated as the State Coordinator. The State Coordinator shall be appointed by the Secretary of the Department of Administration and shall receive a salary commensurate with State government pay schedules for the duties of this office, or such salary to be set by the State Human Resources Commission pursuant to G.S. 126-4. Necessary travel allowance or reimbursement for expenses shall be authorized for the State Coordinator in accordance with G.S. 138-6. Sufficient clerical staff shall be provided under the direction of the Secretary of the Department of Administration.

(b) This State Coordinator shall have administrative experience and the recommendation of the North Carolina Rape Crisis Association and the North Carolina Council for Women. If possible, the State Coordinator shall have public speaking experience, training in rape crisis intervention and education in a related field. (1977, c. 997, s. 1; 1991, c. 134, s. 5; 2013-382, s. 9.1(c).)

§ 143B-394.3. Office of Coordinator of Services for Victims of Sexual Assault - duties and responsibilities.

The duties of the State Coordinator shall include the following:

(1) To establish an office to facilitate and coordinate all programs and services which deal with the victim of sexual assault;

(2) To research the needs of the State and already existing programs for sexual assault services;

(3) To create a liaison between public services and private services with which victims of sexual assault normally come in contact;

(4) To be an information clearinghouse on all aspects of sexual assault services;

(5) To develop model programs and training techniques to be used to train medical, legal, and psychological personnel (both in the public and private sectors) who deal with the victims of sexual assault, and to aid in implementing these programs to suit the needs of specific communities;

(6) To be available to aid and advise sexual assault services on operational and functional problems; and

(7) To develop and coordinate a public education program for the State of North Carolina on the phenomenon of sexual assault. (1977, c. 997, s. 1.)

Part 10B. Displaced Homemakers.

§§ 143B-394.4 through 143B-394.10: Repealed by Session Laws 2013-360, s. 30.2(c), effective July 1, 2013.

§§ 143B-394.11 through 143B-394.14. Reserved for future codification purposes.

Part 10C. Domestic Violence Commission.

§ 143B-394.15. Commission established; purpose; membership; transaction of business.

(a) Establishment. - There is established the Domestic Violence Commission. The Commission shall be located within the Department of Administration for organizational, budgetary, and administrative purposes.

(b) Purpose. - The purpose of the Commission is to (i) assess statewide needs related to domestic violence, (ii) assure that necessary services, policies, and programs are provided to those in need, (iii) strengthen the existing domestic violence programs which have been established pursuant to G.S. 50B-9 and are funded through the Domestic Violence Center Fund, and (iv) recommend new domestic violence programs.

(c) Membership. - The Commission shall consist of 39 members, who reflect the geographic and cultural regions of the State, as follows:

(1) Nine persons appointed by the Governor, one of whom is a clerk of superior court; one of whom is an academician who is knowledgeable about domestic violence trends and treatment; one of whom is a member of the medical community; one of whom is a United States Attorney for the State of North Carolina or that person's designee; one of whom is a member of the North Carolina Bar Association who has studied domestic violence issues; one of whom is a representative of a victims' service program eligible for funding by the Governor's Crime Commission or the North Carolina Council for Women; one of whom is a member of the North Carolina Coalition Against Domestic Violence; one of whom is a former victim of domestic violence; and one of whom is a member of the public at large.

(2) Nine persons appointed by the General Assembly, upon recommendation of the President Pro Tempore of the Senate, one of whom is a member of the Senate; one of whom is a district court judge; one of whom is a district attorney or assistant district attorney; one of whom is a representative of the law enforcement community with specialized knowledge of domestic violence issues; one of whom is a county manager; one of whom is a representative of a community legal services agency who works with domestic violence victims; one of whom is a representative of the linguistic and cultural minority communities; one of whom is a representative of a victims' service program eligible for funding by the Governor's Crime Commission or the North Carolina Council for Women; and one of whom is a member of the public at large.

(3) Nine persons appointed by the General Assembly, upon recommendation of the Speaker of the House of Representatives, one of whom is a member of the House of Representatives; one of whom is a magistrate; one of whom is a member of the business community; one of whom is a district court judge; one of whom is a representative of a victims' service program eligible for funding by the Governor's Crime Commission or the North Carolina Council for Women; one of whom is a representative of the law enforcement community with specialized knowledge of domestic violence issues; one of whom provides offender treatment and is approved by the North Carolina Council for Women; one of whom is a representative of the linguistic and cultural minority communities; and one of whom is a public member.

(4) The following persons or their designees, ex officio:

a. The Governor.

b. The Lieutenant Governor.

c. The Attorney General.

d. The Secretary of the Department of Administration.

e. The Secretary of the Department of Public Safety.

f. The Superintendent of Public Instruction.

g. The Secretary of Public Safety.

h. The Secretary of the Department of Health and Human Services.

i. The Director of the Office of State Human Resources.

j. The Chair of the North Carolina Council for Women.

k. The Dean of the School of Government at the University of North Carolina at Chapel Hill.

l. The Chairman of the Governor's Crime Commission.

(d) Terms. - Members shall serve for two-year terms, with no prohibition against being reappointed, except initial appointments shall be for terms as follows:

(1) The Governor shall initially appoint five members for terms of two years and four members for terms of three years.

(2) The President Pro Tempore of the Senate shall initially appoint five members for terms of two years and four members for terms of three years.

(3) The Speaker of the House of Representatives shall initially appoint five members for terms of two years and four members for terms of three years.

Initial terms shall commence on September 1, 1999.

(e) Chair. - The chair shall be appointed biennially by the Governor from among the membership of the Commission. The initial term shall commence on September 1, 1999.

(f) Vacancies. - A vacancy on the Commission or as chair of the Commission resulting from the resignation of a member or otherwise shall be filled in the same manner in which the original appointment was made, and the term shall be for the balance of the unexpired term.

(g) Compensation. - The Commission members shall receive no salary as a result of serving on the Commission but shall receive per diem, subsistence, and travel expenses in accordance with the provisions of G.S. 120-3.1, 138-5, and 138-6, as applicable. When approved by the Commission, members may be reimbursed for subsistence and travel expenses in excess of the statutory amount.

(h) Removal. - Members may be removed in accordance with G.S. 143B-13 as if that section applied to this Article.

(i) Meetings. - The chair shall convene the Commission. Meetings shall be held as often as necessary, but not less than four times a year.

(j) Quorum. - A majority of the members of the Commission shall constitute a quorum for the transaction of business. The affirmative vote of a majority of the members present at meetings of the Commission shall be necessary for action to be taken by the Commission.

(k) Office Space. - The Department of Administration shall provide office space in Raleigh for use as offices by the Domestic Violence Commission, and the Department of Administration shall receive no reimbursement from the Commission for the use of the property during the life of the Commission.

(l) Staffing. - The Secretary of the Department of Administration shall be responsible for staffing the Commission. (1999-237, s. 24.2(b); 2001-424, s. 7.7; 2006-264, s. 29(o); 2009-342, s. 1; 2011-145, s. 19.1(g), (i); 2013-382, s. 9.1(c).)

§ 143B-394.16. Powers and duties of the Commission; reports.

(a) Powers and Duties. - The Commission shall have the following powers and duties:

(1) As recommended in the January 15, 1999, final report of the Governor's Task Force on Domestic Violence, to develop and recommend to the General Assembly the "Safe Families Act" and to promote adequate funding to promote victim safety and accountability of perpetrators.

(2) To develop and recommend domestic violence training initiatives for law enforcement and judicial personnel and for all persons who provide treatment and services to domestic violence victims.

(3) To develop training initiatives for and make recommendations and provide information and advice to State agencies in the areas of child protection, education, employer/employee relations, criminal justice, and subsidized housing.

(4) To provide information and advice to any private entities that request assistance in providing services and support to domestic violence victims.

(5) To design, coordinate, and oversee a statewide public awareness campaign.

(6) To design and coordinate improved data collection efforts for domestic violence crimes and acts in the State.

(7) To research, develop, and recommend proposals of how best to meet the needs of domestic violence victims and to prevent domestic violence in the State.

(8) To adopt rules in accordance with Article 2A of Chapter 150B of the General Statutes for the approval of abuser treatment programs as provided in G.S. 50B-3(a)(12). The Commission shall adopt rules to establish a consistent level of performance from providers of abuser treatment programs and to ensure that approved programs enhance the safety of victims and hold those who perpetrate acts of domestic violence responsible.

(b) Report. - The Commission shall report its findings and recommendations, including any legislative or administrative proposals, to the General Assembly no later than April 1 each year. (1999-237, s. 24.2(b); 2002-105, s. 1.)

§ 143B-394.17. Reserved for future codification purposes.

§ 143B-394.18. Reserved for future codification purposes.

§ 143B-394.19. Reserved for future codification purposes.

§ 143B-394.20. Reserved for future codification purposes.

Part 10D. Sexual Assault and Rape Crisis Center Fund.

§ 143B-394.21. Sexual Assault and Rape Crisis Center Fund.

(a) The Sexual Assault and Rape Crisis Center Fund is established within the State Treasury. The fund shall be administered by the Department of Administration, North Carolina Council for Women, and shall be used to make grants to centers for victims of sexual assault or rape crisis and to the North Carolina Coalition Against Sexual Assault, Inc. This fund shall be administered in accordance with the provisions of the State Budget Act under Chapter 143C of the General Statutes. The Department of Administration shall make quarterly grants to each eligible sexual assault or rape crisis center and to the North Carolina Coalition Against Sexual Assault, Inc. To be eligible to receive funds under this section, a sexual assault or rape crisis center shall meet the following requirements:

(1) Have been in operation on the preceding July 1 and continue to be in operation.

(2) Offer all of the following services: a hotline, transportation services, community education programs, daytime services, and call forwarding during the night; and fulfill other criteria established by the Department of Administration.

(3) Be a nonprofit corporation or a local governmental entity.

(4) Have a mission statement that clearly specifies rape crisis services are provided.

(5) Act in support of victims of rape or sexual assault by providing assistance to ensure victims' interests are represented in law enforcement and

legal proceedings and support and referral services are provided in medical and community settings.

(b)   Funds appropriated from the General Fund to the Department of Administration, North Carolina Council for Women, for the Sexual Assault and Rape Crisis Center Fund shall be distributed in two shares. The North Carolina Coalition Against Sexual Assault, Inc., and sexual assault or rape crisis centers whose services are confined to rape crisis or sexual assault services shall receive an equal share of thirty-five percent (35%) of the funds. Organizations whose services contain sexual assault or rape crisis services and domestic violence services or other support services shall receive an equal share of the remaining sixty-five percent (65%) of the funds. (2008-107, s. 19.1.)

Vision Books Order Form

Fax Orders:	1-980-299-5965
Phone Orders:	1-704-898-0770
E-mail Orders:	www.visionbooks.org
Mail Orders:	Vision Books, LLC P.O. Box 42406 Charlotte, NC 28215

Shipp To:
Name_____
Address_____
City_____State_____Zip_____
Phone_____Fax_____
Email_____@_____

Bill To: We can bill a third party on your behalf.
Name_____
Address_____
City_____State_____Zip_____
Phone____(_____)_____Fax_____
Email_____@_____

Pamphlet Number ($15.00 Each)	Qty	Total Cost
_____	_____	_____
_____	_____	_____
_____	_____	_____
_____	_____	_____
_____	_____	_____
_____	_____	_____
_____	_____	_____
_____	_____	_____
Full Volume Set 1-92	92 Pamphlets	1,380.00

Free Shipping & Handling on Full Volume Orders
Add $1.00 Shipping & Handling Per Pamphlet $_____

Total Cost $_____

Thank you for your support. Management!

DID YOU ENJOY THIS BOOK?

Vision Books, LLC would like to hear from you! If you or someone you know has been fasely imprisoned, we would like to hear your story. If the 'North Carolina Criminal Law and Procedure' has had an effect in your life or if you have suggestions, we would like to hear from you. Send your letters to:

Vision Books, LLC
Attn: Staff Writers
P.O. Box 42406
Charlotte, NC 28215
Email: staff@visionbooks.org

Order Additional Copies:

Fax Orders:	1-980-299-5965
Phone Orders:	1-704-898-0770
E-mail Orders:	www.visionbooks.org
Mail Orders:	Vision Books, LLC P.O. Box 42406 Charlotte, NC 28215